Fictional Theories and the Three Great Novels

Fictional Theories and the Three Great Novels

Asha Kanwar

PRESTIGE

Published by
Prestige Books
3/28, East Patel Nagar, New Delhi 110 008
in association with
Indian Society for Commonwealth Studies
New Delhi

ISBN : 81-85218-23-4
1991

Jacket design by
Three-A Corporation
New Delhi 110 002

Phototypesetting by
Laser Impressions
New Delhi 110 028
Ph. 537296, 537756

Printed at
Mehra Offset Press
New Delhi 110 002

Contents

Part I: Theory

Part II: Practice

Introduction

> ... the only starting-point for research lies in isolated empirical facts; the only valid criterion for deciding on the value of a critical method . . lies in the possibility which each may offer of understanding these facts, of bringing out their significance and the laws governing their development.
>
> Lucien Goldmann, *The Hidden God*

The present book is primarily a consideration of the fictional criticism of two English critics Arnold Kettle and Raymond Williams. With the recent emergence of a post-Althusserian, deconstructionist Marxist criticism, the work of these earlier critics, especially Kettle, has been somewhat marginalized.[1] The aim, then, is to study the origins, development and achievement of this earlier enterprise locating it within the context of English studies.

For a better understanding and assessment of their project, it will be necessary to undertake two directions of analysis – a setting of the context from which their work emerged and the practical application of their concepts. In order to trace the origins of their work, it will be necessary to go back to the 1930s the period during which both Kettle and Williams were initiated into critical writing.[2] The thirties was also a period of great political turbulence that initiated a wide variety of committed Left-Wing writing in various spheres, a trend that escalated to nearly the end of the decade when the mood changed with the imminent war. Kettle entered Cambridge in 1937, just two years before Williams, yet the time lag was enough to effect a marked change in their respective perspectives. Also potent in that period was the voice of Leavis heard particularly in the pages of *Scrutiny*. The extent to which these major politico-cultural currents affected the work of these two critics will set the context for a detailed analysis of their work.

Once the terms of analysis have been established, the next step will be to apply the concepts to the three novels selected from the *corpus* of the nineteenth-century novel. The novels selected are

Wuthering Heights, Middlemarch and *Tess of the d'Urbervilles,* which may be taken as marking three distinct moments in the development of the nineteenth-century novel. A hypothetical graph of the historical background of the development of the Victorian novel would ascend from 1848 to its apogee in 1871-72 with a decline to 1891 when the transition from Victorianism to modernism begins.

The selection has also been dictated by the fact that of the three novels under study, two are the works of women writers. This is of course immediately problematized by the fact that both assume male pseudonyms. George Eliot is undoubtedly a male pseudonym while Ellis Bell is rather unusually androgynous. It was only two years after *Wuthering Heights* (December, 1847) was first published that the author's gender was revealed in a 'Biographical Notice' by Charlotte Bronte, who explained:

> we did not like to declare ourselves women because – without at that time suspecting that our mode of writing and thinking was not what is called "feminine" – we had a vague impression that authoresses are liable to be looked on with prejudice; we had noticed how critics sometimes use for their chastisement the weapon of personality, and for their reward, a flattery, which is not true praise.[3]

This passage declares the fundamental problem that will be examined in its complexity, but I might add, briefly. However, the fact that two of the writers are women and that women are historically and socially structured differently from men, cannot be ignored and it is part of the task of this book to consider the significance of gender as a consideration in the criticism of literature.

Overall, the novels are appropriated as testing sites for the theories of the two critics whose epistemologies can be broadly said to be based on realistic models; therefore, these texts would seem likely to provide a way of examining these theories by looking at their strongest points (rather than, as is often the case, at their weakest links). In simple terms, the book then can be seen as an imposed exercise which will broadly undertake to perform three functions. It will broadly undertake to perform three functions, 1) it will provide a detailed analysis of the fictional criticism of Kettle and Williams, 2) it will undertake a fresh reading of the selected texts by counterposing the positions of not only the two said critics but also using suitable perspectives that could help in a better understanding of the texts and 3) of providing a method and procedure for examining critical theories in their practical aspect.

The choice of focusing the study on the works of Kettle and Williams as the two critics under discussion, needs to be explained at this stage. The primary concern is to examine their work as particular instances of a certain kind of Marxist criticism. Neither critic, it must be admitted, figures centrally in more recent maps of the Marxist literary "canon," as in, for example, Eagleton's list:

> Let us review some of the names of the major Marxist aestheticians of the century today: Lukacs, Goldmann, Sartre, Caudwell, Adorño, Marcuse, Della Volpe, Macherey, Jameson, Eagleton.[4]

However, within Marxist criticism, there can be many different perspectives according to correspondingly different needs. One recent account notes three, in particular:

> those people who wish to relate their interest in literature to their socialist commitment; those who wish to explore Marxist literary criticism as opposed to the dominant critical tradition; and those engaged in the development of Marxist aesthetic theory itself.[5]

Kettle's enterprise is primarily based on the first need while Williams's work shows elements of the second and third categories. However, Williams's work marks a constant process of development that corresponds to his shifting relationship with Marxism, a development of which I hope to outline a part, in the course of the study.

The second and related reason for the choice of these particular critics arises from my previous experience in research and higher education in India. The two major critical texts discussed in this book (Kettle's *An Introduction to the English Novel* and Williams's *The English Novel from Dickens to Lawrence*) are not only widely influential but they also point to the problem of how styles of criticism are mediated in a different cultural context. In India, very few readers are conscious of the ideological framework of the books or consider their identity as Marxist works of criticism. It is interesting to note that *An Introduction to the English Novel* is far more popular than *The English Novel from Dickens to Lawrence.* Kettle's book was a key text in Britain in the fifties and early sixties, and that it is still in the foreground within the context of English studies in India shows both the delays involved in the retailing of English texts in India, especially in provincial universities, and also the need for simple, comprehensive yet authoritative texts. Thus, the question of this widespread appeal is intriguing, given the fact that these books did not set out to address a post-colonial readership.

Equally, the popularity of the nineteenth-century novels in India is also a subject of debate. They were first disseminated to the colonial subjects on the basis of their moral/didactic content which made them useful tools for extending the imperialist ideology. (The importance of English literature in colonial administration is further evident from the fact that it was included in "the competitive exams that were instituted for the Indian civil service in 1855 and for the home service somewhat later."[6] They were read largely by a public which had never seen a moor or the wild heath or even snow. Was this phenomenon simply a case of cultural imperialism or did it have some connection (the alleged "universality" of great art that transcends barriers of history and culture) with this alien culture? Ekambaram puts forward one view:

> Of all the writers of English fiction Thomas Hardy was most popular among both the high-brow and the low-brow readers for different reasons. . . . while the British audience would have appreciated Hardy's dramatic description of stormy scenes (Egdon Heath), convincing narration of improbable situations, characteristic humour and behavior of rustic characters like Diggory Venn, Indian intellect appreciates that which closely resembled his own tradition of thinking in life. Hardy's view of life (viz. Man's unsuccessful attempt to meet the circumstances of life) comprising fatalism and the dignity of man even in the dark moments of life, would reasonably impress the Indian high-brow.[7]

This fatalism relates closely to the Hindu notion of "karma" and the Muslim one of "kismet." The popularity of Hardy can be judged from the fact that a film based on *Tess of the d'Urbervilles* and transposed to the Indian context entitled *Dulhan Ek Raat Ki* (literally, "Bride of One Night"—released in the early sixties) was watched with delight throughout the country. Ekambaram lists Dickens second in order of popularity because his social criticism was immediately understood by the Indian who recognized similar problems in his own life.

Literature, in so far as its practical aspect is concerned, can either serve to extend the consciousness in a progressive manner or it can be used for the purposes of establishing and maintaining subservience in ex-colonial societies. In view of the fact that most students hardly have any proficiency in the English language, the mediation of critics, especially if they are English, is essential. Most conservative critics have stressed the universality of the human experience, but human experience is never apolitical or acultural. Leavis's call for an "organic past" is an assertion for older values.

This further reinforces the fatalism that is so deeply rooted in the Indian psyche. Therefore, in India, there is the need for a more radical approach, leading to a heightened awareness of the present-day social situation. It was necessary to touch upon the problem as the future of English studies in India is so closely allied to that of critical developments in England. Kettle's work provides a useful link between Leavisism and the work of Williams, while the latter's work borders on the new approaches and developments in literary criticism that are beginning to gain ground in India.

The book is structured in two parts, with the first comprising four chapters, dealing with the Marxist criticism of fiction in the thirties, the hegemony of Leavis and *Scrutiny*, the work of Kettle and finally that of Williams. Part II consists of a systematic analysis of the three novels focusing on particular statements and concerns of Kettle and Williams. Other critical positions are also requisitioned, but the primary focus is on the refinement and clarification of the positions of Kettle and Williams in actual analysis. The final question, however, will be an examination of the merits and limitations of the respective approaches of these critics, so that a new direction in the field of critical analysis may be proposed. This could either mean looking in the alternate fields of post-structuralism, deconstruction, feminism or theories of colonial discourse (which would be particularly valid within a Third World context) or it could lead to a synthesized or pluralistic discourse which would incorporate the major critical concerns of the eighties not only from a Eurocentric perspective or from a global transcendentalist ahistorical standpoint, but one which will be culture-specific and non-hierarchical. At this point it would be possible to answer the question whether a macro theory of the novel is possible or whether instead of looking for a broad all-encompassing poetics, it is better to leave the question open-ended so as to allow for variations of culture, history and the socio-economic specificities of each context.

NOTES

1. In the case of Williams, it is the earlier works that have been marginalized whereas texts like *Marxism and Literature* (1977), *Problems in Materialism and Culture* (1981), *Culture* (1981), and *Writing in Society* have had some recognition.
2. Williams's writing career was initiated much earlier, "By the time I was sixteen, I was writing plays which were performed in the village. . . . I also wrote a novel which nobody is ever going to see, called *Mountain Sunset.*" *Politics and Letters* (London:Verso, 1981), p. 30.
3. "Biographical Notice of Ellis and Acton Bell," *Wuthering Heights: An Annotated Text with Essays in Criticism*, William M. Sale, Jr., ed. (New York: W.W. Norton, 1963), p. 4.
4. *Walter Benjamin or Towards a Revolutionary Criticism* (London: NLB, 1981), p. 96. However, Eagleton has since changed his stance vis-a-vis Williams as is evident in his book *Function of Criticism* (London: Verso, 1984).
5. Editorial Comments, *Red Letters,* Vol. 3, p. 2.
6. Richard Altick,. *The English Common Reader* (Chicago: University Press, 1967), p. 183.
7. Ekambaram, *Fiction and the Reading Public in India,* C.D. Narasimhaiah ed. (University of Mysore: Wesley Press, 1967), p. 13.

Marxist Criticism of Fiction in the Thirties

> My whole work was affected by the atmosphere of the thirties. I realized, as I grew older, how much we're the products of the thirties.
>
> Arnold Kettle[1]

> My first contacts with Marxist literary argument occurred when I came to Cambridge to read English in 1939. . . . What I really learned from, and shared with, the dominant tones of that English Marxist argument was what I would now call, still with respect, a radical populism. It was an active, committed, popular tendency, concerned rather more (and to its advantage) with making literature than with judging it, and concerned above all to relate active literature to the lives of the majority of our own people.
>
> Raymond Williams[2]

The 1930s then constituted a common starting-point for the intellectual development of Kettle and Williams; and it was, for them, a particular 1930s; one dominated by Left-Wing politics—and the problem of its relation to literary practice and literary study. However, this is not to underestimate the complementary and substantial influence of Leavis and *Scrutiny,* an area to be dealt with, in the next chapter. Here the focus will be primarily on the "Red" aspect of the decade. The thirties's Marxist criticism of fiction will be seen in three different contexts—(a) literary creativity in its historico-political background, (b) Marxist literary theory in the Soviet Union and Germany, gauging its impact in Britain, and, (c) the general state of literary criticism in Britain. This will be followed by a section analysing Marxist criticism of fiction in Britain with specific reference to relevant critical texts published in 1937. The conclusion will survey the general position of the Marxist critics and of how Kettle and Williams inserted themselves within this historical "moment."

I

While no historical decade can be characterized in isolation, the launching of the Communist paper, the *Daily Worker* in January 1930, can be taken as symbolic of the beginning of the distinct political character of the decade[3] that saw a steady increase in Left literary activity, reaching its peak in 1937 and then declining to end in 1939 with the Hitler-Stalin pact. Towards the end of the thirties, the political mood becomes more diffuse, in the sense that the Popular front against Fascism incorporated people of different political persuasions rather than limiting itself to the communists alone.

The reasons for this swing to the Left by the thirties intellectuals – for in the 1926 General Strike, many students played the role of strike breakers – has characteristically been attributed to the general situation of the period. Economic Depression, hunger, unemployment, public expenditure cuts, the defeats of the Labour Party (particularly in 1931), the rise of fascism and the Spanish Civil War provided the incentive for committed action. The General response to the crisis is voiced by the central figure of one of Caudwell's unpublished autobiographical stories: "We both need a religion, but what religions are there nowadays? Communism remains, I suppose."[4] Samuel Hynes interprets the adoption of this surrogate religion as the tendency among the young of the thirties to the "will to believe" rather than to the "will to change" the world.[5] This does not seem wholly true, for many young intellectuals of the period engaged their physical and mental energies to the cause of effecting social change. The founding of Left journals, dramatic societies, book clubs and above all participation in the Spanish Civil War (Cornford, Fox, Caudwell), which, for them, was not an ordinary war, but a fight for principles, is ample evidence of this.

At that time, within the wider Soviet-European context there were various theories regarding the function and value of art in a socialist state. Realism was generally regarded as the essence of good art.[6] This was the basic premise behind the doctrine of socialist realism in the Soviet Union. Just as Marx and Engels were not against *Tendenzpoesie* but did not want explicit attention drawn to the tendency,[7] Mehring and Plekhanov believed that conscious introduction of tendentiousness reduced art to propaganda. Lenin, however, was of the opinion that

> Literature must become part of the common cause of the proletariat, "a cog and screw" of the one single great Social-Democratic mechanism set in motion by the entire politically-conscious vanguard of the entire working-class.[8]

Lenin's perspective is practical rather than aesthetic and his primary concern was with the spread of mass literacy and the diffusion of political consciousness. Proletkult, a group headed by A.A. Bogdanov, organized "creative writing" studios all over the country with the express purpose of training working-class writers and artists.[9] On the other hand, Trotsky believed that proletarian art was not possible because the cultural level of the class was too low and that the notion, in a future classless society, was unsound. The Formalists studied linguistics and were allied to the *avant garde* Constructivists in their rejection of traditional art. With Mayakovsky's pamphlet in the 1920s, Osip Brik's "social command" came into currency. This implied the artists's intervention in political matters and wished to do away with the "myth of an apolitical art."[10]

These various trends were superseded by the concept of "socialist realism" which was installed as official party policy with the First Congress of the Workers's Union in 1934. The key speeches were delivered by Gorky, Bukharin and Zhdanov with the latter defining socialist realism as follows :

> It means in the first place, that you must know life in order to be able to depict it truthfully in artistic creations, to depict it neither "scholastically" nor lifelessly, not simply as "objective reality," but rather as reality in its revolutionary development.[11]

Brewster observes three aspects of this definition saying that it is the socialist realist *method*, not the socialist realist *style*, that it is "realism that is mimesis, but not naturalism," and that "realism had to be tempered with revolutionary romanticism."[12] These aspects can be found in the thirties's fictional practice in England. While many deviations occurred within its framework, socialist realism continued to wield powerful influence until 1956, reinforced as it was by the work of Lukacs.

The work of Lukacs himself was not available in the thirties Britain, as Kettle confirms, "Lukacs began to be translated in the fifties

I think, whereas in the thirties and forties he was very esoteric."[13] But Lukacsian influence filtered into Britain via the Soviet Union disguised in the tenets of socialist realism. Indirectly, the main oppositional force to socialist realism and directly to Lukacs was Brecht, who shared the same ideology with Lukacs, and believed, also with Lukacs, that the end of art was the widening of political consciousness, yet took recourse to a different means of achieving this end. Lukacs's definition of realism is a fuller exposition of the Engelsian one. For Lukacs, the work of art should provide a Hegelian "totality":

> an image of reality in which the opposition of appearance and essence, of the individual case and the general rule, of the immediacy of the senses and the abstract conceptualization etc. are resolved. The immediate effect of the work of art is to dissolve the oppositional elements into a spontaneous whole, so that they form an inseparable unity for the reader.[14]

The reader is taken as a passive consumer to whom the artist feeds a pre-prepared "unity." The contrast with Brecht is obvious:

> Our concept of realism must be wide and political, sovereign over all conventions. Realistic means: discovering the causal complexes of society/unmasking the prevailing view of things as the view of those who rule it/writing from the standpoint of the class which offers the broadest solutions for the pressing difficulties in which human society is caught emphasizing the element of development/making possible the concrete and making possible abstraction from it.[15]

For Brecht, the work of art must be open-ended so that the reader/viewer is an active producer in constructing the artistic experience. In the case of Lukacs, the artist's presentation of the solution serves as an example to be emulated by the reader in changing social reality. Brecht believes that

> the contradictions of existence under capitalism must be highlighted, not reconciled . . . the work is seen as a product and this implies the moment of consumption as well as production.[16]

Chris Pawling points out that the theories of Benjamin and Brecht are useful correctives to Lukacs, for, "by examining art as production, they expose Lukacs's commitment to 'high culture' and the 'classics'."[17] Brecht's technique, in a bid to deconstruct hierarchical systems, involves use of montage, reportage and alienation effects.

By recent standards, the thirties's Marxist position is regarded as theoretically crude yet it laid the foundations for the future of a sophisticated Marxist aesthetics in Britain. In fact, this pioneering work is all the more important when one considers Kettle's observation:

> But in the 1930s, when Alick West and Christopher Caudwell, Edgell Rickword and Douglas Garman, Cecil Day Lewis, Edward Upward, Ralph Fox . . . were among those who came into the Communist Party and pioneered a British Marxist literary-critical practice, the work of the Continental Marxists was scarcely known and much of it not yet written.[18]

Leavis was evidently not interested in Marxism and considered the English Marxists "an easy match" with the sole exception of Christopher Hill, who was treated with respect.[19] It was a debate easily won by the Leavisites, and Williams, admitting this, explains:

> Marxism, as then commonly understood, was weak in just the decisive area where practical criticism was strong: in its capacity to give precise and detailed and reasonably adequate accounts of actual consciousness: not just a scheme or a generalization but actual works, full of rich and significant and specific experience.[20]

Historically speaking, criticism can be divided into two categories--criticism as specialist literary discourse (academia today) or criticism as dealing laterally with wider socio-cultural issues as in the days of Addison and Steele. Neither the Left, nor the Leavisite school was narrowly specialist. Eagleton suggests that Leavis desired for himself a Samuel Johnsonian, sage/prophet kind of position, whereas the Marxist school was more overtly political.[21] Overall, the literary situation of the thirties can be tentatively summed up in the words of L.C. Knights, who, opening a review of Spender's *Life and the Poet* (1942), believes in the potency of the following factors:

> the existence of a vast amorphous reading public caring little or nothing for poetry, the consequent organization of "serious" writers in small self-supporting groups, and the attraction for the young of the confident orthodoxy of communism.[22]

II

Left literary-critical activity reached its zenith in 1937. The publication of *Illusion and Reality, The Novel and the People, Crisis and Criticism,* among others, prompted David Margolies to respond enthusiastically:

> an extraordinary outpouring of Marxist literary theory at one time, and all in one way or the other responding to the crisis, especially as it was reflected in literature.[23]

Christopher Caudwell, Ralph Fox and Alick West shared with many writers of their time, a clear anti-Fascist, revolutionary Communist perspective. In Caudwell's view, it was not necessary to adopt a politically militant attitude to effect social change, for the effecting of social change was inherent in the nature of literature itself. He explains further, that in the process of artistic creation, the desires of the subject are projected in the form of an "illusion." It is on the basis of this illusion that individuals are inspired to create a corresponding "reality" which results in social change. Art performs the function of helping the instincts to adapt to the environment.

Maurice Cornforth suggests that Caudwell is attempting to synthesize Freudian and Weismannian theories with Marxism.[24] Whatever the truth of this observation, it is a fact that Caudwell believes that no field of study is mutually exclusive and calls for the establishment of interdisciplinary studies where there is action and interaction between various fields. He tries to dismantle the duality between "illusion" and "reality": "romance" and "realism," "subjective" and "objective," an enterprise that Williams approves of and endorses when he states "we have to think, rather, of human experience as both objective and subjective, in one inseparable process" and goes on to quote from Caudwell: "Every part of the body not only affects the other parts but is also helpful in determining relations with the rest of reality."[25]

Illusion and Reality deals primarily with poetry while *Romance and Realism* (*RR*) is concerned with 'bourgeois literature' in general, and especially with the development of the novel from Defoe to Joyce. Caudwell's project is to trace the economic changes in society and to relate them to the literary forms that then arise:

> It will then be noticed that so far our revolutionary periods have been poetical periods (Shakespeare, Milton . . .). The novel tends to be conservative and satisfied. (*RR*, 68-69)

The hallmark of the typical bourgeois novel is that the author believes it possible to:

> construct a closed absolute world of art from which the observer is excluded, a world of absolute values existing in themselves, not a world of values for the observer. (*RR*, 119)

This tendency arises because the writer is not conscious of the determinate character of social relations. Instead, the writer should recognize this material fact and acquire a positive world-view. It is only then that the novelist can create the proletarian novel on the lines laid by the Socialist realists in Russia. While Caudwell stresses the importance of the aesthetic element in literature, he relies heavily on the ideological – arguing for example that, "it is Lawrence's final tragedy that his solution was ultimately Fascist and not Communist."[26] He sounds narrowly prescriptive when he criticizes "fellow travellers" like Auden, Day Lewis and Spender and recommends that they become "real Communists" if they are to help create "a new vital poetry." (*RR*, 138)

Similarly, Caudwell's evaluation of the work of women writers is based on ideological rather than aesthetic criteria. George Eliot is passed over quickly as "a smaller and yet significant figure" (*RR*, 71) while the Brontes represent the "final phase of bourgeois culture in which woman revolts against her subjection" (*RR*, 72) – with no word at all about specifically artistic achievement. However, his views on the gender question, in general, are distinctive and worthy of attention in the light of more recent feminist thought. Caudwell recognizes the fact of physiological inequality between the sexes, and says that the solution does not lie in the female accepting male values (Marian Evans becoming George Eliot) but "this equality can be achieved only in a culture whose values are contributed jointly by men and women." (*RR*, 72)

In fact, Caudwell is almost the only Marxist who is regarded with any respect by recent critics who tend to take a generally denigratory view of the thirties's enterprise. However, in his own day, Christopher St. John Sprigg (alias Caudwell) was not even well-known enough to merit an obituary, whereas to his contemporary, Ralph Fox, already a writer of "international repute," a full issue of the *Left Review* was dedicated on his death in January 1937. In February 1937, *The Novel and the People* was published posthumously and reviewed alongwith Philip Henderson's *The Novel Today*. Reviewing the books, Jack Lindsay points out that both provide a Marxist approach, and are complementary in that *The Novel and the People* (*TNTP*) deals with the novel from Rabelais and Henderson continues where Fox leaves, that is, with the post Great-War novel.[27] The discussion here will, however, be limited to *The Novel and the People*.

In *The Novel and the People,* Fox begins by trying to clarify the misconceptions regarding Marxism by explaining its basic tenets, for he is interested in establishing its position as the "most humanist of all world outlooks."[28] Fox's major importance lies in the fact that he was able to recognize and dismiss the crude base-superstructure models that his contemporaries like Caudwell were subscribing to, for he acknowledged the fact that "art is most farther from the basis, responds far less easily to the change in it." (*TNTP*, 30) It is clear that Fox has the "law of uneven development" in mind as also the letter that Engels wrote to J. Bloch in 1890:

> According to the materialist conception of history, the determining element in history is *ultimately* the production and reproduction of real life.... If therefore somebody twists this into the statement that the economic element is the only determining one, he transforms it into a meaningless, abstract and absurd phrase.[29]

While Fox isolates the problem, he does not undertake further explanations. This particular issue has resulted in theories of "mediation," "homologous structures" and more sophisticated explanations of the base-superstructure model.

In *The Novel and the People*, the key concept is that of the "epic structure" of the novel, a concept Fox shares with Hegel who describes the novel as "the epic of the middle class world"[30] and with Lukacs who calls it "great epic" *(die Grosse Epic)*.[31] It is only in the capitalist world that there is a conflict between "the hero [who] asserts his freedom and self development within a world which denies it." (*TNTP*, 7) Furthermore, "the creative process is the struggle between the creator and external reality," (*TNTP*, 28) observations that can be linked to Lukacs's description of the realist novel. In fact, the other concept that Fox shares with Lukacs and Engels are those of "realism," "type" and "totality." While it cannot be proved whether Fox was or was not aware of the work of Lukacs, it is possible that *The Soul and the Forms* (1911) and the *Theory of the Novel* (1916) were accessible to him during his two-year sojourn at the British section of the Marx-Engels Institute in Moscow. For an explanation of the nature of the epic character of the novel, it is best to turn to Fox himself:

> It must show man not merely critical, or man at hopeless war with a society he cannot fit into as an individual, but man in action to change his conditions, to master life, man in harmony with the course of history and able to become the lord of his own destiny. This means the heroic must return to the novel, and with the heroic its epic character. (*TNTP*, 100)

Fox observes that the loss of the "heroic" has brought the novel to its current state of disintegration in the twentieth century, a generalization that can of course be challenged.[32] According to Fox, the function of art is to extend man's consciousness and to heighten his sensibility. To achieve this, a writer must have a progressive world-view and working-class sympathies. In other words, Fox is advocating a move to socialist realism in the manner of Caudwell.

If Fox has generated the impression that he is reducing art to class ideology, he is quick to add that a novel is an "artistic creation" with form as well as content, and even though "primacy is on the side of content, form reacts on content and never remains passive." (*TNTP*, 40) He then embarks on a valuable discussion of style. Condemning the use of an ornamental, affected style, he suggests that the writer strive to create a "living style" which must have conformity of word and thought, for example, "the romantic thought will demand a romantic style and the realist thought the plain 'prose'." (*TNTP*, 133) He points out that modern prose has become "anaemic" and can only be revitalized by fresh importations from America or working-class speech. He wants language to express life rather than to "conceal" it, as in the case of B.B.C. usage. Fox seems to be condemning elitist notions of language, that is, standard language or Received Pronunciation (R.P). He believes that a democratic use of language alone can infuse art with life and colour. Therefore, the absorption of fresh terms of slang into artistic language is needed in order to signify the changing experience of life in modern society. (This somehow harks back to Wordsworth's call for linguistic secularization in art).[33]

Very often the dominant trend in the thirties's Left literary-thinking is an amalgam of Marxism and Romantic values. The revolutionary zeal evoked by the Spanish Civil war in the young Marxists is parallel to that felt by the Wordsworth generation in the face of the French Revolution, so that the Auden generation might easily echo the words of its predecessors:

> Bliss was it in that dawn to be alive,
> But to be young was very heaven.

The Romantic attitude of viewing art in its aesthetic aspect as well as in its role of being the voice of humanity against oppression and exploitation – are strikingly similar to the thirties's perspective. But the crucial difference lies in the fact that, as Alick West argued, "the Romantic poets were unable in their particular circumstances to give a material meaning to their social conception."[34]

West also believes in the continuity of Marxism and Romantic discourse and, as Graham Pechey points out, he insists that "any Marxist criticism or cultural theory will need to carry out a transformation of romanticism parallel to Marx's transformation of Hegel."[35] The importance of West lies in the fact that his book *Crisis and Criticism* (*CC*) is the most serious attempt to confront *Scrutiny* and addresses itself to questions of bourgeois critical practice.

West was able to recognize the bourgeois dichotomy between "work" and "culture" and hence the elitist bias of all literary evaluation which is primarily subjective and ultimately ideological. The shifting popularity of a work of art does not affect its intrinsic worth :

> The value of literature springs from the fact that it continues and changes the organization of social energy; we perceive value through the awakening of the same kind of energy in ourselves. (*CC*, 101)

Literature may evoke two kinds of responses – consumer or productive, "consumer" pointing to passive reception whereas productive energy can arouse men to make their own history and "change, be it ever so little, in ever so limited a degree, life itself," (*TNTP*, 33) a sentiment shared by both Fox and West. It is interesting to note that in this general remark of "consumer" and "productive" response lie the seeds of the sophisticated "reception-aesthetic" theories of such later critics like Wolfgang Iser, Stanley Fish, Michael Riffaterre and others.[36]

Not wishing to appear one-sided in judging a work of art in relation to socio-economic determinants alone, West turns to judging aesthetic value in terms of language. He removes language from its "idealist" sphere as expression of thought and places it in the field of "action, both in its purpose and origin." (*CC*, 75) As we have already seen, there is an increasing interest in questions of language among the thirties writers. West goes on:

> All good literature has richness and vigour in its style . . . the use of idiomatic expression . . . *the more it uses them idiomatically, in violation of the laws of grammar and logic, the more it approaches art.* (*CC*, 81)

The emphasized section of this quote is all the more interesting if one recalls Jan Mukarovsky's distinction between standard and poetic language--the latter depending for its effects upon the deliberate distortion of linguistic items to achieve maximum foregrounding against a standard background.[37]

The relation between form and content in literature parallels that of language:

> the form of the words and sentences expresses and appeals to the previous experience of the social organism; the content of the particular act of speech indicates a particular activity; the excitement of energy is the result of both processes. (*CC*, 98)

While both form and content are inseparable, it is the content which determines the form, for example, when a writer wishes to write a poem, the conventional form that he has accessible to him is modified by his present content and what emerges is something new. The similar process can be transformed to novelistic forms.

In *Crisis and Criticism*, West is preoccupied with poetry and literature in general rather than with fiction in particular to which only the final chapter "James Joyce: *Ulysses*" is devoted. In spite of his enlightened views on the aesthetic aspects of literature, what West in practice actually does is to look for "clear reflection of social conditions," (*CC*, 96) for example, he analyzes *Paradise Lost* in the best traditions of "vulgar" Marxism referring to "the feudal organization of heaven." (*CC*, 96) Joyce is dismissed on the grounds that *Ulysses* "does not organize social energy; it irritates it, because it gives it no aim it can work for." (*CC*, 127) West is basically looking for the "effect" literature has on the reader with regard to the generation of progressive/retrogressive energy.

West's remark, "Literature is therefore propaganda. But not all propaganda is literature," (*CC*, 98) more or less sums up the position of the writers under discussion. Auden's distinction between propaganda and art in *The Poet's Tongue* (1935) is useful in this context:

> The propagandist, whether moral or political, complains that the writer should use his powers over words to persuade people to a particular course of action . . . But poetry is not concerned with telling people what to do, but with extending our knowledge of good and evil . . . leading us to the point where it is possible for us to make a rational and moral choice.[38]

Caudwell, Fox and West were all members of the Communist Party, sharing admiration for Soviet literature and socialist realism. They view literature from a materialist standpoint and evaluate it according to its functional value, that is, in how far it can ultimately effect social change. For Fox, art must in the end serve an epistemological function:

> The revolutionary task of literature today is to . . . bring the creative writer face to face with his only important task, that of winning the knowledge of truth, of reality. Art is one of the means by which man grapples with and stimulates reality. (*TNTP*, 31)

West "was more obviously a practising critic than Fox or Caudwell and his conclusions are more fully argued and supported than theirs."[39] He nad the additional advantage of having time at his disposal for revising and extending his theses whereas Fox and Caudwell had died before realizing their full potential.

III

In reviewing the achievement of the thirties, one's attention is drawn to the notion that history is not an "objective" fact but an ideological "construct." It is for this reason perhaps that no one picture of the period can be declared authentic, final or complete. For example, the major writers discussed so far have been men. However, feminist historians have revealed that women's issues were being discussed not only in the pages of the *Left Review*, but were the major focus of attention in *Time and Tide*, a feminist journal that declared its intention to "treat men and women as equally part of the great human family."[40] This version of the thirties has presented a threefold picture of women--as excluded, misrepresented but also as "actively organizing together, culturally and politically, alongside men and sometimes against them."[41] Obviously, this dimension is missing from more overtly official historical accounts.

However, the aspect of thirties history that is our primary concern here, is that of the Marxists and their relation to the "Scrutineers." The primary reason for their marginal position was, as Williams has pointed out, the dogmatic nature of their enterprise which resulted in reducing the autonomy of literature thereby pushing it into the sphere of political propaganda.[42] The second major reason was the ambivalent position of many thirties's literary Marxists in relation to the working-classes. Rooted in the bourgeoisie, and having traversed the public-school-Oxbridge circuit, they wanted to support, but also experienced a feeling of guilt, towards the working-classes. Morever, within a predominantly conservative culture, Left-Wing activities could only remain peripheral and transient.

Yet the crisis of the time had an immediacy that stimulated these writers to militant positions. This pressure demanded a practical approach rather than the conventional one of viewing literature as only a scholarly pursuit. The main problem of this generation was that they lacked the perspective of time to be able to synthesize ideology and reality in order to achieve a more balanced outlook. The achievement of these writers lies in the fact that they laid the foundation of a hitherto non-existent Marxist tradition of literary criticism in Britain. And it is within this context that the work of later critics like Kettle and Williams can be assessed.

In the case of Kettle, West was the main influence whereas for Williams, the central work of the thirties debate was Fox's *The Novel and the People*.[43] This is not to underrate the influence of Fox on Kettle or of West on Williams. For example, in the Open University course Unit on *The Late Nineteenth Century Novel*, Kettle discusses the relation between the epic and the novel, taking his cue from Fox. Similarly, Williams develops the "Westian emphasis on the materiality of art."[44]

However, to trace only the Left literary-critical influence on the overall formation of the position of Kettle and Williams would be to present a one-sided picture. For though Leavis was the major oppositional force, he helped shape even subsequent Left literary theory and practice. Kettle's work has often been regarded as a form of Left-Leavisism while Williams's work on the novel has been an implicit acknowledgement of this influence. In general terms, the work of Kettle and Williams can be seen as a convergence of English Marxism and *Scrutiny* in different degrees. The extent of this interaction will be the subject of the following chapter.

NOTES

1. Asha Kanwar "An Interview with Arnold Kettle," Milton Keynes, 1984.
2. Raymond Williams, *Marxism and Literature* (Oxford: Oxford University Press, 1977), pp. 1-2.
3. Alun Howkins, "Class against Class: The Political Culture of the C.P.G.B., 1930-35" in Frank Glovesmith, ed., *Class Culture and Social Change*

(Brighton: Harvester, 1980, p. 248). Howkins sees the *Daily Worker* as "part of the culture of British communism," p. 248.

4. Samuel Hynes, "Introduction," in Christopher Caudwell, *Romance and Realism* (Princeton: Princeton University Press, 1970), p. 6.

5. *Loc. cit.*

6. According to Helga Gallas, such a premise leads to reductionism. Instead, she proposes the alternate notion that "artistic activity is one of the modes of production and is subject to the laws of production." This suggests 2 methods of procedure; (1) "the literary *product* is seen as a commodity which follows the laws of the capitalist market." (2) "The literary *production process* is conceived of as praxis, in the Marxist sense of the word." *Working Papers in Cultural Studies,* Vol. 4, Spring 1973, p. 117.

7. Lee Baxandall and Stefan Morawski, *Marx and Engels on Literature and Art* (New York: International General, 1977), p. 85.

8. Quoted in Ben Brewster, "The Soviet State, the Communist Party and the Arts 1917-36," *Red Letters,* Vol. 3, 1976, p. 4.

9. Though the *Left Review* (1934) did invite working-class writing, Proletkult was unknown in Britain until 1935 as Edgell Rickword reminisces in an interview with John Lucas (1974).

10. Dave Laing, *The Marxist Theory of Art* (Brighton: Harvester, 1978), p. 32.

11. *Ibid.*, p. 41.

12. Brewster, p. 8.

13. Kanwar.

14. Quoted in Laing, pp. 48-49.

15. *Ibid.*, pp. 56-57.

16. Chris Pawling, Translator's Preface to Helga Gallas, "The Part Played by Lukacs in Working out a Marxist Theory of Literature in the Leauge of Revolutionary Proletarian Writers," *W.P.C.S.*, p. 106.

17. *Ibid.*, p. 108.

18. A. Kettle, "Introduction," Alick West *Crisis and Criticism* (London: Lawrence and Wishart, 1975), p. 2.

19. Kenneth Trodd, "*Scrutiny* in the 30s," *The Review,* Nos. 11-12, p. 10.

20. Raymond Williams, *Problems in Materialism and Culture* (London: Verso, 1980), pp. 18-19.

21. Terry Eagleton, "Criticism and the Public Sphere," Lecture at the University of Sussex, April 1984. Subsequently published in *The Function of Criticism* (London: Verso, 1984).

22. Quoted in Trodd, "*Scrutiny* in the 30s," *The Review,* p. 9.

23. David Margolies, "*Left Review* and Left Literary Theory," Jon Clark et al eds., *Culture and Crisis,* p. 72.

24. Mauriuce Cornforth, "Caudwell and Marxism," *Modern Quarterly,* Vol. 6, Winter 1950-51, pp. 16-33. Caudwell uses the Weismannian concept of "genotype" which would be roughly equivalent to the Freudian "id."
25. R. Williams, *The Long Revolution* (London: Chatto and Windus, 1961), p. 20.
26. D. Margolies, p. 78.
27. *Left Review,* Vol. III, No. 1. Feb. 1937, p. 52.
28. Ralph Fox, *The Novel and the People* (London: Lawrence and Wishart, 1937), p. 34.
29. *Basic Writings on Politics and Philosophy,* Lewis S. Feuer, ed. (N.Y. : Collins, The Fontana Library, 1969), pp. 436-37.
30. Alan Swingewood, *The Novel and Revolution* (London: Macmillan, 1975), p. 7.
31. G.H.R. Parkinson, *George Lukacs* (London: Routledge and Kegan Paul, 1977), p. 25.
32. In a contemporary context, it can be said that the epic hero has given way to the more secular "protagonist" and even the anti-hero. The novel as a genre is not in a state of decline but co-exists with other cultural forms like television and film.
33. In the Preface to the *Lyrical Ballads* (1805), Wordsworth advocates the depiction of incidents and situations from "common life" in a "selection of language really used by men" (21) because such men "convey their feelings and notions in simple and unelaborated expressions." (220) Derek Roper, ed. (London: MacDonald and Evans, 1976).
34. A. West, *Crisis and Criticism,* p. 76.
35. Graham Pechey, "*Scrutiny,* English Marxism and the Work of Raymond Williams," *Literature and History,* Vol. II, Spring 1985, p. 70.
36. Reader response criticism is not a conceptually unifiable category but even within its field, perspectives can range from formalism to post-structuralism.
37. In "Standard and Poetic Language," (1932) *A Prague School Reader in Esthetics: Literary Structure and Style,* Paul L. Garvin, ed. and trans. (Georgetown: University Press, 1964).
38. S. Hynes, *The Auden Generation,* p. 14.
39. J. Clark, *Culture and Crisis,* pp. 74-75.
40. Dale Spender, ed., *Time and Tide Wait for No Man* (London: Pandora Press, 1984), p. 7.
41. Batsleer et al, p. 160.
42. E. Upward, *In the Thirties* (London: Heinemann, 1962), p. 42.
43. R. Williams, *Politics and Letters,* p. 44.
44. G. Pechey, p. 72.

F. R. Leavis and *Scrutiny*

> The new-comer already threatened to be a nuisance in the shape of rivalry, and was certainly a nuisance in the shape of practical criticism.
>
> George Eliot, *Middlemarch*

Having studied the Marxist antecedents of Kettle and Williams in the last chapter, I will now turn to the other major discourse that has shaped their epistemologies. The *Scrutiny* enterprise, spearheaded by F.R. Leavis, saw itself in the thirties as an *avant garde* oppositional movement which challenged the Establishment – Cambridge University, and the literary press on a range of issues, the chief being the lack of seriousness hitherto attributed to English studies. It is important that at that time, Leavis and *Scrutiny* were not as central as they have subsequently become. The *Scrutiny* position in no sense occupied the central place within the discipline that it came to occupy in the post-War period. For while it not only had the upper hand in the lively and uncompromising debate that it engaged in with the thirties Marxists, it also managed to outlive the decade, lasting well into the fifties. By the 1940s, *Scrutiny* and Leavis were established well enough to exert an almost institutional influence. Leavis's pupils were dispersed all over the country and a sort of Leavisite hegemony took over the practice of literary criticism. The post-War generation believed that the study of literature would exert a humanizing influence, an assumption called into question by George Steiner who points out that "literary values and the utmost of hideous inhumanity could co-exist in the same community, in the same individual sensibility."[1] In spite of the pluralism of literary critical discourses, Leavisism came to stand for a kind of meta-discourse which has been challenged from time to time by New Criticism, structuralism, a variety of Marxisms and more recently, deconstruction but has not yet been displaced completely as a central reference point within English literary criticism.

This chapter includes a brief survey of the history of *Scrutiny*, in the sense of examining what gave rise to this quarterly journal and sustained it over twenty one years of its existence, the range of interests it covered and what factors contribute to its lasting influence. The primary focus, however, is on an attempt to piece together F.R. Leavis's theory of fiction in order to understand the subsequent works of Kettle and Williams and their relation to it.

Leavis relates the inception of *Scrutiny* in 1932 specifically to its Cambridge milieu. He says, "Only at Cambridge could the idea of *Scrutiny* have taken shape. . . . It was . . . . a product, the trimuphant justifying achievement, of the English Tripos."[2] The first editors were L.C. Knights and D.W. Harding who were subsequently joined by F.R. Leavis and Denys Thompson. But to the modern reader, *Scrutiny* evokes associations primarily to the fact that gradually the other editors dispersed to various parts of the country, leaving F.R. and Q.D. Leavis to keep the journal going at Cambridge.

Literary criticism is not the only discourse to be found within the pages of *Scrutiny*. Articles covered various subjects like education, advertising, ballet, architecture, politics, economics and arts among others. Contributors like Wilfrid Mellers wrote brilliant criticism of music whereas Q.D. Leavis criticized cinema for its disruptive influence on the traditional working-class culture. (In fact, this mistrust of contemporary art forms is one of the major weaknesses of the *Scrutiny* position.) As Leavis pointed out in the Manifesto, besides publishing articles on literature and the arts, *Scrutiny* would deal with "various significant aspects of contemporary life."[3] To begin with, *Scrutiny* was as good as its word, keeping an open forum to accommodate varying viewpoints. For instance, it carried reviews by Auden, Edmund Blunden (members of what was later designated "the Gang"). Gradually however, the moment passed and, as C.B. Cox puts it, "the *Scrutiny* attitudes hardened into a creed."[4] In trying to combat the insistent pressure of Marxist ideology during the thirties, *Scrutiny* attitudes came to be associated with a particular ideology that became its specific creed. While not wishing to be labelled, Leavis grudgingly concedes that the *Scrutiny* position could be termed "liberal," not in the sense of *laissez-faire,* but in that it stood for the promotion of a "humane tradition."[5]

Scrutiny's main bone of contention with Left writing was its tendency to subordinate culture to economic and political considerations. A.L. Morton, a Left historian, tried to conciliate Leavis (without any success), by pointing out that the cultural objectives of *Scrutiny* and of socialism were the same.[6] This is not to say that *Scrutiny* did not have its share of the Marxist element, for example L.C. Knights, though this influence disappeared in 1937 when Marxism, in any case, was retreating at all levels. In a bid to remain neutral, *Scrutiny* held a symposium, in accordance with readers's demands in 1939, entitled "The Claims of Politics" featuring eight intellectuals. Though overtly anti-capitalist, it never took to socialism. It aimed for a communism of a wider kind, that is, an "organic community," for as Leavis claimed what has disintegrated is not merely "bourgeois" or "capitalist" civilization, it is the "organic community."[7]

The "organic community" referred to was a past rural community based on natural laws and certain social values that had been destroyed with the advent of industrialization. The "homogeneous society" was now irretrievable though both Leavis and Thompson asserted that keeping the memory of the old order would prove helpful in achieving a new one.[8] This nostalgia for the lost order has laid *Scrutiny* open to censure from various quarters. Kenneth Trodd calls it its "ideological weak-spot."[9] In *The Country and the City,* Williams dismisses it as a pastoral myth while Terry Eagleton calls it "reactionary."

Discarding political commitment as the solution to contemporary problems, *Scrutiny* emphasized the "need to establish a criterion of seriousness"[10] and hoped to achieve its effect by bringing about reform in the educational system. A constant theme throughout its career was:

> the belief that education, a potentially "humanizing" activity, was at present complicit with the "economic process"; that it should be reformed as a centre of opposition to the latter; and that in this effort, the role of literary training was paramount.[11]

Education must be made democratic and hence accessible to a Carlylean "aristocracy of talent" rather than to the privileged few. This concern for revolutionizing education goes back to another distinguished Cambridge don Hector Chadwick and to Matthew Arnold before him. In critical heritage and cultural concerns, Leavis seems to be a direct descendant of Arnold.[12] Not only Arnold, but Leslie Stephen is acknowledged by Q.D. Leavis as one of his precursors:

> He seemed to us to be in the direct line of the best tradition of our literary criticism, to exemplify the principle [sic] virtues of a literary criticism, and to exhibit a tone, a discipline and an attitude that were desirable models to form oneself on.[13]

It is this literary integrity that is the hallmark of Leavisian criticism. By displacing the claims of politics and dismissing the influence of "external general systems" like psychoanalysis, theology or philosophy, he aimed "to vindicate literary criticism as a distinct and separate discipline."[14] He popularized practical criticism of the "words on the page kind" as advocated by I.A. Richards. Leavis dismissed the value-free approach of traditional academic scholarship where the primary concern was with the establishing of "facts" on empirical grounds. The Leavises opposed both "positivist or speculative concerns"[15] in literary studies and called for authentic critical judgement, which Mulhern describes as :

> The typical gesture of Leavisian criticism . . . was recognition . . . and where appropriate, affirmation of what was immanent in the concrete literary word. This criticism was therefore, a form of intuitionism: specifically, it was considered in *the intuition of moral values in literary experience*.[16]

While theoretically Leavis dismisses the claims of positivist and speculative conerns in literary criticism, his own methodology is a blend of both. It is this ambivalence that makes it difficult to categorize Leavis's criticism.

In order to read poetry, Leavis suggests a procedure saying that "Words in poetry invite us not to 'think about' and judge but to 'feel into' or 'become'--'realize a complex experience' that was 'given in the words'."[17] The critic must evaluate the piece before him sensitively and ask the questions "Where does this come? How does this stand in relation to . . . ? How relatively important does it seem?"[18] There should be no given norms according to which a piece is to be evaluated. Leavis was willing to concede that after a set of particular judgements had been made, it was possible to deduce norms from them but such generalizations hardly had any significance in criticism for they encouraged rigidity and mechanical reading. In his own hands, Leavis's critical evaluations are genuine, invigorating as well as flexible whereas in those of his followers, they tend to rigidify into Leavisism.[19]

During the thirties, *Scrutiny* concentrated mainly on discussions of poetry while the novel and drama were relatively marginalized. It was only after 1940, that the balance tilted in favour of the novel and Leavis's essays on George Eliot, Henry James and Joseph Conrad, which had been published in *Scrutiny,* were compiled in *The Great Tradition* (1948). This shift in emphasis is related by Mulhern to the fact that only when the possibility of developing political affiliations had been discounted could "*Scrutiny* turn to . . . the novel."[20]

A study of *The Great Tradition* alone may lead to the impression that Leavis is a shade too eclectic in his re-drawing of the novelistic canon. His later publications, however, prove that his tradition could be broadly categorized as "the English novel from Dickens to Lawrence," (though it should be pointed out that there are basic differences between the traditions of Williams and Leavis, a point to be taken up in a subsequent chapter). Leavis's "tradition" extends as in the case of Dickens, who is seen as primarily an entertainer in *The Great Tradition,* but is later vindicated in a book-length study entitled *Dickens, The Novelist* (1970) and declared as equal in stature with Shakespeare. Lawrence is similarly canonized in the study *D.H. Lawrence, Novelist* (1955).

The Great Tradition opens with the announcement that "The great English novelists are Jane Austen, George Eliot, Henry James and Joseph Conrad." (*TGT,* 9) These writers have been short-listed on the basis of the fact that

> they not only change the possibilities of the art for practitioners and readers, but they are significant in terms of the human awareness they promote; awareness of the possibilities of life. (*TGT,* 2)

Leavis further points out that "to be important historically, is not, of course, to be necessarily one of the significant few." (*TGT,* 3) It is these "significant few" that constitute the tradition, which is a trans-historical category relating the past to the present. With the increasing industrialization of society, traditional conventions disintegrate. As Leavis and Denys Thompson put it :

> What we have lost is the organic community with the living culture it embodied. Folk songs, folk dances . . . an art of life, a way of living.[30]

Hence the survival of a literary tradition becomes all the more important since "the continuity of consciousness, the conservation of the collective experience is the more dependent on it."[22] Only novels of distinction can be included in the "tradition" and writers aspiring to greatness must be, to put it rather simply, innovators in form and must possess a profoundly serious interest in life. (*TGT,* 18) The tradition of the English novel begins with Jane Austen, who provides "an exceptionally illuminating study of the nature of originality, and she exemplifies beautifully the relations of 'the individual talent' to tradition." (*TGT,* 5) The idea of tradition here has close affiliations with T.S. Eliot's theory that the individual is not only part of the tradition, but, however subtly, alters it. While Leavis agreed with Eliot on this score, he rejected the idea of "impersonality," according to which Eliot implies that the poet should submit to the objective demands of tradition and to "certain imputed characteristics of poetic production, in which 'the man who suffers' and 'the mind which created' were ideally 'distinct'."[22]

By focusing attention on *The Great Tradition,* some of the basic concepts of Leavis's fictional theory like "language," "morality and the novel," "affirmation of life" and "the novel as dramatic poem" will be discussed. Referring to Blake in his lecture at the London School of Economics, Leavis says:

> His individuality has developed in terms of the language, with the ways of experiencing as well as of handling experience, that it involves. The mind and sensibility that he has to express are of the language.[23]

Instead of looking for direct social evidence in literature in the manner of Taine, Leavis regards language as an aspect of the social nature of the individual. In this, Leavis was greatly influenced by C.H. Rickword's "Notes on Fiction" in *The Calendar.* Mulhern points out that for Rickword, to speak of "character," "situation" and "incident" was to misconceive the very nature of the novel--for the novel is basically an art of language. According to Leavis, "literary study . . . means a study of the words and their order."[24] For instance, in *The Great Tradition,* Leavis uses this approach, quoting long passages from texts and analyzing the verbal texture closely. But linguistic dexterity is not the sole criterion for Leavis, in whose work there is a close juxtaposition of the moral and the aesthetic. The form of the book is moulded by the moral preoccupation of the author.

In *The Great Tradition,* however, the main criteria of greatness in novelists are their "vital capacity for experience, a kind of reverent openness before life, and a marked moral intensity." (*TGT*, 9) By contrasting Flaubert's preoccupation with formal perfection on account of which he falls short of achieved greatness, with Jane Austen's "moral preoccupations," (*TGT,* 8) Leavis seems to be privileging the moral over the aesthetic. David Lodge, however, shifts the emphasis to the other end of the scale:

> In the last analysis, literary critics can claim special authority not as witnesses to the moral value of works of literature, but as explicators and judges of effective communication, of "realization."[25]

What he suggests is that critics should allow the aesthetic experience to control and modify the moral perspective. Though Leavis tries to see the moral and the aesthetic as complementary, yet the emphasis inevitably falls on the moral. Of Jane Austen, Leavis says, "The vitality of her art is a matter of a preoccupation with moral problems that is subtle and intense because of the pressure of personal need." (*TGT,* 32) Similarly George Eliot is praised on account of her "profound insight into the moral nature of man." (*TGT,* 123) As R.P. Bilan points out :

> There can be no significant form apart from this kind of radical moral inquiry into life, and the organization that results--the inclusive scheme--is that of the moral fable or moral pattern.[26]

It is with reference to *Hard Times* that Leavis defines the moral fable, even though *Nostromo, The Secret Agent, The Europeans* and *The Portrait of a Lady* are all described as "moral fables." He defines it, saying that:

> in it the intention is peculiarly insistent, so that the representative significance of everything in the fable--character, episode and so on--is immediately apparent as we read. (*TGT,* 227)

By "moral fable," Leavis does not mean its didactic aspect nor does he mean that a moral essence is deducible from the work of art. For Leavis, 'in a successful work . . . values are not stated but enacted by the whole work; the concept of "enactment" is at the centre of Leavis's thinking about morality and the novel.'[27] Q.D. Leavis, in her last public engagement at the Cheltenham Festival Annual Literature Lecture in 1980 stresses the distinction saying that "the English novel had from its start an essentially and profoundly moral (I dont mean moralistic) framework and intention."[28] Bilan points out that the distinguishing feature of a "moral fable" is its insistence on "concentrated, or inclusive significance" and that "the characters in the novel are limited to their place in this scheme."[29] The latter is seen as a drawback by Bilan who says that it is the typical way in which Leavis deals with character, that is, referring to the values they represent whereas ideally, "exploration of character as well as values . . . must be given their due."[30]

The affirmation of life is the other major concept in Leavis's novel criticism. The Lawrentian influence is evident from the fact that Leavis quotes approvingly from the former's *Letters* saying, "one must speak of life and growth amid all this mass of destruction and disintegration." (*TGT,* 26) It is not an abstract concept of life that Leavis is looking for, but life as presented in concrete terms.

The test of excellence in fiction depends not on the values depicted but on the way the values are enacted and dramatized. Praising *Nostromo,* Leavis says:

> The impressiveness lies in the vivid reality of the things we are made to see and hear, and the significance they get from their relations in a highly organized and vididly realized whole.(*TGT,* 196-7)

The focus in thus on the experience of life communicated by literature. This vitality is a positive quality that Leavis picks out in his assessment of *Hard Times.* Talking about the contrast between Sissy the "dark eyed and dark-haired" girl and Bitzer "so unwholesomely deficient in natural tinge," (*TGT,* 230) Leavis points out:

> The moral and spiritual terms are rendered here in terms of sensation, so that the symbolic intention emerges out of metaphor and the vivid evocation of the concrete. . . . Sissy stands for this vitality as well as goodness . . . she is generous impulsive life. (*TGT,* 230-31)

But obviously this presentation of life is very different from that referred to by critics who consider that "the mark of the master is external abundance--he gives you lots of life." (*TGT,* 227) But the "life" Leavis values "must be controlled art."[31] Great art is recognizable by the "awareness of the possibilities of life" (*TGT,* 2) that it engenders as also by the "human potentialities" (*TGT,* 12) that it celebrates. Thus the novelists with a positive attitude to life are elevated to canonical status. But as Bilan rightly points out, this is not to suggest that Leavis is advocating the novel with a happy ending, for even though *The Portrait of a Lady* is tragic, the final result is the affirmation of human values.[32] The problem with this concept arises when Leavis tends to make it the universal criterion of value. For instance he "struggles" to present Conrad, with reference to *Nostromo,* as an "affirmer of life"[33] when there are hardly any positive values in it.

This touchstone of "life affirmation" is brought from the realm of drama to that of the novel. It explains to an extent Leavis's formulation of the novel as a "dramatic poem." Leavis designates Henry James as a poet-novelist not because of his use of symbolism but because of "the determining and controlling interests in his art engage what is 'deepest' in him (he being a man of exceptional capacity for experience), appeal to what is deepest in us." (*TGT,* 128) Similarly, Dickens is regarded as a poetic dramatist on account of "the possibilities of concentration and flexibility in the interpretation of life such as we associate with Shakespearean drama." (*TGT,* 242) In both cases the emphasis is on the capacity to respond to life, to interpret it and finally to transmute it into art with great linguistic dexterity.

The other quality that Leavis admired in a writer's craft is her/his maturity which is closely tied up with impersonality as opposed to the "ego" when the writer is unable to distantiate her/himself from the work of art. This comes across most strongly in the analysis of George Eliot whose work fluctuates "between the poised impersonal insight of a finely tempered wisdom and something like the emotional confusions and self-importances of adolescence." (*TGT,* 75)

In spite of the basic ideological difference between Leavis on the one hand, and Kettle and Williams on the other, there are visible links in their critical practice in some respects. The three critics share a common profession and their literary criticism is based on their teaching practice. Kettle and Leavis are both primarily critics and their achievement does not include creative writing. Their methodology is not theory-centred but based on an analysis of specific texts.

Kettle has adopted certain key concepts used by Leavis, not *in toto* but with certain modifications. "Moral fable" is one of them. In the Preface to *An Introduction to the English Novel,Vol.I,* Kettle says:

> I have used throughout the book to describe a particular kind of novel the term "moral fable." The phrase, as far as I know, is Defoe's, but it has been used and . . . developed in recent years by Dr. F.R. Leavis.[34]

A detailed discussion of Kettle's use of the term will be found in the following chapter. Here, it is sufficient to point out the connection. In general terms, Kettle's use of "life" and "experience" recall Leavis's criteria of judging great novelists according to their "vital capacity for experience, a kind of reverent openness before life, and a marked moral intensity." (*TGT,* 9) Kettle further shares with Leavis the terms "concrete" and "positive values." His use of "concrete" is evident in the following passage:

> the realization is intensely concrete: we seem to smell the kitchen of *Wuthering Heights*, to feel the force of the wind across the moors, to sense the very changes of the seasons. Such concreteness is achieved not by mistiness but by precision.[35]

Kettle's "positive values" amounts to life-enhancing values which in turn is roughly equivalent to Leavis's "human values."

In the early years of the Second World War, when Williams was first at Cambridge, he reminisces that Bloomsbury and *Scrutiny* were both commonly dismissed as a "bourgeois cult."[36] Yet the article he wrote for the Socialist Club bulletin was entitled "Literature and the Cult of Sensibility" and in retrospect Williams admits that "one key term in Leavis's criticism had obviously filtered through to me."[37] This instance is symptomatic of the whole Leavis-Williams relationship which in lay terms would count as one alternating between love-hate, censure-praise. When Williams started his journal *Politics and Letters* in post-War Cambridge, the guideline behind its inception was to "unite radical left politics with Leavisite literary criticism."[38] Williams was attracted to Leavis on account of his "cultural radicalism," "practical criticism" and his "great stress on education."[39]

Reading and Criticism (1950) is generally regarded as a restatement of Leavis's critical judgement and in the Preface to this book, Williams acknowledges his debt to Leavis and *Scrutiny* "for the intelligent development of critical analysis as an educational discipline."[40] As Watson points out, "the title of his book clearly implies the equation that Leavis had made a decade earlier: 'the ideal critic is the ideal reader'."[41] Even though Williams argues that the methods of practical criticism suitable to analyzing poems cannot be carried over into the novel, yet the Leavisite influence is apparent in his particular pronouncements. For example, in the introductory note, he says that "criticism is concerned with evaluation, with comparison, and with standards."[42] The final paragraph in *Reading and Criticism* is again a restatement of the Leavis position, "Literature is communication in written *language.... The importance* to the quality of our lives of a rich, vital and constantly renewed language is inestimable."[43]

The other common ground of interest that Williams shares with Leavis is "tradition." Both believe that it is not something that is handed down from one generation to the next but is a highly selective process that needs to be revised by each subsequent generation. Kettle and Williams also share with Leavis a concern for the "specific Englishness"[44] of the novel. In practice, all three critics have a problem dealing with modern fiction though in each case for different reasons, a question to be dealt with in later chapters. When not adequately synthesized, the pull towards Leavis and that towards Marxist ideology marks the tendency towards idealism and materialism that is discernible from time to time in their works.

In reviewing the achievement of Leavis and *Scrutiny*, it is necessary to summarize the merits and demerits of their enterprise. Critics of *Scrutiny* generally draw attention to the fact that the "Scrutineers" assumed the role of the conscience-keepers of public morality in what they termed a "technologico-Benthamite" (Leavis's phrase) society, based on the query, "If *Scrutiny* doesn't do something about it, who else is likely to?"[45] This made them authoritarian and closed to other points of view. It resulted in a failure to select and appreciate good contemporary literature for they firmly believed that "a Fall had taken place round about the end of the 1920s."[42] It also induced them to take a rather condescending and simplisitic view of Marxism, believing that it meant a subordination of the individual to the economic.

Leavis's criticism often borders on the cryptic and intuitive. For example, he says:

> Jane Austen, in fact, is the inaugurator of the great tradition of the English novel and by "great tradition" I mean the tradition to which what is great in English fiction belongs. (*TGT*, 7)

This idealist position has called into question the very nature of the validity of practical criticism. However, to be fair to Leavis an examination of the following passage is essential.

> For to insist that literary criticism is, or should be, a specific discipline of intelligence is not to suggest that a serious interest in literature can confine itself to the kind of intensive local analysis associated with "practical criticism" to the scrutiny of the "words on the page" in their minute relations, their effects of imagery and so on; a real interest is an interest in man, society and civilization, and its boundaries cannot be drawn.[47]

Leavis thus reveals the full potential range of his project – one that has often been narrowly interpreted.

The major importance of Leavis lies in the fact that he was able to establish the centrality of English studies whereas previously it had often been regarded as a non-serious discipline to be palmed off on dilletantes and women. Leavis emphasized the fact that "literary criticism is not a mystic rapture but a process of the intelligence"[48] and that it was not only "a discipline . . . but a social and moral force."[49] The reason for *Scrutiny's* success can be attributed to the fact that the "Scrutineers" were single-minded and consistent in their purpose.

Leavis has thus had a great impact on the reading habits of the English speaking public for "criticism, when it performs its function, not merely expresses and defines the contemporary sensibility, it helps to form it."[50] And even if practical criticism now seems "provincial and etiolated":

> our present and larger critical situation cannot be understood except as the outcome of contradictions within its underlying philosophical--or aggressively *anti*-philosophical position.[51]

A direct offshoot and extension of this position is what is termed "Left Leavisism" by Terry Eagleton in connection with his teacher Raymond Williams's critical practice. In fact, Williams has pointed out that his concept of "structure of feeling" was conceived as an attempt to overcome the weaknesses of the Leavisite and the "vulgar" Marxist positions. Recognizing this conjuncture as Left-Leavisism, Pechey says that "the criticism of Arnold Kettle stands as a demonstration that this label may be worn without shame,"[52] thus negating the negative connotations linked to the term by Eagleton. The implications and validity of Pechey's statement will be the subject of a detailed discussion in the next chapter.

NOTES

1. *Language and Silence* (Harmondsworth: Penguin, 1969), p. 83.
2. F.R. Leavis "*Scrutiny:* A Retrospect," *Scrutiny*, XX (Cambridge University Press, 1963), p. 1.
3. F.R. Leavis, "*Scrutiny*: A Manifesto," Eric Bentley, ed., *The Importance of Scrutiny* (New York: University Press, 1964), p. 4.
4. C.B. Cox, "*Scrutiny*: A Revaluation," *Spectator,* Oct. 25, 1963, p. 531.
5. F.R. Leavis, "Retrospect of a Decade (1940)," *A Selection from Scrutiny,* Vol. I, p. 175.
6. F. Mulhern, *The Moment of Scrutiny* (London: NLB, 1979), pp. 66-67.
7. F.R. Leavis, "A Serious Artist," *Scrutiny*, I, 2, Sept, 1932, p. 177.

8. Mulhern, p. 59.
9. Kenneth Trodd, "*Scrutiny* in the 30s," *The Review,* Nos. 11-12, p. 10.
10. Denys Thompson, "What Shall We Teach?," *Scrutiny,* VII, 4, March 1939, p. 404.
11. Mulhern, p. 101.
12. Like Arnold, Leavis felt that an educated minority was necessary to safeguard the cultural standards of the nation.
13. Mulhern, p. 129.
14. F.R. Leavis, *The Common Pursuit* (Harmondsworth: Penguin, 1978), p. 212.
15. Mulhern, p. 157.
16. *Ibid.*, p. 171.
17. "Literary Criticism and Philosophy: A Reply," VI, 1, June 1937, pp. 60-61.
18. *Ibid.*, p. 61.
19. Williams, *Politics and Letters,* p. 68.
20. Mulhern, p. 218.
21. *Ibid.*, p. 117.
22. *Ibid.*, p. 132.
23. *The Common Pursuit,* p. 124.
24. Bentley, "The Importance of *Scrutiny,*" in Walsh, p. 96.
25. David Lodge, *The Language of Fiction* (London: Routledge and Kegan Paul, 1966), p. 68.
26. R.P. Bilan, *The Literary Criticism of F.R. Leavis* (Cambridge: University Press, 1979, p. 124.
27. *Loc. cit.*
28. Q.D. Leavis, *Collected Essays,* G. Singh, ed., (Cambridge: University Press, 1983), p. 310.
29. Bilan, p. 119.
30. *Ibid.*, p. 120.
31. *Ibid.*, p. 119.
32. *Ibid.*, p. 127.
33. *Ibid.*, p. 128.
34. Williams, *Politics and Letters,* p. 265.
35. *Ibid.*, p. 13.
36. *Ibid.*, p. 139.
37. *Loc. cit.*

38. *Politics and Letters*, p. 44.
39. *Loc. cit.*
40. *Ibid.*, p. 65.
41. *Loc. cit.*
42. *Ibid.*, p. 66.
43. *Reading and Criticism*, p. 3.
44. *Ibid.*, p. 107.
45. *The English Novel*, p. 122.
46. Q.D. Leavis, "Charlotte Yonge and Christian Discrimination," (1944) *A Selection from Scrutiny*, Vol. I, p. 159.
47. Williams, *Problems in Materialism and Culture*, pp. 17-18.
48. *The Common Pursuit*, p. 200.
49. Q.D. Leavis, "Leslie Stephen: Cambridge Critic," *A Selection from Scrutiny*, Vol. I, p. 25.
50. Bentley, ed., *The Importance of Scrutiny*, XXVI.
51. Cox, "*Scrutiny:* A Revaluation," p. 532.
52. Graham Pechey, "*Scrutiny*, English Marxism and the work of Raymond Williams," *Literature and History*, Vol. 11, 1, Spring 1983, p. 65.

Arnold Kettle

Kettle's book *An Introduction to the English Novel, Vols. I and II* has had international currency, yet it is worth recording that he has not had that central influence within the British academic world that is attributable to Leavis. There could be several reasons for this. First, unlike Leavis, Kettle did not have a journal which he could use as a platform for disseminating his ideas (it might be argued that he had been on the editorial board of *Marxism Today* until recently, yet his influence was not of the dominant kind that characterized Leavis's in relation to *Scrutiny,* nor was he located at Oxbridge the traditional centre of British academia but in provincial universities which perhaps relegated his enterprise to the sidelines. The general assumptions underlying Kettle's critical practice may be broadly defined as liberal humanist. Since Kettle's approach is eclectic and moderate, it does not command the attention that radical theories are liable to. For example, the more recent influential contemporary books on literary theory like Tony Bennett's *Formalism and Marxism* (1978), Catherine Belsey's *Critical Practice* (1980), and Eagleton's *Literary Theory* (1983) do not include a reference to him.

Roughly speaking, Kettle's writing career can be said to span a period of forty three years, if one takes as a starting point his article "Marxism and Literature," written as a student at Cambridge and published in *University Forward* in 1939, to its culmination in the Course Units on the nineteenth century novel at the Open University in 1982, when he retired after a long career as a teacher. His publications include a range of subjects from literature to education, politics, book and film reviews. Kettle's major book, however, is *An Introduction to the English Novel, Vols. I, II* (1951, 53) though he has also written *Karl Marx, Founder of Modern Communism* (1963, second ed. 1968) which has been translated into Norwegian, Italian and Swedish. Another book that is not so well known is Kettle's *Communism and the*

Intellectuals(1965). He has edited *Shakespeare in a Changing World* (1964) and *The Nineteenth Century Novel: Critical Essays and Documents* (1972, revised ed. 1981), the rest of his output being evident in articles and lectures for the Open University. *An Introduction to the English Novel, Vols. I, II* has attained wide currency all over the world, wherever English is spoken and taught. According to Margot Kettle, his wife, it is recommended in schools and colleges in Australia. Similarly, it is available in most college libraries and bookshops in India. Hutchinson have, moreover, published a cheap edition for students costing ten rupees which is approximately sixty five pence in sterling. In terms of popularity, I would rank it above *The Great Tradition* and Walter Allen's *The English Novel* even though it belongs to the same category, that is, a basic authoritative book on the English novel. The reason for this is that *The Great Tradition* is too selective whereas *The English Novel* is too general. Morever, *The Great Tradition*, like *The English Novel from Dickens to Lawrence* is primarily structured on specific authors whereas *An Introduction to the English Novel, Vols. I, II* deals more overtly with specific texts, that is, "Emily Bronte: *Wuthering Heights* (1847)," "George Eliot: *Middelmarch* (1871-72)."

It is perhaps for this reason that the book is so popular in India, where the whole educational system is exam-oriented and to show familiarity with and quote from an English author is a definite advantage. Secondly, the style is simple, direct and easily comprehensible – a major plus point in the Indian context where the majority of students receive their first initiation into the English language in or after class V. This clearly fulfils Kettle's intention of reaching out to as many people as possible and he admits that "its great advantage is that students understand it."[1] Most students and even teachers in India seem, however, to be unaware of the Marxist background of the book. The main reason for this could be the lack of Marxist awareness within the Indian political scene and secondly, the "tone" is not overtly Marxist for as Kettle puts it, "The last thing I had in mind was to write Marxist literary criticism."[2]

However, Kettle himself does not regard *An Introduction to the English Novel* as his claim to fame:

> More than anything else I would like to be associated with the material I have prepared for the Open University. That has been my most productive period and a task I was most suited to do.[3]

The fact that these units would hardly be accessible to students outside Britain, indicates that Kettle considers himself an educationist first and only then a literary critic. By taking this keen interest in education, he hoped "to help people improve their lives, to become more politically conscious . . . [to discover] new possibilities."[4] Even as a literary critic, he has practical aims, that is, to help people enjoy the study of literature and to help the "reader to re-examine and question some quite basic assumptions in their way of reading."[5]

In writing *An Introduction to the English Novel, Vol. I, II,* Kettle did not consciously try to synthesize Leavisite and Marxist positions both of which were in the forefront in the thirties Cambridge milieu. But Kettle acknowledges his debt to Alick West, recognizing him as:

> the main single influence on me because he too combined this great respect for literature because of its quality of the use of language and the need to analyse particular pieces of literature rather than to make general statements about them and this he combined with a Marxist outlook.[6]

This is not to ignore Leavis's influence for as Kettle says, "although Leavis did not have a progressive attitude, yet he took literature seriously and he was concerned to link the judgement of literature to the judgement and values of life."[7] *The Great Tradition* is almost a central reference point for most critics of fiction (Williams, Eagleton) and Kettle is not free from the influence as the editors of *The Uses of Fiction* point out that Kettle incorporated central elements of that sequence, such as *The Portrait of a Lady* (which had been virtually nobody's book and now became everybody's book)."[8] Kettle also agrees with Leavis that literature though affected by ideology was more than ideology and "has a reality of its own."[9]

Apart from being labelled a Left-Leavisite, Kettle is also called an orthodox Marxist by George Steiner in his essay "Marxism and the Literary Critic." Steiner makes a distinction between orthodox Marxists and "para-Marxists," using Michael Crouzet's phrase.[10] These distinctions are based on the one hand on Engels's letters to Margaret

Harkness (1885, 1888) stating that "the more the opinions of the author remain hidden, the better for the work of art"[11] while on the other hand, on Lenin's essay "Party Organization and Party literature" (*Novaia Jizn*, Nov. 1905) proclaiming that "Literature must become part of the general cause of the proletariat."[12] Steiner defines the "para-Marxists":

> But however committed they may be to dialectical materialism, para-Marxists approach a work of art with respect for its integrity and for the vital centre of its being. They are at one with Engels in regarding as inferior the kinds of literature which, in Keats's phrase, have a palpable design upon us.[13]

It might seem that this definition is easily applicable to the approach of Kettle and hence he should be rightly placed with the para-Marxists who include Lukacs, Goldmann and Benjamin. But Kettle's position is, in fact, somewhere between the two for he shares with the orthodox Marxists the view that the Party must exert suitable pressures on the regulation of artistic activity.[14] Hence it appears that Kettle's position is a kind of *via media* between the two fundamental principles that affect Marxist literary theory. To test the validity of this hypothesis, we will turn to an analysis of *An Introduction to the English Novel.*

This book exemplifies Kettle's attempt to trace the trajectory of the English novel over the three centuries of its development. He deals with the question of the emergence of the English novel and the conditions which contributed to its development. Kettle's book, in two volumes, is further subdivided into separate parts, each dealing with a specific period. Volume I consists of three parts, the first entitled the "Introductory" defines categories like "life and pattern," "realism and romance" which are the basic tools of his analysis. Part II is devoted to an analysis of the eighteenth century novel and introduces the concept of the "moral fable." The final part concentrates on the nineteenth century novel discussing specific texts rather than making general statements about the *corpus* of a particular writer's work. For example, he discusses *Emma* rather than giving an overview of Jane Austen's writings. He then takes up the *The Heart of Midlothian* followed by a very perceptive analysis of Dickens's *Oliver Twist*, Emily Bronte's *Wuthering Heights* rounding off the volume with George Eliot's *Middlemarch.* Volume II is similarly divided into two parts--the first dealing with the "last Victorians," Henry James, Samuel Butler and Thomas Hardy while the second focuses on the "first quarter" of the twentieth century including writers like Joseph Conrad, D.H. Lawrence, James Joyce and E.M. Forster. It also devotes a chapter to writers as diverse as Arnold Bennett, H.G. Wells, John Galsworthy and Virginia Woolf. The third part takes us into the "second quarter" of the century, drawing attention to Aldous Huxley, Graham Greene, Joyce Cary, Ivy Compton-Burnett, concluding with Henry Green's *Party Going.* The reason for cataloguing this long list is to emphasize the range of Kettle's interest. Unlike Leavis and Williams, he includes the eighteenth and twentieth century novels. His "tradition" is hardly narrow nor can it be said to overlook the achievement of twentieth century writers, a problem that is exemplified in the works of both Leavis and Williams.

Kettle defines the novel as "a realistic prose fiction complete in itself and of a certain length." (*I*, 26) This broad but vague definition may be somewhat clarified by Kettle's definition of realism. According to him, "realism means being 'relevant to real life' as opposed to romance, escapism, wishful thinking, unrealism." (*I*, 28) For instance, he defines *Gulliver's Travels* as realistic, because even though it has a large percentage of fantasy, "it has to do with the actual problems and values of life." (*I*,28) This yardstick again is rather vague in that it can be invoked to categorize almost any kind of writing as "realistic." Realism, for Kettle, is not only evaluative but a generic term as well. It differs from naturalism in that while naturalism is almost equivalent to photographic representation, realism probes the surface appearance to get to the underlying essence.

He attributes the rise of the novel in eighteenth century England to a number of factors.[15] Its emergence could be seen as a realistic reaction to the tales of medieval romance prevalent in the sixteenth and seventeenth centuries: or it could be put down to the rise of a wide reading public, for whom the novel was the perfect form of entertainment; or the novel form could be said to have grown with the rise of the middle-classes. While none of these alternatives constitutes the absolute truth, the seventeenth century revolution is an important factor, for it destroyed feudalism and ushered in the era of the bourgeoisie. According to Kettle:

> great revolutions in human society change men's consciousness and revolutionize not only their social relationships, but their outlook, their philosophy and their art. (*I*, 28)

Here Kettle's theory of the relationship between the literary and historical development seems rather close to the position of the orthodox Marxists. It implies a one to one base/superstructure model that overlooks the complexity of "uneven development," "mediation" and "over-determination." However, Elmer Borlund says that "readers who feel that Marxist criticism is necessarily dogmatic should read Kettle's chapter on Bunyan or his eloquent essay on *The Portrait of a Lady*."[16]

For Kettle, the value of great literature lies in its capacity to change men's consciousness. Art does not have any direct impact on social change but by changing our perceptions, it indirectly encourages the process. It does not solve problems but is in itself a solution. As Kettle points out:

> And indeed it is foolish to talk glibly of the "solution" offered by a work of art, the experience of the work of art is in itself a kind of solution, a synthesis, a discovery of the nature of the problem (*II*, 74)

Literature is not primarily concerned with knowledge but with the imagination. For example, *Uncle Tom's Cabin* may direct the reader's attention to certain facts regarding the question of human freedom, yet *Wuthering Heights* is a greater novel because it "can change men's *consciousness* and make them aware of what they had not even guessed." (*I*, 13) Kettle seems to be judging value according to the affective power of a novel--a criterion that is highly subjective and variable for each reader is affected according to his individual and cultural experience. (However, this issue was not a live one at the time he was writing.) Besides, how is this effect achieved?

In order to answer this question, an examination of Kettle's critical methodology is necessary. In Kettle's view, instead of judging the novel under various headings of "character," "plot" or "narrative," it is best to get an overall view of the book: "We have to see each novel whole before we can attempt to assess the parts or even to decide the criteria relevant to our judgement." (*I*, 7) It must be judged in terms of its "relevance to life" (*I*, 12) but it is the novel to be judged rather than its author's intentions or the general philosophical principles underlying it. Evidently the *modus operandi* is Leavisite but it is worth asking how far these guidelines are followed consistently in Kettle's practice. It would appear that there are frequent lapses into a simplistic Marxist outlook that, for example, makes him reject George Eliot's world-view in *Middlemarch* as being deterministic (*I*, 173) and hence weakening the novel. Kettle believes that the novel must not be judged according to extra-literary criteria like sociology, psychology or philosophy. The best method would be to incorporate extra-literary criteria with the criteria derived from the work itself. Kettle's method consists in first finding out what kind of novel a particular work is, what it is about and finally taking the cue from the book itself.

Central to Kettle's theory is the concept of the life-pattern relationship. These elements, separable and yet inseparable are essential to any great novel. Novels must be able to transmit a sense of life. But "the good novel does not simply convey life, it says something about life. It reveals some kind of pattern in life. It brings significance." (*I*, 13) Kettle defines pattern as that "quality of a book which gives it wholeness and meaning, makes the reading of it a complete and satisfying experience." (*I*, 14) In great novels the synthesis and balance of these two elements is perfectly achieved. Life and pattern sound remarkably like the conventional labels of content and form but Kettle reminds us that this is not so:

> "Form" is important only in so far as it enhances significance, and it will enhance significance just in so far as it bears a real relation to, that is to say symbolizes or clarifies, the aspect of life that is being conveyed. (*I*, 15)

Pattern is the direct outcome of the writer's vision. How a writer will select and present his material depends on his point of view. His knowledge does not matter to the extent his sensibility does for that regulates even his sentence construction. Here again, the Leavisite influence is evident.

Kettle believes that the artistic vision of a writer can transcend his conscious philosophy as in the case of Scott who as a "benign aristocrat" was able to adopt the viewpoint of the peasantry. (*I*, 114) The connections with Lukacs are evident, who, following Engels, called Balzac a great writer on the grounds that for all his sympathies with the aristocracy, he was able to attain a progressive understanding. By emphasizing this aspect, Kettle seems to be substantiating the fact of the autonomy of art and the individuality of the writer who is a character in history.

Parallels with Engels and Lukacs are further in evidence if an examination is made of his remarks on the art of sucessful characterization. For in order to portray life realistically, a novelist needs to portray characters who are individuals and at the same time more than individuals, that is "types." To Kettle:

> The artistic type . . . is not an average, not a lowest common multiple of human characteristics, but rather the embodiment of certain forces which come together in a particular social situation to create a peculiar kind of vital energy. (*I*, 157)

Here one is reminded of Engels's letter to Minna Kautsky when, congratulating her on her characterization, he says "Each of them is a type but at the same time also a definite individual."[17] Lukacs has developed and explained this concept at greater length:

> The central category and criteria of realist literature is the type, a particular synthesis which organically binds together the general and the particular both in characters and situations. What makes a type a type is not its average quality, nor its mere individual being, however profoundly conceived; what makes it a type is that in all the humanly and socially essential determinants are present in their highest level of development, in the ultimate unfolding of the possibilities latent in them . . . rendering concrete the peaks and limits of men and epochs.[18]

Even though Lukacs was fairly esoteric at that time Kettle mentions him in *An Introduction of the English Novel, Vol. I.* As Kettle refers to Lukacs, it is evident that he was familiar with his first book to be translated into English, *Studies in European Realism*, which was published in 1950. According to Lukacs:

> The *typical* is not to be confused with the *average* (though there are cases where this holds true), not with the *eccentric* (though the typical does as a rule go beyond the normal). A character is typical, in this technical sense, when his innermost being is determined by objective forces at work in society.[19]

It is significant that the concept of "type" originated from Balzac's letter to Eve Hanska, written in 1834:

> Also, in the *Etudes de moeurs,* there will be *individuals* treated as types, and in the *Etudes philosophiques* there will be *types* depicted as *individuals*. Thus I shall have brought all aspects of life, the type by individualizing it, the individual by typifying him. I shall have invested the fragment with thought and given to thought the life of an individual.[20]

This concept, as we have seen, has been taken up by Engels and further developed by Lukacs and is germane to Kettle's "life/pattern" relationship. Lukacs, however, has defined this concept in a complex way according to the dimensions of the "breadth *(Breite),* essentiality *(Wesentlichkeit),* enhancement *(Steigerung),* and self-awareness (Selbsbawusstheit)."[21] Demetz explains that by breadth, Lukacs means that "the writer must equip the hero with a number of tangible details and specific character traits" and "in order to be essential, the literary type must, in its individuation, substantially represent the dominant forces of changing society."[22] "Enhancement" and the capacity to depict "potential or latent character of a situation that has not yet developed and is only remotely suggested in present reality" while "self-awarenes" implies that "the type must clearly articulate his connection with the essential and make himself a sounding board for universal propositions."[23] Without going into the loopholes of these criteria, it is clear that Kettle has not thought of these philosophical implications.

In general terms, "life" and "pattern" constitute the Leavisite strand in Kettle's *oeuvre* and as mentioned in the previous chapter, these are not the only terms. "Life" can be said to symbolize the experiential aspect of art whereas pattern can be taken as its ethical angle. The other Leavisite terms that are recurrent in Kettle's works are "moral fable," "positive values" and "symbolic quality."

In the development of the early English novel, Kettle traces two parallel trends--that of the moral fable and non-allegorical fiction. Kettle regards Defoe and Nashe as pioneers of the non-allegorical tradition. Unlike the exponents of the moral fable, their concern is with the surface texture of life and not with the moral significance behind it. Instead of judging and evaluating bourgeois morality, these writers merely observe and record it. Among the precursors of this tradition rank the writers of the picaresque. The picaresque novel was born because early bourgeois man had not found his roots, nor did he know what he was up against. As such, his literary adventures had to be a series of disconnected events, lacking a central pattern. Kettle says:

> Just as a moral fable fails unless the writer imbues his original concept with the stuff of life, so will the non-allegorical novel, which begins with the writer's undefined "sense of life" fails unless he gives his "slice of life" a moral significance, a satisfying pattern. (*I*, 23)

In the moral fable, pattern is the dominant factor. Here the central discovery seems to have been made by the writer prior to his conception of the book. This can illustrate an idea, a precept or a view of life. But if the philosophy of life is over-simplified or not wholly true, the whole structure will crumble. So, in order to avoid this, the writer should illustrate a "truth" so profound that it can withstand deep probing. Alternately, it should fill his creation with the breath of life in such a way that the fable transcends the idea that evoked it. While evaluating a novel, one should concentrate on the work itself rather than on the moral principle behind it. The writer of a moral fable faces an additional danger of beginning with a prior conception and of trying to mould his matter to illustrate it. This would result in an inadequate expression of life. And as we have seen, for Kettle, the sense of life is of paramount importance. For example, Kettle admits that Swift's philosophy is sterile, yet *Gulliver's Travels* succeeds because of the "vitality of his observation." (*I*, 19)

The moral fable is different from "moral discovery" as used by Conrad. According to Conrad, some kind of "moral discovery" should be the object of "every tale." (*II*, 63) This discovery is made in the "very act of artisitic creation" (*II*, 63) whereas in the moral fable the discovery has already been made. Kettle describes *Tess of the d'Urbervilles* as a moral fable because "it is the expression of a generalized human situation in history" (*II*, 48) as opposed to being "a purely personal tragedy" or a "philosophic comment on life in general and the fate of woman in particular." (*II*, 48) At the beginning of this chapter, this book is referred to as a *roman a these* and it might seem at first sight that this could be equated with the moral fable. However, there is a crucial difference, for the thesis of the novel may not be moral, but for either to be successful, it must be infused with the breath of "life." Yet "life" in itself is not enough, for it must be complemented with "pattern." Secondly, this vitality must be controlled by art for Kettle attributes the weakness of Godwin's *Caleb Williams* to the fact that "the vitality it brings the book is a sort of hysteria, something uncontrolled, unrealized, neurotic." (*I*, 54) This once again takes us back to Leavis's belief that life "must be controlled art."[24]

Kettle's preoccupation with "life is not only traceable to Leavis but to Virginia Woolf, Henry James and D.H. Lawrence as well. He discusses Woolf's comment that "life escapes " (*II*, 93) in the work of Bennett, Wells and Galsworthy. For her, the presentation of minute and accurate details does not constitute "life," for life is not "a series of gig lamps symmetrically arranged, life is a luminous halo, a semi-transparent envelope."[25] Kettle applauds her capacity to present "a certain intimate quality of felt life." (*II*, 93) In his chapter on Lawrence's *The Rainbow,* Kettle quotes form Henry James's *The Ambassadors,* "Live all you can; it is a mistake not to." (*II*, 115) He refers to Lawrence as having said in the *Phoenix*: "To be alive, to be man alive, to be whole man alive; that is the point." (*II*, 115) Commenting on the work of these two very different writers, Kettle points out that its value lies:

> in this passionate striving after life and the sense in both that the world into which they and their characters are pitched denies the potentialities of living. It is this positive sense of human aspiration which goes so far to counteract the unsatisfactory–and indeed life-denying – elements in their own philosophies. (*II*, 115)

It is clear that the concept of "life" has a positive connotation and often Kettle uses the term "positive values" to indicate his appreciation of a particular aspect of a novel whether in terms of character or in terms of the writer's conscious philosophy. Kettle defines it as "life-enhancing values very much in terms of changing historical and social reality."[26] For example, Heathcliff is seen as an embodiment of moral superiority because he is "a conscious rebel," and is able to carry the positive values of human aspiration on his shoulders." (*I*, 14) But a mere presentation of these values is not enough. As Kettle points out:

> The weakness of all Forster's novels lies in a failure to dramatize quite convincingly the positive values which he has to set against the destroyers of the morality of the heart. (*II*, 45)

Kettle rejects the emphasis of "life" in favour of "living." For "life" by itself is an abstract concept whereas Kettle is a believer in the "concrete" depiction of experience and characters and he measures the success of a writer in relation to his achievement of this "concreteness." *Wuthering Heights* is distinguished by this characteristic and it is achieved "not by mistiness but by precision." (*I*, 139) Precision does not mean "naturalistic description" (*I*, 140) in the sense of minute details nor does it mean that the writer should work in certain ideas. What it indicates is the use of symbols, "concepts which have significance and validity on a level different from that of logical thought." (*I*, 140)

"Symbolic" is another term of value found in the work of Kettle. To him:

> The symbolic novel is an advance on the moral fable just in the sense that a symbol can be richer--can touch more of life--than an abstract moral concept. (*I*, 140)

A symbol stands for something beyond the immediate referent and therefore, it adds an extra dimension to a specific work. As Kettle points out, in *Ulysses*, "Father Conmee and the 'viceroy'–besides contributing to the Dublin scene have a symbolic importance: they represent the Church and the State." (*II*, 131) Similarly, the symbolic quality of *The Portrait of a Lady*, contributes to the fact that the characters "though unmistakably individuals, are more than individuals." (*II*, 23) Kettle offers a broad guideline for judging what kind of novel a particular work is by referring to the different names that are typical of a particular genre. He says that in allegory and the novel of "humours" the names signify the character, such as Squire Allworthy, whereas in the non-symbolic novels of Jane Austen, the names like Emma Woodhouse are totally without significance. But in symbolic fiction, "the names of characters have a particular rightness of their own: Heathcliff, Noah Claypole, Henry James's characters." (*I*, 141) This is rather a broad generalization but keeping in mind the fact that the book is primarily meant as an introduction, it is easy to see that such categories are useful for the student in getting a hint about the kind of novel a particular book is.

Discussing the trends in the twentieth century novel, Kettle relates them to the overall changes taking place in modern society. The twentieth century witnessed the great divide between the "good" and the "popular" literature. While the former is restricted to a select coterie of the elite, "popular" or "middlebrow" best-sellers are devoured by the masses. Kettle skirts round the problem of "popular" literature, focusing attention only on the "good." However, he does include a specimen of "middlebrow" fiction, for example, John Galsworthy's *The Man of Property.* The idea is that it must never shake "certain secure complacencies." (*II*, 87) Galsworthy's novel "has its core of seriousness, its spark of genuine insight which is not merely incidental but central to its very conception." (*II*, 87) Even though Kettle does not mention the word "tradition," he is using the term "seriousness," which is a key term in the construction of the Leavisian tradition. However, in spite of its "seriousness" *The Man of Property* is dismissed as a "museum piece, not as a living work of art." (*II*, 90)

Kettle states that pessimism and narrowness have become the hallmark of twentieth century literature. It is not due to lack of "raw material" but because experience has become fragmentary and therefore the picture that emerges from the novels of Aldous Huxley, George Orwell, Arthur Koestler, Graham Greene and Evelyn Waugh "is in the last degree unhopeful and, as a result, unhelpful. . . . They are not simply writers describing decadence, they are decadent writers." (*II*, 159) This might appear unsympathetic but Kettle deals with each novel in a sensitive and perceptive manner and ascribes them more attention than either Leavis or Williams has done. If the novels of the thirties and forties are not great, it is because they fail to substantiate positive human values. *Ulysses* is seen as "a revolutionary development" and is regarded as being "in one of the main traditions of the English novel," (*II*, 122) but it is "unsatisfying" because of Joyce's "sterlity of . . vision of life." (*II*, 134) The decisive common denominator in all these novels is either a lack of life or an inadequacy in the writer's philosophy of life. This seems to be the most potent factor in Kettle's criteria. The future of the English novel does not lie with the writers from the middle-classes but with novels written from a working-class perspective. Kettle is of the opinion that:

> The test of the future novelist like that of his predecessor, will lie in the depth and sincerity of his responses to the profoundest and most perilous issues of the time. (*II*, 177)

I will now try to assess the contribution of Kettle to the field of literary criticism. The most striking aspect of *An Introduction to the English Novel, Vols. I, II* is the wide area of the novel that Kettle has undertaken to discuss. By doing so, he is secularizing the "canon" thereby giving due importance to writers like Scott, Dickens and Hardy who have often been bypassed by the dictators of tradition. Though Kettle begins with certain concepts that he shares with Leavis on the one hand and Engels and Lukacs on the other, his analysis of each text goes beyond the limits of this framework and illustrates the fact that rigid principles are of no avail in a literary-critical context and implies that the call for scientism can only be relative. Above all, his use of simple language encourages the common reader. His emphasis may seem, to some, sociological, but his stand can be summed up in his own words:

> Today we feel the need for a new attitude to the traditional divisions of knowledge. It can be summarized in Forster's phrase — "only connect." And Marxism certainly seeks to connect. We seek a connection between politics and literature, between the arts and the sciences — we seek to study each separate discipline within the context of human development.[28]

Kettle's emphasis is pragmatic and his belief is that literary criticism is the necessary complement to the reading of a book for it heightens the appreciation and understanding of it.

Rather than catering to a select student body in one of the conventional universities, Kettle decides to address a wider audience from all walks of life who had the opportunity to learn late in life such as students in the Open University. Thus his career as a teacher has been meaningful not only to students in Britain but to students of literature all over the world. He has thus extended the function of criticism from an academic exercise to one with a wider socio-political impact.

Summing up Kettle's achievement, the editors of the *The Uses of Fiction* point out that his practice actualizes the prescription of Walter Benjamin:

> The task of the Marxist literary critic then is to be able to respect the relative closure of the novel, to be able to detect those points of openness where the character of the epoch and its illusions have a direct and unavoidable bearing on our understanding of it, and to be able to account for its persistence as a living force beyond its age.[29]

However, the similarity ends here for Kettle is quite different from Benjamin, who is:

> undeniably a difficult figure partly because much of his writing is extremely concise and opaque, and partly because his opinions do not always appear to be consistent.[30]

Moreover, Benjamin's significance lies in his very sophisticated adaptation of Marxism to cultural criticism.[31] It is mainly on account of this last feature that he seems closer to Raymond Williams whose work on fiction will constitute the main part of the following chapter.

NOTES

1. Asha Kanwar, "Interview with Arnold Kettle," Milton Keynes, March 4, 1985, *Social Scientist,* 1987, pp. 54-61.
2. *Ibid.*
3. *Ibid.*
4. *Ibid.*
5. *The Nineteenth Century Novel* (Milton Keynes: Open University Press, 1982), p. 5.
6. Interview with Arnold Kettle.

7. *Ibid.*
8. Douglas Jefferson and Graham Martin, eds., *The Uses of Fiction* (Milton Keynes: The Open University Press, 1982), p. 1.
9. Interview with Arnold Kettle.
10. George Steiner, "Marxism and the Literary Critic," *Language and Silence* (Harmondsworth: Pelican, 1969), p. 273.
11. *Loc. cit.*
12. *Ibid.*, p. 271.
13. *Ibid.*, p. 276.
14. Kettle, "The Artist and Politics," *Marxism Today*, Vol. 3, No. 5, May 1951, p. 143.
15. Ian Watt assigns several reasons for the rise of the novel but above all attributes it to "the great power and self-confidence of the middle class as a whole." According to him, the reading public was extending to include the tradespoeple, tastes were shifting from the religious to the secular, prose was favoured as opposed to verse, circulating libraries were established in 1742, and publishers who now controlled the production and distribution of books, replaced the patrons of nobility who had hitherto influenced the writing profession. *The Rise of the Novel* (London: Chatto and Windus, 1963), p. 59.
16. E. Borlund, *Contemporary Literary Critics* (Hongkong: Macmillan, 1982), p. 327.
17. B. Krylov, ed., *Marx and Engels on Literature and Art* (Moscow: Progress, 1976), p. 90.
18. *Studies in European Realism* (London: Grosset and Dunlap, 1977), p. 85.
19. Georg Lukacs, *The Meaning of Contemporary Realism* (London: Merlin, 1969), p. 123.
20. A. Maurois, *Prometheus: Life of Balzac*, p. 255. Referenced in Frederick Anthony Barnett, "The Holy Ghost; Lukacs's 'Marxism': The Concepts of Class Consciousness and Realism in the Works of G. Lukacs: Toward a World-View Analysis," Unpublished D.Phil. Thesis, University of Sussex, October 1972.
21. Peter Demetz, *Marx Engels and the Poets*, trans. Jeffrey L. Sammons (Chicago: University Press, 1967), p. 209.
22. *Ibid.*, p. 209.
23. *Ibid.*, p. 210.
24. R. P. Bilan, "From Leavis to Marx," *Queens Quarterly*, p. 119.
25. *The Common Reader* (London: Hogarth, 1968), p. 189.
26. Interview with A. Kettle.

27. Kettle, like the other critics of Joyce, "preserves him as unread." C. McCabe, *James Joyce and the Revolution of the Word* (London: Macmillan, 1981), p. 3.
28. Kettle, *Crisis and Criticism,* p. 2.
29. Jefferson and Martin, eds., *The Uses of Fiction,* p. 3.
30. Julian Roberts, *Walter Benjamin* (London: Macmillan, 1982), p. 3.
31. *Ibid.*, p. 9.

Raymond Williams

Raymond Williams is influential in various fields—English studies, sociology, politics, cultural and media studies and his achievement is comparable in range and scope to that of Lukacs or Benjamin, as Eagleton has rightly observed.[1] Among the socialist writers in contemporary Britain, he is what E.P.Thompson calls "our best man" and Anthony Barnett praises him on the grounds that he "stands for a kind of truthfulness."[2] Not only in India, but even within the context of British academia, Williams's concepts are requisitioned, modified, developed but certainly not ignored. His work has generated research in different areas though the present discussion will deal with a particular sector of his work--the field of fictional criticism. In this chapter, the focus will be on his concepts of the "knowable community," "structure of feeling" and "realism," these being key terms in his fictional methodology. However, these terms are not narrowly literary-critical but have a direct bearing on his analysis of culture. Therefore, a brief look at Williams's understanding and definition of the term "culture" is relevant here.

According to Williams, "literary theory cannot be separated from cultural theory, though it may be distinguished within it."[3] In the early sixties, when Williams tried to establish his position in regard to the notion of culture, he saw it as "creative activity" and as "a whole way of life."[4] In the seventies, he moved to the theory of cultural materialism which he defines as "the analysis of all forms of signification, including quite centrally writing, within the actual means and conditions of their production." This can be seen as the rapprochement of his earlier ideas to Marxism.[5] But his approach is eclectic in the sense that he takes up what he considers are the positive aspects of Marxism and combines them with the traditional liberal outlook that can be traced back to F.R. Leavis and Matthew Arnold. However, Williams's enterprise aims at the supercession of the notion of an elite culture replaceable by a democratic common culture that will ultimately overcome the class distinctions in society. The process must enlist the efforts of the people themselves:

> The struggle with which that process confronts us now is, I believe, the struggle to create public meanings which are authentic forums: to create a society whose values are at once commonly created and criticized, and where the discussions and exclusions of class may be replaced by the reality of common and equal membership. That, still, is the idea of a common culture.[6]

In his call for the democratization of culture, Williams is breaking away from the tradition of Arnold and Leavis, key figures in any discussion of "culture." For Arnold, culture is the "pursuit of our total perfection by means of getting to know . . . the best that has been thought and said in the world."[7] Leavis, on the other hand, finds himself facing a modern industrial society with its attendant phenomena of mass production and mass media which in turn have created mass society, where the decline in the quality of life and standards of aesthetic value can only be deplored in the strongest terms, "what we have lost is the organic community."[8] In *The Country and the City*, Williams dismisses the notion of "organic community" as a pastoral myth. In fact, Leavis's concept is a sort of utopia in retrospect. In order to regain this lost community, the elite would have a specific role to play. By the elite, Leavis refers neither to the religious nor the political leaders but the intellectuals believing that "in any period it is upon a very small minority that the discerning appreciation of art and literature depends."[9] For Arnold, the appreciation of art and literature is the means by which culture can be attained but in Leavis art *is* culture whereas Williams takes culture to mean an ever-evolving process, arising out of "a whole way of life." In *The Long Revolution*, Williams points out that there are three levels of culture operative at any particular point in time—"the lived culture" of a certain period that is only experienced by the people then alive, "the recorded culture" evident in art, buildings or dress and the culture of the "selective tradition."[10] The hegemonic process involved in the selection or rejection of a tradition depends upon the effective dominant culture which operates at all levels of society in subtle ways:

> The processes of education; the processes of a much wider social training within institutions like the family; the practical definitions and organization of work; the selective tradition at an intellectual and theoretical level: all these forces are involved in a continual making and remaking of an effective dominant culture, and on them, as experienced, as built into our living its reality depends.[11]

More specifically, the same process is evident in the construction of literary traditions and canons.

Williams began his career as a literary critic with *Reading and Criticism* (1950) although it was not until 1971 that he again published a consolidated book on the novel *The English Novel from Dickens to Lawrence* (hereafter cited as *TEN*), which is a transcription of the eleven lectures that he delivered in Cambridge from 1961 to 1968. (This is not to suggest that he did not work on the novel in the interim). If the former book is overtly Leavisite, the gap of twenty one years seems to have sustained the influence. Eagleton believes:

> *The English Novel from Dickens to Lawrence* is an implicit riposte to *The Great Tradition* . . . the book is a *rewriting* of the "great tradition" from an alternative standpoint, rather than a total displacement of that critical terrain.[12]

Although Williams extends the tradition, he adheres to the main course charted by Leavis and had it not been for this particular influence, he would not start his assessment of the novel "at the 1840s but in the 1790s."[13] It would then hardly seem a coincidence that he discusses mainly canonical texts in most of his discussions of the novel, that is, in *The English Novel*, in *Modern Tragedy* and *The Country and the City*, However, the latter includes a discussion of working-class novels as well. While he is working within the "dominant literary paradigm"[14] in *The English Novel*, in *The Country and the City* he takes up literature not for the purpose of literary analysis but as historical evidence to expose the ideology that would maintain the country/city dichotomy.

Highly selective, Leavis opens *The Great Tradition* with the announcement: "The great English novelists are Jane Austen, George Eliot, Henry James and Joseph Conrad."[15] Williams discusses these writers at some length with the sole exception of James whom he brackets with Wells. At the same time he accords a place of honour to the writer, who had been referred to patronizingly by James as "the good little Thomas Hardy."[16] Leavis and Williams both install George Eliot as the superior novelist as compared to Jane Austen. Leavis then discusses the early phase of Eliot's development, paying special attention to *Middlemarch* and *Daniel Deronda*, whereas according to Williams *Adam Bede* is the novel of primary merit. James is treated with reverence by Leavis while Williams finds Wells superior in some respects. After studying the novels of Conrad, Williams focuses attention on the trauma of being "alone in the city" with reference to the city novelists, Gissing, Dickens, Mrs. Gaskell, Joyce and Lawrence, praising *Sons and Lovers* and *Lady Chatterley's Lover*, taking up for censure the very novel that Leavis praises, *Women in Love*. So while Williams's alternate tradition implicity takes off from the earlier one, the emphasis has changed. It is clear that the differing perspective is based on the ideological position of the two critics. For example, critics have traced Williams's favouring of Hardy to his own working-class origins. This may not be strictly true, but throughout his preoccupation with the tension between the "educated" and the "customary" one can see his own life situated in the "border country" between Wales and Cambridge and between middle- and working-class consciousness. (Williams's attempt to maintain his Welsh links is especially evident in his novels). Throughout his work, Williams is trying to resolve a series of basic dichotomies—between high and common culture, between the individual and the social and the country and the city and it is this attempt that perhaps contributes to the difficulty that is involved in understanding his work. It is this search for totality that leads to the inception of the term "knowable community."

I

"Knowable community" may be the binding principle in *The English Novel*, but it is only defined in *Politics and Letters:*

> Those novels which can attain an effective range of social experience by sufficiently manifest immediate relations possess a knowable community.[17]

Commenting on the spurt of novels written during those twenty months between 1847-48, Williams says that the experience common to all the novelists of this generation is the "exploration of community, the substance and meaning of community." (*TEN,* 11) It involves the question of examining relationships in a particular society and the ways these are manifested in concrete ways in fiction. In fact, it is this bearing that is dominant from Dickens to Lawrence.

Conventionally, the novel would depict people and their relationship on the assumption that the reader and the author shared a common knowledge that social relationships are a reliable index through which persons can be known. But as a result of the rapid changes taking place in the nineteenth century society this confidence gave way to the sense that people are only potentially knowable. It became extremely difficult to apprehend the complex urban society that was causing the fragmentation within communities. Thus, "an important split takes place between knowable relationships and an unknown, unknowable, overwhelming society."(*TEN,* 15) Society is no longer viewed as a passive background against which the drama of lives unfolded itself, but as "an agency, even an actor, a character . . . a process that entered lives to shape or to deform." (*TEN,* 13) When dealing with individual novelists, Williams tries to find out how and to what extent the novelist is able to apprehend the crisis of this time and to give it shape in his novels.

Explaining the concept further, Williams say that the "knowable" is not an objective category alone, in the sense that it is not only "what is there to be known" (*TEN,* 17) but also what the observers desire and need to know. Thus "knowable community" incorporates both social fact plus the consciousness of the author. For "novelists did not simply react to the conformation of the social crisis, but subjected them to intricate processes of redefinition."[18] What is important then is the writer's defining consciousness, Referring to George Eliot, Williams differentiates between the "knowable" and the "known" community:

> The knowable community is the common life, which she is pleased to record with a necessary emphasis, but the known community is something else again – an uneasy contract, in language with another interest and another sensibility. (*TEN,* 82)

This "uneasy contract" is the tension between the "narrative idiom of the novelist and the recorded language of her characters." (*TEN,*

79-80) It is on this continuous conflict between "customary" and "educated" language that Williams traces the tradition from George Eliot to Hardy to Lawrence. Williams suggests that Lawrence, in his early short stories, succeeds where Hardy and Dickens before him had failed, that is in resolving the tension between the language of the novelist and that of the characters. On the other hand, it would seem that this disruption is conducive to creative activity, for example, because of this problem, George Eliot had to create almost a new form each time she wrote.

From the 1890s to 1914, there is a growing awareness of the split between the individual and society. The isolated consciousness creates its own community and this is manifested in the "internal disturbance of language and form." (*TEN,* 124) The language that emerges to articulate this experience is then ordinary, divested as it is of conventional trappings (trappings that could be associated with traditional forms) as in *Ulysses* which Williams praises for "community of speech." Alternate critical positions would contend that there was precisely this community of speech lacking in *Ulysses.*[19]

One can guage the importance that Williams assigns to language from his statement that "the most deeply known human community is language itself." (*TEN,* 167) But language does not necessarily entail an analysis of style but is an index through which human relationships can be gauged. Thus the concept of knowable community not only embodies a depiction of social experience by the defining consciousness of the writer, but also its articulation in language, that is seen as "historically and socially constituting."[20] However, all social experience is not recorded for there is also that intangible, elusive experience which because it is still in process is not yet articulate. Williams describes this as the "structure of feeling" from which all art is made. (*TEN,* 192)

II

"Structure of feeling," a socio-cultural term is an important element in Williams's methodology and one he uses frequently in his discussion of drama and the novel. Though sparingly used in *The English Novel*, it occurs fairly often in *The Country and the City*. It is explained at length in *The Long Revolution* and dealt with theoretically in *Marxism and Literature* though it was first used by Williams in *Preface to Film* (1954):

> To relate a work of art to any part of that observed totality may, in varying degrees be useful but it is a common experience, in analysis, to realize that when one has measured the work against the separable parts, there yet remains an element for which there is no external counterpart. This element, I believe is what I have named the structure of feeling of a period and it is only realizable through experience of the work of art itself.[21]

Here the main emphasis is on experience. But to speak of experience in the past, as a fixed entity, is to imply that it is a static finished product. All experience is a process and to express this sense of continuity, Williams has devised the term--"it is as firm and definite as 'structure' suggests, yet it operates in the most delicate and least tangible parts of our activity."[22] Though a very complex term, the only way to simplify it is to say that it corresponds roughly to the culture of that time. It is not necessary for the structure of feeling of a particular period to be common to all members of the community yet it is a "very wide possession"[23] and all communication depends upon it.

At any point in time, there are three levels of structure of feeling in operation, corresponding roughly to the three generations living at that time.[24] Each generation creates its own structure of feeling in response or reaction to the world it inherits, taking up, abandoning, changing the values of its predecessors. According to Williams, the structure of feeling is not to be equated with the documentary culture or the social character of the period. Documentary culture, like fashions and buildings provides a direct evidence of the period whereas the structure of feeling is not so easily accessible, it can elude people even in close contact with it. The structure of feeling can be said to correspond in part to the dominant social character but the structure of feeling is related to the effect that this does or does not have on the life of the people. Thus the social character is the "ethic" while the structure of feeling is the "experience,"[25] which without being articulate can exert "palpable pressures."[26] While still in solution, a structure of feeling has elements of the dominant, residual and emergent characteristics of a culture and is at first taken as personal.[27] It is only later that this takes shape as an institution or a formation that it can be recognized as social. In fact, the term structure of feeling incorporates subjective and objective aspects. For "feeling" can be equated with the Leavisite "experience" and the Lawrentian "felt life" while "structure" implies pattern or form as opposed to content. It might be possible to see a parallel here in the life-pattern categories designated by Kettle. Richard Dyer *et al* are of opinion that:

> The pattern of experience, however is not defined in terms of a set of explicit beliefs--e.g., an ideology but in terms of the implicit structure which the social life exhibits at the level of experienced values: thus, structure of feeling, an apparently paradoxical concept.[28]

They further find points of reference between Williams's "structure of feeling," Lukacs's "potential consciousness" and Goldmann's "world vision."[29]

According to Alistair M. Duckworth, the phrase "structure of feeling" seems to imply:

> an outlook shared by a number of writers in a period, to some extent limited by historical consciousness, class allegiance, and a common inheritance of traditional topics, genres and styles, but capable nevertheless in individual instances of pushing throughout these limits to the picturing of things as they are.[30]

Duckworth points out that the view expressed here approximates to that of Lukacs when he argues that great realist writers, in spite of their conscious political views, however reactionary they might be, are able to depict social actuality.[31]

Referring to structure of feeling, Eagleton says that "what this concept designates, in effect, is ideology."[32] But by stressing "feeling," that is the very charge that Williams wishes to avoid. Ideology may be broadly defined as the "system of ideas appropriate" to a particular class or it may mean "illusory or merely abstract thought."[33] While this sense of ideology can have connections with the dominant social character of a period, it is different from the structure of feeling which cannot be equated with "ideas" or "thought," for it refers to:

> specifically affecting elements of consciousness and relationships; not feeling against thought, but thought as felt and feeling as thought.[34]

It is possible to see close connections between structure of feeling and Gramsci's concept of hegemony. For hegemony does not mean overt political control but is merely a subtle way of influencing and shaping human nature and relationships. Hegemony is a "realized complex of experiences, relationships and activities, with specific and changing pressures and limits."[35] This differs from ideology in that it does not solely "depend for its hold in its expression of the interests of the ruling class but also on its acceptance as 'normal reality' or 'common sense' by those in practice subordinated to it."[36] Hegemony thus penetrates to all levels of society and exerts pressures on all relationships. By adopting this concept, Williams is able to examine the political angle of "culture." Hegemony is primarily concerned with domination and subordination and while it may influence the structure of feeling, it cannot be equated with it.

Eagleton has suggested that structure of feeling is similar to Goldmann's "transindividual structures." In his theory of genetic structuralism, Goldmann says that all human beings try to respond meaningfully to the problems that they encounter in the course of social life. The collective response is structured as a world-view. These world-views are not static or fixed but in a constant state of structure of feeling, while a world-view is structured by the social class collectively, it is articulated by the writer who:

> achieves a coherent awareness of what, among the other members of his group, remains vague and confused, and contradicted by innumerable tendencies.[37]

Williams too sees the writer as naming the new responses, perceptions and interests of an age. But whereas in Goldmann, this is an unconscious process, in Williams, the writer is conscious of the reality he is depicting. For the perception of the knowable community is a matter of conscious choice on the part of the writer. Not only does he articulate, but he also directs our attention to new ways of seeing ourselves and the world. For both Goldmann and Williams there is no direct relationship between society and the novel in terms of content but the relationship exists between the ideology of a society and the fictional world the writer is able to create.

Williams again shares Goldmann's view that "cultural creation as a sector [is] privileged perhaps, but nonetheless of the same nature as all other sectors of human behaviour."[38] While similarities do exist between the two critics, structure of feeling is different from transindividual structures. According to Williams at any given time, there are three structures of feeling operative corresponding to the three generations then alive. The structure of feeling of the senior group has been articulated in the previous generation whereas that of the younger generation has yet to be articulated. Therefore, it is only the "dominantly culturally productive group,"[39] which articulates the structure of feeling of its age. (This age specification seems rather arbitrary. Moreover, it ignores the psychological aspects of the situation.) It would then seem that structure of feeling is generation-specific whereas transindividual structure is class-specific. Later, however, Williams changes his position, admitting that he would now use the concept "more differentially between the classes."[40] In spite of this, the difference remains, for transindividual structures are related to world-views, which are already crystallized collective responses, whereas structure of feeling is experience "still in solution." Goldmann's concept can be seen more as a "structure of thought" for it is a tangible philosophical position as opposed to Williams's fluid experiential category. This could well be symptomatic of their overall historico-cultural positions – French classicism on the one hand and British romanticism/ empiricism on the other.

There is yet another change in Williams's position in relation to this concept. In *The Long Revolution*, he had said that structure of feeling is easier to recover in the present than in the past. But, as the interviewers point out in *Politics and Letters*, it would be easier to recover in the past rather than the present which is still in a state of flux. Williams concedes this, saying that "while a structure of feeling exists in the present, so to speak, grammatically, I do not now think it more recoverable."[41]

What then is the relation of structure of feeling to art and literature? Williams believes that "all art is made" from "the structure of feeling that is lived and experienced but not quite arranged as institutions and ideas." (*TEN,* 192) In fact a literary text can be taken as a concrete instance of the structure of feeling of a particular society in a specific historical moment. It would be easy to relate the structure of feeling to the content of a literary artefact, but it cannot be simply reduced to it. As Williams says:

> The idea of a structure of feeling can be specifically related to the evidence of forms and conventions --semantic figures which in art and literature, are often among the very first indications that such a new structure is forming.[42]

It is through relationships that are presented as "lived" and "felt" that a work of fiction can indicate the formation of new structures. The novelist does not merely depict these changes in social formations but makes us "live" and "experience" them through his art. Commenting on this concept, Eagleton says:

> *The English Novel from Dickens to Lawrence*, puts the notion to superb use: the novel, for Williams, is one medium among many in which men seek to master and absorb new experience by discovering new forms and rhythms, grasping and so constructing the stuff of social change in the living substance of perceptions and relationships.[43]

III

Williams has been charged with being "ideologically bound to the moment of nineteenth century realism."[44] In the nineteenth century, realism as a method in literature or art came to mean accurate representation and to describing things as they actually exist.[45] Before the end of the century, there was a separation between realism and naturalism. Naturalism as opposed to supernaturalism, implies the exclusion of God and attention to the poor and sordid details of life. But for Williams, the term realism has no such simple connotations:

> When I think of the realist tradition in fiction, I think of the kind of the novel which creates and judges the quality of a whole way of life in terms of the qualities of persons.[46]

What Williams is stressing is the balance between the personal and the social; as both being coeval; with neither having priority over the other. He emphaizes:

> Every aspect of personal life is radically affected by the quality of the general life, yet the general life is seen at its most important in completely personal terms.[47]

This synthesizing process is what marks the moment of high realism not only in the nineteenth century novel, but also endows the abstract events of history with a concrete quality.

According to Williams, in the twentieth century, the realist novel faced a rupture between the "social" and the "personal."[48] On the basis of emphasis, the "social" can be further sub-divided into the "social-descriptive" and the "social-formula" novels. The "social-descriptive" category places its main stress on the way of life at a particular time and place rather than on individuals. In the "social-formula" novel, the writer abstracts a pattern from his observation of social experience and creates a whole fictional world according to this "formula." What is missing here is real society and real persons for the characters created are merely functional. Again the "personal" can be similarly sub-divided. In the "personal descriptive" novel, society is subordinated to individual perceptions while in the "personal formula," characters are created in accordance with the formula derived from the author's experience. The world is created through the consciousness of a single character. This can also be termed "the fiction of special pleading"--a narrative mode that depicts only a few people from the perspective of one or a few characters and it relies on a rather direct contact with the reader, making him empathize with the character/characters. What is lacking in all these categories is the crucial balance.

This call for balance and relationships of a whole kind, links him to Lukacs and his concept of totality. For Lukacs as well, the personal is not separable from the social and what the writer expresses is not just his own thoughts and feeling but must be able to "grasp society as a totality."[49] which must then be depicted in a concrete way. According to Lukacs:

> The hallmark of the great realist masterpiece is precisely that its intensive totality of *essential* social factors does not require, does not even tolerate, a meticulously accurate or pedantically encyclopaedic inclusion of all the threads making up the social tangle; in such a masterpiece the most essential social factors can find total expression in the apparently accidental conjunction of a few human destinies.[50]

The writer of the realist masterpiece must create characters and situations, which Lukacs, following Engels, calls "types." For Lukacs, the author who succeeds in creating "types" is a realist and the criterion of literary value is realism for only realist works of art are genuine works of art.[51]

In his "Lecture on Realism," Williams says: "the three emphases which are often consciously described as realism are the secular, the contemporary and the socially extended."[52] While discussing the TV film *The Big Flame,* he adds another dimension to this tripartite definition, which is "the consciously interpretative in relation to a particular political viewpoint."[53]

Williams's commitment to the moment of nineteenth century high realism (classic realism) prevents him from doing full justice to the modernist text. However, it guides his own creative practice as is evident from his attempt to recreate the balance of the paradigmatic Victorian novel in his own fiction, particularly the Welsh trilogy, *Border Country* (1960), *Second Generation* (1964) and *The Fight for Manod* (1978). Williams admits that his problem was to find a suitable form that would "allow the description both of the internally seen working-class community and a movement of people, still feeling their family and political connections out of it."[54] The solution then lay in turning to the nineteenth century novel which he sees as "successful studies of one kind of mobility, the uncertainty of moving between two kinds of life."[55] Explaining his practice further, Williams says that "writers commit themselves to certain rhythms – in my case the rhythms of certain kinds of Welsh speech,"[56] a fact that is true of all his novels. While Williams agrees that the twentieth century cultural forms are undoubtedly drama, TV and film but that does not make the novel an anachronism for "there are certain feelings, certain relationships . . . which can be conceived in the novel." (*TEN*, 190)

In discussing individual novelists, Williams does not apply traditional methods of analysis like focusing on the plot, theme, characterization, symbols or narrative techinques. Nor does he employ the "words on the page" methodology that the *Scrutiny* school modified from New Criticism. Williams places an emphasis on the social base of literature though he does not subscribe to the crude reflectionist mode of criticism. In other words, the effects of social crises are not directly redeemable in literature of value but are mediated and overdetermined in complex and subtle forms in actual personal relationships. While this method reduces reliance on evaluation to a minimum by a change in emphasis, the judgement can easily slip from the literary to the ideological. (However, it might be pointed out that no judgements, literary or otherwise, are free from ideological dictates.) Williams does not dispense with evaluation but attempts to secularize the process as is evident from his observation, "criticism leads to the hypostatization of the critic *above* the process making judgements *inside* the process, in the way people do in everyday contemporary argument is very different."[57]

The English Novel from Dickens to Lawrence is Williams's contribution to putting the English novel in its proper perspective, for the Continental theoreticians of the novel like Lukacs and Goldmann deal chiefly with French, Russian and German novels. The term "English" is not merely a geographical distinction for writers of other origins—Scots, Irish, Welsh and Polish have contributed to its tradition. In the nineteenth century novel, Williams finds a very "specific Englishness" which he defines as "the common consciousness, the common culture, a very specific set of common concerns."(*TEN*, 122) At another level, the concept of Englishness is rejected by Williams when it is "congruent with much more general reflexes and campaigns of the English ruling class as a whole."[58] and it is this constant dialectic within Williams's thought which has been characterized by Parrinder as his "negativity."[59]

Williams's position has been an evolving one and so demands a brief review because *The English Novel from Dickens to Lawrence* has to be seen as part of a larger process and body of work. Before the Second War, Williams was a member of the Communist Party at Cambridge, a position he did not resume after the War. In his journal

Politics and Letters, and the book *Reading and Criticism,* he adopts a humanist position in the manner of Leavis "on such things as the need for cultural standards and for the training in resistance to the environment."[60] In *Drama from Ibsen to Brecht*, Williams is still on Leavisite terrain with the "words on the page" methodology. It is only in *Culture and Society* and *The Long Revolution* that he begins to found his own position, when he turns from literary to social concerns and more specifically to cultural concerns. During the fifties and sixties, Williams remains in close association with the New Left (in fact, he can be seen as a key figure in its formation, along with Stuart Hall and E.P. Thompson), while keeping a distance from Marxism, certain aspects of which, like the base/superstructure model he could not accept. It is only in 1973, with the publication of *The Country and the City,* that his acceptance of Marxism becomes evident and is finally consolidated in *Marxism and Literature* (1977). His return to Marxism can in fact be traced to the last years of the sixties. This acceptance is not sudden but according to Anthony Barnett:

> it can be shown that virtually all of Williams's book contains a strong materialist moment as well as a recongnisable idealist one. It is the altering relationship between the two which provides a basis for comprehending the remarkable evolution of his thought.[61]

Stuart Hall sums up the development of Williams's thought by categorizing it into three stages. He calls Raymonds Williams I of the period of *The Long Revolution* a "mixed case."[62] During this time Williams is still under the influence of Leavis. Raymond Williams II, "juxtaposes the new found Continental Marxist tradition and the English literary tradition."[63] Raymond Williams III of the essay on 'Base and Superstructure' engages in a dialogue with European Marxism, opposing Althusser, Barthes and the linguists in general.

Throughout his work, Williams is trying to resolve a series of basic dichotomies–between high and common culture, between the individual and the social, the country and the city and the educated and the customary. This is what constitutes the basic tension of his work. His concern is with the whole way of life rather than with any one aspect of it. It is this which leads him to look for a totality within the novelistic community. His quarrel with Marxism has been on account of his inability to accept the straightforward base/superstructure relationship as understood by most thirties Marxists.

Unlike Leavis, Williams does not accept the mythicized image of a past society. In *The Country and the City,* instead of a retrospective outlook, Williams tries to project such a community into the future. He does not believe that literary history is a matter of :

> placing individual works in relation to traditional topics, genres or styles, but a means of evaluating the ways in which English literature records through its eras the slow transformation--the "long revolution" of English society from feudalism through agrarian and industrial forms of capitalism to the democratic capitalism of today.[64]

This clearly indicates a Marxist model of history. Williams feels that it is the critic's duty to expose the false models of society that sometimes emerge from literary evidence and to correct this view so that a social structure, based on reality, may be constructed. In *The Country and the City,* Williams disposes of two myths--that of the past organic community and that which suggests that "God made the country and man made the town."[65] Williams does not use literary evidence for an assessment of historical facts alone, but uses it as an index to gauge the structure of feeling of its time. He differs from Kettle in that he does not relate historical and literary developments in the deterministic base/superstructure mode and instead of looking for the social content of literature alone, fixes his focus on the forms and conventions that are shaped by social considerations, for, as he says, "conventions have social roots, that they are not simply formal devices of writing."[66]

While within the field of cultural studies Williams is highly influential, his impact in other fields is diffuse. The reason for this could be that since he has written so widely on such varied topics, his impact is dispersed. His work on drama may be regarded by some as valuable while others may see his work on the novel as being of superior quality. His literary criticism is no doubt shaped by the Leavis influence but it is unfair to dismiss it as Left-Leavisism. For he has extended it to include strands of the Continental Marxist tradition, investing it with a theoretical bent that is somewhat uncommon within the English tradition. It is in this that he differs greatly from Kettle who is averse to theory and theorizing. The difference can be traced back to their early days at Cambridge when Kettle was more in alignment with the thirties Marxists whereas Williams admits that "We were pretty critical of socialist realism—our interests were very much more in modernism."[67] These differences in their critical practice will be further highlighted in the second section that will be based on an examination of selected nineteenth century novels.

NOTES

1. *Criticism and Ideology* (London: Verso, 1976), p. 24.
2. Quoted in Garry Watson, "Criticism and the English Idiom: The Significance of Raymond Williams," *New Universities Quarterly*, Vol. 31, No. 4, Autumn 1977, p. 468.
3. *Marxism and Literature* (Oxford: University Press, 1977), p. 145.
4. *The Long Revolution* (London: Chatto and Windus, 1961), p. 41.
5. During the 50s and 60s, Williams remains in close association with the New Left (in fact, he can be seen as a key figure in its formation, along with Stuart Hall and E.P. Thompson) while keeping a distance from Marxism, certain aspects of which, like the base/ superstructure model, he could not accept. It is only in 1973, with the publication of *The Country and the City*, that his acceptance of Marxism becomes evident and is finally consolidated with *Marxism and Literature* (1977).
6. Williams, "Culture and Revolution: A Response" in Terry Eagleton and Brian Wicker, eds., *From Culture to Revolution* (London: Sheed and Ward, 1968), p. 308.
7. Matthew Arnold, *Culture and Anarchy*, J. Dover Wilson, ed. (Cambridge: University Press, 1963), p. 6.
8. Leavis and Denys Thompson, *Culture and Environment* (London: Chatto and Windus, 1965), p. 143.
9. F.R. Leavis, *Education and the University* (London: Chatto and Windus,1965), p. 143.
10. *The Long Revolution*, p. 49.
11. *Problems in Materialism and Culture* (London: Verso, 1980), p. 39.
12. *Criticism and Ideology*, p. 36.
13. *Politics and Letters* (London: Verso, 1981), p. 245.
14. See "Crisis in English Studies," *Writing in Society* (London: Verso, 1983), p. 203.
15. *The Great Tradition* (Harmondsworth: Penguin, 1962), p. 9.

16. *Ibid.*, p. 39.
17. *Politics and Letters*, p. 247.
18. Jacob Korg, Rev, *TEN, Modern Fiction Studies* (18), p. 263.
19. C. McCabe, *James Joyce and the Revolution of the Word* (London: MacMillan, 1981).
20. *Marxism and Literature*, p. 44.
21. *Politics and Letters*, p. 159.
22. *The Long Revolution*, p. 48.
23. *Loc. cit.*
24. See *The Long Revolution*, p. 65; *Politics and Letters*, p. 157.
25. *Ibid.*, p. 65.
26. *Marxism and Literature*, p. 132.
27. *Ibid.*, p. 121-27.
28. "Literature/Society: Mapping the Field," *Working Papers in Cultural Studies*, Vol. 4, Spring 1973, p. 30.
29. *Ibid.*, p. 30.
30. "Raymond Williams and Literary History," *Papers in Language and Literature*, 1974, Vol. II, p. 426.
31. *Loc. cit.*
32. *Criticism and Ideology*, p. 33.
33. *Keywords* (London: Fontana, 1983), p. 157.
34. *Marxism and Literature*, p. 132.
35. *Ibid.*, p. 112.
36. *Keywords*, p. 145.
37. Goldmann, *The Hidden God* (London: Routledge, 1964), p. 315.
38. Goldmann, *Towards a Sociology of the Novel* (London; Tavistock, 1975), p. 156.
39. *Politics and Letters*, p. 157.
40. *Ibid.*, p. 158.
41. *Ibid.*, p. 163.
42. *Marxism and Literature*, p. 133.
43. *Criticism and Ideology*, p. 34.
44. *Ibid.*, p. 36.
45. *Keywords*, p. 259.
46. *The Long Revolution*, p. 278.
47. *Loc. cit.*

48. *Ibid.*, p. 280.

49. Parkinson, *Georg Lukacs* (London: Routledge, 1977), p. 88.

50. *Studies in European Realism* (New York: Grosset and Dunlap, 1964), p. 148.

51. According to Istvan Meszaros, "Realism is the central notion of Marxist aesthetics . . . for Marx realism is not just one among the innumerable artistic trends . . . but the only mode of reflection of reality which is adequate to the specific powers and means at the disposal of the artist." *Marx's Theory of Alienation* (London: Merlin, 1970), p. 198. Even within a Marxist framework, realism has not had a uniform definition or unproblematic character. The two opposing perspectives on realism, broadly classic realism and neo realism, can be generally situated in the debates between the Formalists and Socialist Realists in the Soviet Union in the 1920s and 1930s and the celebrated Lukacs/Brecht debtate also in the 30s.

52. *Screen,* Vol. 18, No. 1, Spring 1977, p. 65. Lecture given by Williams at the SEFT/*Screen* weekend school held in London, Oct. 8-10, 1976.

53. *Ibid.*, p. 68

54. *Politics and Letters*, p. 272.

55. *Ibid.*, p. 273.

56. *Ibid.*, p. 279.

57. *Ibid.*, p. 336.

58. "Raymond Williams and Marxism: A Rejoinder to Terry Eagleton," *New Left Review*, Sept-Oct. 1976, p. 50.

59. P. Parrinder, "The Accents of Raymond Williams," *Critical Quarterly*, Vol. 26, Nos. 1 and 2, p. 50.

60. Bilan, p. 211.

61. Barnett, p. 63.

62. "A Critical Survey of the Theoretical and Practical Achievements of the Last 10 Years," in *Literature, Society and the Sociology of Literature*, Francis Barker et al, eds. (Univ. of Essex, July 1976), p. 1.

63. *Ibid.*, p. 2.

64. Alistair M. Duckworth, "Raymond Williams and Literary History," *Paper on Language and Literature*, 1974, Vol. 11, p. 422.

65. Duckworth, p. 423.

66. *Politics and Letters*, p. 306.

67. *Ibid.*, p. 45.

The Three Great Novels

According to Williams, the series of novels written in the 1840s marked "a new kind of consciousness" (*TEN,* 9) and "for the next eighty years the novel was to be a major form in English literature." (*TEN,* 9) In fact, for both Kettle and Williams, the nineteenth century novel is the primary reference point on which they base their fictional theories. As Bradbury points out:

> At different points in its evolution, literary criticism seems to take up different prototypical forms, genres, or groups of works, as the central object of attention, according them exemplary status and asking of them that they show us just what it is that literary art most typically is.[1]

The enterprise of both Kettle and Williams can be broadly termed as "realist-centric" and while they can deal fairly adequately with the novels falling within its scope, they are less successful in analyzing the modernist text.

Wuthering Heights (1848), *Middlemarch* (1871-72) and *Tess of the d'Urbervilles* (1891) have all withstood the "test of time," that is, they are now "canonical" texts. However, this is not to suggest that their reputations have been stable throughout. On the contrary, they have been subject to epochal fluctuations. For example, *Wuthering Heights*, upon publication, owed its fame to the misunderstanding that it had been written by Charlotte Bronte (who, by then was already an established name with the remarkable success of *Jane Eyre*). But its present success, as Williams observes, can be attributed to "change in twentieth century literature, moving towards the theme and language of *Wuthering Heights* and away from the main fictional tradition of the decade in which it was written."[2] *Middlemarch* suffered an eclipse from the 1920s to the 1940s on account of the wide currency that the

Jamesian aesthetic of "showing" rather than "telling" had gained.[3] More recently, following McCabe, it is at the centre of controversial concerns dealing with "classic realism." *Tess of the d'Urbervilles* offended certain moralistic quarters in its time, but its appeal continues as is evident from the results of the survey carried out by the *Times Educational Supplement* (2.1.81) when most entrants to the University named Hardy as their first choice, thus prompting Antonia Byatt to conclude that "Hardy Rules O.K."[4] All this goes to prove Widdowson's thesis that texts should be seen:

> not merely as productions of their period, nor, then, as receptacles of historical messages from that period which criticism decants, but as cultural productions of the 1980s.[5]

Nor is the "canon" sacrosanct, for each period structures and restructures its own, according to the interests and needs of dominant social groups. As Eagleton has noted:

> "Survivability," as Brecht saw, is in any case a profoundly suspect criterion of literary value: the history of the life, death and resurrection of literary texts is part of the history of ideologies.[6]

However, the three selected novels constitute what may be termed as the major representative instances of the nineteenth century novel. They can be seen both as landmarks in the development of the novel as a literary genre and in terms of their modes of commentary on the patterns of social and historical change that marked the society from which they originated. So far we have examined the fictional theories of the two critics. By applying these to the selected texts it is hoped that (a) a clearer picture of the theory and practice of the two critics will emerge, (b) a better understanding of the novels under study will result and (c) an assessment of the validity and the value of critical approaches in general will be initiated.

In discussing the novels, I will be making use of the key critical concepts expounded by Kettle and Williams. Kettle's categories of "realism" and "romance," his "life-pattern relationship," his concept of the "moral fable" will be further scrutinized in the next three chapters. Williams's terms "knowable community," "structure of feeling" and "realism" have already been discussed at length in Chapter IV, but how far they help to clarify our understanding of specific texts is a question that can only be answered with the kind of detailed analysis which follows. As we have seen, there is a considerable difference of emphasis in their respective approaches, yet the binding factor is not only the ideological but their basic preoccupation with the nineteenth century novel and with "realism." According to Istvan Meszaros:

> Realism is the central notion of Marxist aesthetics . . . for Marx realism is not just one among the innumerable artistic trends . . . but the only mode of reflection of reality which is adequate to the specific powers and means at the disposal of the artist. The inimitable masters of Greek art are the great realists, and so is Balzac. There is absolutely nothing *stylistically* common to them. But despite the centuries, social, cultural, linguistic barriers, etc. that separate them, they can be brought to a common denominator because, in accordance with the specific traits of their historical situations, they achieve an artistically adequate depiction of the fundamental human relations of their times.[7]

Even within a Marxist framework, realism has not had a uniform definition or an unproblematic character. This has given rise to various controversies and equally numerous schools of thought. Yet:

> The label "realism" has always claimed some value in and of itself, whatever its specific operational definition, however it is said to be recognized.[8]

For instance, even the German Expressionists, who distorted the fabric of the real world, wished to retain their claim on realism for they believed that by extricating an object from its context, they were exposing "true" reality.[9] However, this can be classified as neo-realist as opposed to the classic realist position that Kettle and Williams subscribe to. These two opposing perspectives on realism can be generally situated in the debates between the Formalists and Socialist Realists in the Soviet Union in the 1920s and 1930s and the celebrated Lukacs/Brecht debate also in the thirties, as already discussed in Chapter 1.

As Kettle and Williams both belong to the realist school, it would therefore be appropriate to determine the merits and demerits of this position, of not only what they *do* see but also what they *do not* see. In order to do this I will take up different critical perspectives, for example, that of feminism, formalism and structuralism in order to highlight the assumptions and omissions of the two critics. When Kettle and Williams wrote their major works on the novel [*An Introduction to the English Novel* (1951) and *The English Novel from Dickens to Lawrence* (1971) respectively], some of these approaches were still not current and so, by throwing light on hitherto ignored areas, they will contribute to a fresh and more diverse view of the texts. Indirectly, it will also draw attention to not only the changing fashions in literary criticism, but also the ideological motivations behind critical judgements.

Part II is divided into three chapters, each dealing with *Wuthering Heights, Middlemarch* and *Tess of the d'Urbervilles*. Each chapter will be further sub-divided into sections, each of which will deal with selected statements made either by Kettle or by Williams, which will then generate a discussion dealing with specific key issues at various levels.

NOTES

1. *Possibilities* (London: OUP, 1973), p. 3.
2. R. Williams, *The Long Revolution*, (London: Chatto and Windus, 1961), p. 5.
3. D. Lodge, "*Middlemarch,* The Idea of a Classic Realist Text," *The Nineteenth Century Novel,* Kettle, ed. (London: Heinemann, 1981), p. 222.
4. Also referred to in Widdowson, "Hardy in History: A Case Study in the Sociology of Literature," *Literature and History,* Vol. 9, 1, Spring 1985.
5. *Ibid.*, p. 5.
6. *Criticism and Ideology* (London: Verso, 1978), p. 178.
7. *Marx's Theory of Alienation* (London: Merlin Press, 1970), p. 198.
8. Andrew Tudor, "The Many Mythologies of Realism," *Screen*, Spring 1972, Vol. 13, No. 1, p. 27.
9. *Ibid.*, p. 32.

Wuthering Heights

Wuthering Heights, the first and only novel by Emily Bronte is frequently acclaimed as a work of idiosyncratic "genius" and it is a measure of this "genius" that the novel apparently "pre-empts the utterings of . . . commentators."[1] How far the text eludes or submits to the analysis of its commentators, Kettle and Williams in particular, will be the main concern of this chapter. In order to explore this, I will take up three selected statements – two from Kettle and one from Williams and though a detailed analysis of these touches upon various aspects of this complex novel, this disproportion is no indication of the superiority of the one critic over the other but is rather attributable mainly to the fact that while Kettle devoted a complete chapter to *Wuthering Heights,* Williams in *The English Novel from Dickens to Lawrence* entitled his chapter "Charlotte and Emily Bronte," giving equal attention to both writers. Each statement will be dealt with in a separate section, but not in isolation, and in the light of some of the alternative critical perspectives on the novel.

In Section I, the focus is on Kettle's statement proclaiming Heathcliff as a member of the working-class. This has been a common assumption among Marxist critics, for example David Wilson, who insists: "whether Emily Bronte was fully conscious of it or not, we can see in Heathcliff a true representation of the working men of her time."[2] This raises questions of how far the context of the novel encourages such an interpretation and if the author actually wanted to champion the cause of the working-classes or whether Heathcliff is being explained by "substituting the vocabulary of liberalism with the language of Marxism."[3] To what extent can such a powerful character be reduced to this single dimension? For, in spite of his sheer unrelenting, violent, revengeful nature, Heathcliff enlists the reader's sympathy and admiration. Williams, certainly, does not believe in explaining Heathcliff's enigma in class terms, for he believes: "the real problems then remain, often forgotten or put aside or postponed behind the confidence of the class account."[4]

Section II will begin with Kettle's definition of *Wuthering Heights* as "concrete yet general" and "local and yet universal." (*I*, 130) This leads to questions of what constitutes the "concrete" and to the central problem of defining realism as not only a method but also a term of value. A review of the techniques used for achieving this effect such as the role of the narrators will also be undertaken. Is realism a "pure" convention or is it compatible with the romantic, the Gothic and the fantastic modes? By investigating this problem we can suggest some perspectives which Kettle and Williams ignore by their preoccupation with realism. It may be a fact that "the power and intensity of *Wuthering Heights* need no additional emphasis" (*TEN*, 63) yet how do Kettle and Williams account for it?

Having considered the problems of character and realism, section III will attend to questions of structure, initiated by a statement in which Williams relates *Wuthering Heights* to a tradition with "Blake and Lawrence and very specifically with Hardy." (*TEN*, 64) Most critics have seen the novel as being without "antecedents and precedents," therefore it is all the more useful to investigate the grounds on which Williams relates it to the novels of Lawrence and Hardy and how he justifies a cross-generic connection between Bronte and Blake.

Finally, in a brief conclusion, I will draw together the different arguments to summarize the particular achievements and problems in both Kettle's and Williams's analyses of *Wuthering Heights*.

I

> . . . the rebellion of Heathcliff [is] a particular rebellion, that of the worker physically and spiritually degraded by the conditions and relationships of this same society.
>
> Kettle (*I*, 144)

The view that Heathcliff might constitute a figuration of the proletariat did not originate with Kettle. In fact, there had been a tendency amongst earlier Marxist critics to adopt this position. In his essay "Emily Bronte: the First of the Moderns," (1947) David Wilson's interpretation leans heavily upon the evidence of social history:

Whether Emily Bronte was fully conscious of it or not, we can see in the character of Heathcliff a true representation of the working men of her time, after enduring suffering and degradation at the hands of their "betters" turning to defiance and destruction and to the violent movement of the People's Charter.[5]

Here Heathcliff is seen as a representative of the working-class, in an analysis based on a simple reflectionist model. In this passage, Wilson is also broadly following the line of Engels and Lukacs, who praise Balzac for his progressive world-view in spite of his rootedness in a reactionary class. No doubt Emily Bronte was aware of the Chartist movement of her time, as Mrs. Gaskell seems to suggest in her biography of Charlotte Bronte, and the children at Haworth parsonage did have access to current newspapers and periodicals. Yet, is it possible to ascribe Emily Bronte's sympathies (even unconscious) to the working-class movement in this sort of formulation? Clifford Collins, who totally disagrees with Wilson's critique, asks:

> And is there anything in *Wuthering Heights* itself to suggest that Emily Bronte saw Heathcliff "as representing the rebellious working men" and Catherine as typical of "the part of the educated class which feels compelled to identify itself with their cause?"[6]

This implies that Heathcliff is being appropriated as a critical pawn with total disregard to authorial intention and textual evidence.

Kettle enters the debate by stating that Wilson's "identification . . . of Heathcliff with the rebellious working men of the hungry 'forties,'" is "too far removed from the actual impact of *Wuthering Heights* as a novel to be satisfactory." (*I*, 143) It would seem that Kettle will now suggest an alternate reading but in the very next paragraph, Kettle advances a similar interpretation (as already stated in the epigraph) with the added emphasis:

> *Wuthering Heights* then is an expression in imaginative terms of art of the stresses and tensions, conflicts, personal and spiritual of nineteenth century capitalist society. . . . Emily Bronte's novel is at the same time a statement about the life she knew, the life of Victorian England, and a statement about life as such. (*I*, 144)

It is evident that Kettle's position is more complex than that of Wilson and though Heathcliff is seen as representing the working-class at one level, at another, he is seen as the embodiment of positive human values and hence symbolic of the struggle of the "human" against the "non-human." "Non-human" signifies "inhuman" (as opposed to natural) values that are an offshoot of the "false" social system. And by referring to the experience of "life" expressed at various levels, Kettle is achieving a conjuncture of three elements here – the Leavisite, the sociological and the philosophical.

It is interesting to note that Kettle praises Wilson's essay, not because he agrees with it but because:

> Mr. Wilson has done a valuable service in rescuing *Wuthering Heights* from the transcendentalists and in insisting on the place of Haworth (generally assumed to be a remote country village) in the industrial revolution and its attendant social unrest. (*I*, 143-44)

It is clear that Kettle approves of and maintains the same emphasis. This highlights the fundamental difference between the historical and the transcendentalist positions. Kettle seeks to locate the novel in nineteenth century history rather than reading it either in a general romantic way or in an ahistorical, atemporal manner as suggested by E.M. Forster, who advances the proposition that all novelists be viewed "as seated together in a room . . . a sort of British museum reading-room--all writing their novels simultaneously."[7] Kettle's primary emphasis is on situating the novel in a specific time and place not in a transcendental manner but in (as he would say) a concrete way.

In order to consider further Heathcliff's supposed connections with the working class, I will first turn to the manifest "social content" within the text. When Heathcliff gives Nelly an account of his joint misadventure with Catherine at Thrushcross Grange, he is conscious of the fact that "she was a young lady, and they made a distinction between her treatment and mine."[8] Similarly, upon Catherine's return from the Grange, Hindley tells Heathcliff, "You may come and wish Miss Catherine welcome, like the other servants." (*WH*, 53) This class hierarchy is further stressed in Nelly's observation upon Hindley's death, "Hareton . . . lives in his own house as a servant, deprived of the advantages of wages." (*WH,* 194-95) While Hareton was unaware of his subjugation and deprivation, Heathcliff the repressed, exploited and embittered orphan has one ambition, "I want the triumph of seeing my descendant fairly lord of their estates; my child hiring their children to till their fathers" land for wages." (*WH,* 217) It is evident that the social structure involved is highly complex with an interplay of various forces--the economic, the social and the cultural. The interpersonal relationships operate at various levels incorporating the changes taking place in that society due to increased mobility not just in spatial terms but above all in terms of class. Initially Heathcliff and subsequently Hareton are workers without wages, whereas Heathcliff's intention is to reduce the offspring of his enemies to the status of *paid* labourers. This reveals not only Heathcliff's ascent on the social scale, but the general transformation of society from one stage to another, i.e., from a paternalistic ethic to capitalist values based on cash-nexus.[9] What is also evident is that natural rights of *inheritance* leading to power and position are being displaced by more overtly *acquired* power positions. Hence the "natural" master Hareton is dispossessed and displaced by Heathcliff who has reversed the master/servant hierarchy.

Another crucial passage dealing with problems of class is that describing Heathcliff's return after his mysterious absence when Edgar Linton cannot decide how this "gipsy–the ploughboy" (*WH,* 97) is to be entertained at the Grange.[10] Cathy decides: "Set two tables here, Ellen; one for your master and Miss Isabella, being gentry; the other for Heathcliff and myself, being of the lower orders." (*WH,* 98) While administering these instructions, Cathy's tone is "half angry, half laughing" (*WH*, 98) and as the cherished mistress of the Grange, and secure in her position, she is ironic rather than serious. With his transformed appearance, Heathcliff could hardly be referred to, with any justification, as the "lower orders." When Linton condescendingly refers to him, a few lines further, as a "runaway servant," (*WH,* 98) he betrays the insecurity of his threatened class position which is increasingly being called into question.

In any case, "lower orders" and "working-class" are distinct terms and here "lower orders" means common people in general rather than the working-class. Class distinctions are especially crucial in the period between 1770 and 1840, when, as exemplified in E.P. Thompson's *The*

Making of the English Working Class, class relations were both particularly sharp and also in a process of swift transformation:

> Individual mobility could be seen as movement from one *estate, degree, order* or *rank* to another. What was changing consciousness was not only increased individual mobility, which could be largely contained within the older terms but the new sense of a society or a particular *social system* which actually created social divisions, including new kinds of social divisions.[11]

R.S. Neale also tabulates a 5-layered social structure comprising the upper, middle, middling, working-class A and working-class B hierarchy within which there is a constant structuring and restructuring of social positions.[12] The upper class was authoritarian, exclusive and aristocratic, followed by the middle class largely constituted by property owners as well as senior professionals, deferential towards the former. The middling class was composed of the "petit bourgeois, aspiring professional men, other literates, and artisans."[13] While working class A is a label used to designating the industrial workers, working class B incorporates rural labourers, domestic servants, "the urban poor, most working-class women."[14] If Neale's model is requisitioned, it could be said that Heathcliff has been graphically ascending the social scale from working class B position to that of the middle class whereas Hareton has plummeted in a reverse order. As we have seen, a manifest analysis of the *actual* social relations in the text does not relate Heathcliff to the proletariat, for he is not depicted as belonging to the working class A situation. However, there are several opposing sets of relations that render the situation more complex. There is the distinction between the lower orders on the one hand and between the two kinds of working classes on the other. There is the further tension between the residual feudal order and the rising capitalist one along with the rapidly changing conditions of society contributing to the reversal of the master/servant roles and the phenomenon of hereditary and acquired positions. As Neale points out:

> In contemporary opinion authority positions derived from ascribed status generally outweighed income, wealth, and occupation whilst the latter, by themselves, rarely granted status

> and authority. Because of this difficulty in weighing these opposing elements in some rational balance, much of the early nineteenth century literature centred on the problem of social identity.[15]

What is evident in *Wuthering Heights* is the erosion of these traditional positions by the iconoclastic invasion of economic power. It is for this reason that it is difficult to define Heathcliff's social identity.

While Williams does agree that *Wuthering Heights* as a whole should be located within a social context, he does not agree with Kettle's analysis of Heathcliff. According to him, this kind of account overlooks questions of "sexuality and primary relationships"[16] within which the social crisis of the time can be located. Williams seems to be opposing Kettle yet again:

> When I say *Wuthering Heights* is quite central to its time I don't mean its documentary element or what can be called its symbolism; the experience is so direct it doesn't have to be translated. (*TEN*, 69)

By stressing the importance of Cathy's declaration, "Nelly, I *am* Heathcliff,"[17] Williams seems to suggest that Heathcliff and Cathy are alter-egos. The personalities of both are complementary and, as Gilbert and Gubar put it, "androgynous."[18] It is the fragmentation and separation of this unified identity that leads to the central crisis in the novel. Williams seems to suggest that Catherine and Heathcliff represent the marginalized role of gender and class within a capitalist society. However, Williams's position can be further explained in the words of Frankenburg:

> For Williams, *I am Heathcliff* is the core of the novel's exploration of contradictions between desire in and desire for; for Eagleton it is a distancing device. . . . Perhaps it is a dramatically overstated part of the common parlance of romantically illicit love.[19]

Thus in trying to restore the emphasis from the "class account" and a "symbolic" interpretation, Williams has apparently swung in the opposite direction, that is, in reading the relationship in almost mystical terms. This will be discussed at greater length in the next section.

However, Heathcliff can also be seen as a romantic hero who exists as a kind of Byronic misanthrope[20] and his *grand passion* for Cathy and his desire to die with her carry the ultimate connotations of romantic fiction. In his anxiety to stress the social aspect, Kettle states that "Heathcliff was born not in the pages of Byron, but in a Liverpool slum" (*I*, 133) although in fact, Bronte leaves the question of his origins unresolved. Kettle's distinction is not helpful since a Byronic hero could quite plainly have origins in the slum and therefore the two need not be mutually exclusive. Kettle here seems to confuse the question of the *literary* origin of Heathcliff as a type with that of the *real* origins of the character in terms of representation. In fact, clear similarities do exist between Heathcliff and Rochester but while it was the latter who captured the imagination of Victorian readers, Heathcliff was called "a deformed monster" by E.P. Whipple, an American critic,[21] an opinion that seems to have been fairly general among the contemporary readership. This masterful aggressive figure, darkly handsome and intensely passionate, is the forerunner of the "tall, dark and handsome" stereotype of contemporary popular women's romances. However, in the nineteenth century this "dark" man would not necessarily signify exotic eroticism but might also denote the "other" – the unknown evil forces of nature and society that the daughters of a puritanical rector were hardly likely to come in contact with. Eagleton seems to clinch this debate saying:

> No mere critical hair-splitting can account for the protracted debate over whether Heathcliff is hero or demon. . . . The narrative techniques of the novel are deliberately framed to preserve these ambivalences.[22]

This view is corroborated by Nelly Dean's words of consolation to a chastened Heathcliff, "who knows but your father was Emperor of China, and your mother an Indian Queen." (*WH*, 57)

When Mr. Earnshaw first brings Heathcliff from Liverpool, he explains:

> See here wife! I was never so beaten with anything in my life: but you must e'en take it as a gift of God; though it is as dark almost as if it came from the devil. (*WH*, 36)

It is these frequent references to "dark" and "devil" that have directed attention to setting the novel within the Gothic tradition. At various points in the narrative, Heathcliff is referred to as an animal, a "hellish villain" who swears "I would have torn his [Linton's] heart out and drunk his blood" (*WH,* 155) and even though Nelly had tended him in his infancy, she is led to ask, "Is he a ghoul or a vampire?" (*WH*, 342) As Williams acknowledges, to place *Wuthering Heights* in a more familiar tradition would mean including "the fire and madness of romance; the apparitions and dreams of the Gothic." (*TEN,* 62) It is a commonplace to trace the roots of *Wuthering Heights* to the juvenilia of Emily and her sister Anne, the evidence of which remains in the extant Gondal poems. As Winifred Gerin points out:

> Essential to the function of this genre is the insistence on the inhuman nature of the hero/villain. . . . It was a conception or convention obviously attractive to her [Emily Bronte] and one which she adopted whole heartedly to the purposes of her own plot.[23]

In all probability, Bronte was familiar with the horror stories of Mary Shelley, Hoffman and James Hogg. In the Preface to the Haworth edition of *Wuthering Heights,* Charlotte confirms this affiliation to the Gothic tradition saying that "he was child neither of Lascar nor Gipsy, but a man's shape animated by demon-life – a Ghoul – an Afreet." (*WH,* VII) Heathcliff and Frankenstein's monster have several points in common, for example, inexplicable disappearance within the narrative and a return to an orgy of revenge, although these could be dismissed as superficial. The basic similarity is, however, that both are denied love, and it is this that totally distorts their characters. Thus the Gothic element is not metaphysical but explicable in terms of actual fact. Instead of being left at the level of the supernatural, the Gothic is incorporated to the "real" by subtle insertions. For example, even Heathcliff's character, which is heavily grounded in the Gothic convention, is not left at that but related to the "realist" framework by Nelly's comment that Earnshaw's treatment of Heathcliff was enough to convert a saint into a fiend. *Wuthering Heights* has several elements in common with the Yorkshire moors, the forbidding character of Heathcliff and Lockwood's nightmare. Jacques Blondel traces several possible influences from Walter Scott's *The Black Dwarf*,[24] *The Heart of Midlothian* and *Guy Mannering*, the Gothic novel, Byron, Hoffmann's tale "Das Majorat," tales in Blackwood's magazine and finally Shakespeare's *King Lear*. While all these elements are traceable, Blondel says, "one can speak only of an influence of method, not of an influence of feeling."[25]

According to Punter, the Gothic operates between two poles--(i) it rejects the realist mode, (ii) but not wishing the work to degenerate into fantasy alone, "it becomes important to establish its validity within the text itself: thus the increasing complexity of verification techniques."[26] It makes use of various modes like poetic prose, tragedy and expressionism. Punter calls the Gothic both a middle-class and anti-middle-class form because "it both confronts the bourgeoisie with its limitations and offers it modes of imaginary transcendence."[27] In fact, it performs its function by dealing with the bizarre and the "unspoken," thereby raising questions that corrode the complacent surface of accepted and propagated bourgeois values. In fact, Punter goes so far as to say that it "demonstrates the potential of revolution by daring to speak the socially unspeakable; but the very act of speaking it is an ambiguous gesture."[28] Here he seems to be attributing an ideological role to literature, much in the manner of Kettle who believes that art performs its function by changing men's consciousness. Bronte, however, does not leave the Gothic unmediated; it is inserted into the realist mode. According to Kettle:

> All art involves fantasy. A highly fantastic and superficially unlifelike story like *Gulliver's Travels* I class as realistic because it has to do with the actual problems and values of life. (*I*, 26)

While in *Wuthering Heights,* Kettle recognizes the "actual problems" and "values," he chooses to ignore the element of the "fantastic" present in it. As has been discussed already in Chapter 3, Kettle draws attention to the element of the fantastic that co-exists with the overtly "realist," but this seems true only of his theory, for in practice, his reading, in this instance, approximates to the socialist realist position, and the element of fantasy is overlooked. And Gothic is one genre that co-exists along with the realistic in many Victorian novels. Rosemary Jackson explains the strategy:

> A dialogue between fantastic and realistic narrative modes often operates within individual texts, as the second attempts to repress and diffuse the subversive thrust of the first. . . . Ironically, a Gothic tradition is increasingly employed to serve and not to subvert a dominant ideology. Its horrors, transgression and sexual "licence" are exploited by many Victorian novelists to deter a bourgeois reading public from political revolution, even as it provides them with a temporary fulfilment of ungratified desire.[29]

The Gothic element runs throughout the novel in a sort of dialogic tension with the realism and hence it cannot be seen as a "monolithic text" "presented to the reader as a finished, polished, aesthetic object."[30] Britton further explains Bakhtin's thesis that while the monologic text "*affirms* something, the dialogic text creates ambivalences – and also, a sense of infinite expansion of meanings . . . no one ever has the last word."[31] In this sense, *Wuthering Heights* can be taken to be a dialogic text, a point I will come back to in the next section. The novel ends on an ambivalent note. We are told of the appearance of the ghosts of Heathcliff and Catherine to the shepherd lad, and even though it might seem as if a satisfactory ending had been achieved with the Hareton-Cathy story, the tale of the earlier lovers continues uncertainly.

There are frequent references to the colour of Heathcliff's skin. He is "a dirty, ragged, black-haired child" (*WH,* 36) and Mr. Lockwood's first impression of him is that he is "a dark-skinned gipsy." (*WH,* 4) These references are "realistic" enough but given the fact of Heathcliff's marginal position, they lead one to examine the notion of the "other." This tendency to differentiate between individuals on the basis of skin is explained by Homi K. Bhabha:

> Skin, as the key signifier of cultural and racial difference in the stereotype, is the most visible of fetishes, recognized as "common knowledge" in a range of cultural, political, historical discourses, and plays a public part in the racial drama that is enacted every day in colonial societies.[32]

The discourse of the "other" can be characterized by the fear/desire ambivalence – fear on the one hand of the unknown, and desire for the manifestation of the difference that in turn is a gratification for the impulse to power. Within fiction it becomes a problem to represent the "other" and therefore the writer takes recourse to stereotypical images, such as the Gothic villain. Hence, what is thus in operation is a form of imperialist discourse for imperialism is "as much an attitude of mind as it is a description of territorial claims and boundaries."[33] This attitude is asserted over the alien people and in the character of Heathcliff there is the crucial conjuncture of the prejudice against the alien and the contempt for these elements of Western society "delinquents, the insane, women, the poor." As Said says:

> Along with all other peoples variously designated as backward, degenerate, uncivilized, and retarded, the orientals were viewed in a framework constructed out of biological determinism and moral-political admonishment.[34]

What I wish to suggest here is that Heathcliff is inserted as the "other" not as a foreigner or an alienated individual within society, but as the embodiment of an imperialist impulse that was not yet overtly manifest. The "savage" was considered reformable and religion was one institution that helped carry out this project. Yet Heathcliff as a realized literary creation rejects the efforts of religion and to an extent, he transgresses the "otherness" by inverting the Master/Slave dialectic.[35] However, this "otherness" is not totally transcended, for, throughout the novel Heathcliff maintains his identity as the outsider, and even economic power is unable to absorb him within the value system of that society. Even in death, he dispenses with the services of the Church and taking these specific examples, (that is, Joseph's fanaticism and the act of kicking the Bible into the kennel by Catherine and Heathcliff) one can conclude that Bronte is implicitly rejecting the institution of religion as hypocritical and repressive. What Bronte seems to be doing is to portray the social trends of the future at a microcosmic level. Thus the constant presence of the Gothic mode ruptures the fabric of the realist text and the overall structure of the novel exposes the conflictual ideologies in operation within that society. As Paul Brown explains, "the colonialist narrative requires and produces the other--an other which continually destabilizes and disperses the narrative's moment of conviction."[36] Just as Tolstoy was able to articulate the underlying and potential forces that were later to surface in Russian society, so Bronte is able to understand and articulate the world-views that were being structured at a deeper level.

The name Heathcliff itself is rather unusual, like its bearer, serving both as Christian name and surname.[37] The waif Heathcliff becomes Mr. Heathcliff after a mysterious absence, yet the constituent parts Heath and Cliff are strongly representative of the wild and untamed elements of nature rather than of social constraints. Thus Heathcliff, when he has the choice, chooses to live at Wuthering Heights rather than at Thrushcross Grange, the symbol of "civilization." Clifford Collins sees the vital "life-forces" in Heathcliff and this is what links Bronte to D.H. Lawrence. He quotes from one of Lawrence's letters:

> But we must grow from our deepest underground roots, out of the unconsciousness, not from the conscious concept which we falsely call ourselves.[38]

It is this unconscious affinity that forges the bond between Heathcliff and Cathy rather than the sole spirit-of-rebellion explanation that Kettle suggests. Catherine's oft-quoted words will explain the point further, "My love for Heathcliff resembles the eternal rocks beneath: a source of little visible delight, but necessary." (*WH,* 84) Heathcliff and Catherine share the freedom of spirit that marks the world of *Wuthering Heights,* and distinguishes it from Jane Austen's regulated and selective world of social graces.

The two worlds of nature and civilized society are basically irreconcilable, yet both Cathy and Heathcliff accept the values contrary to their deepest desires and are thus ultimately destroyed. By "nature," I do not mean "wildness" or "unrestricted elemental passions" alone but "human values" as well. Catherine, by accepting the values of the Grange, frustrates her chance of happiness forever. She is often accused of making the wrong choice, yet, within an early nineteenth century social context, did she really have a choice? Heathcliff, in order to avenge himself, acquires property and culture to ensure that the same is denied to Hareton.

Heathcliff is a multi-dimensional personality and various facets of his character filter through the varied consciousness of Lockwood, an objective observer, and Nelly Dean, a sensible though somewhat biased participant in the drama of life at Wuthering Heights as well as Thrushcross Grange. In spite of all his negative characteristics, it is clear that much of Bronte's sympathy lies with him.

As we have seen, an examination of the character of Heathcliff has brought to light the various strands that have been brought together not only in his creation but also in structuring the novel as a whole. The elements of romance, the Gothic and the notion of the "other" are not mere conventions but are complex strategies that subvert the ideological thrust of the realist mode. Kettle stresses the importance of social experience and its manifestation "in overt public forms" (*TEN,* 65) (that is, Heathcliff's rebellion). Williams believes that "When there is real dislocation . . . it can appear as radically and as authentically in what is apparently, what is actually personal or family experience." (*TEN,* 65) Kettle and Williams are clearly limited by their instinctive attachment to realism. Kettle negotiates it by taking recourse to a socialist realist position whereas Williams invokes notions of absolute desire. This is a basic difference in their approach to *Wuthering Heights* which will be further discussed in subsequent sections of this chapter.

II

> *Wuthering Heights,* like all the greatest works of art, is at once concrete and yet general, local and yet universal. (*I,* 130)

By positing opposing categories like "concrete" and "general," "local" and "universal," Kettle is making an all-encompassing though somewhat vague statement. Presumably, "concrete" is interchangeable with "particular," and the phrase "concrete and yet general" can be said to include "local and universal" although the latter has specifically spatial connotations whereas the former is a more or less open category. Kettle's use of "concrete" is akin to Leavis's use of it in a tactile way describing the feel of "the mists of the Yorkshire moors." (*I,* 130) In his analysis of *Nostromo,* Leavis commends Conrad's ability of depicting "the vivid reality of the things we are made to see and hear."[39] On the other hand, it is different from Lukacs's use of it, who talks about social reality rather than "felt" experience in this way.[40] "Concrete" can also be taken to dismiss notions of "abstract" and "vague." Kettle continues:

> There is nothing vague about this novel. . . . On the contrary, the realization is intensely concrete, we seem to smell the kitchen of Wuthering Heights, to feel the force of the wind across the moors, to sense the very changes of the seasons. Such concreteness is achieved . . . by precision. (*I*, 130)

Should the word "precision" seem to imply merely naturalistic description, Kettle points out that this is not so. Nor can the novel be fitted into the familiar slots of romance, the picaresque or even the moral fable. According to Kettle, the only novel to which *Wuthering Heights* has any resemblance is Dickens's *Oliver Twist* because its "germ is not an intellectualized idea or concept." (*I*, 131) He clarifies the statement by saying that like Dickens, Emily Bronte "works not in ideas but in images, that is to say concepts which have a significance and validity on a level different from that of logical thought. (*I*, 131)[41] Here Kettle praises this use of images thereby stressing the poetic aspect of the novel in the manner of Leavis. More than that, he points to the symbolic dimension, which it would seem is a different discourse from that of the "concrete." But, as Kettle's concluding statement seems to suggest, "symbolic" can be ultimately related to the "general," "Emily Bronte's novel is at the same time a statement about the life she knew, the life of Victorian England, and a statement about life as such." (*I*, 144) One might observe at this point that the book is set in pre-Victorian England and much of the experience of Bronte is also pre-Victorian. As Q.D. Leavis points out:

> The point about dating the novel as ending in 1801 (instead of being contemporary with the Bronte's own lives) . . . is to fix its happenings at a time when the old rough farming culture based on a naturally patriarchal family life was to be challenged, tamed and routed by social and cultural changes that were to produce the Victorian class consciousness and "unnatural" ideal of gentility.[42]

In a sense then, *Wuthering Heights* is a historical novel not in the sense of using history as spectacle but rather like the novels of Tolstoy. *Wuthering Heights* is not of the magnitude and dimension of the Tolstoyan novels which range over a vast number of concerns, but it embodies a similar sense of historical change even though parallels can be drawn between the two writers, as pointed out in the earlier section. However, by placing her novel in the past, Bronte has not "fixed" the happenings of that society in the sense of depicting them as static, but as dynamic process. As Kettle points out in his chapter on *Middlemarch,* "no society is really static when an artist looks at it." (*I*, 171) This analysis points to Kettle's commitment to dialectical materialism. On the other hand, this chapter on *Wuthering Heights* displays a marked allegiance to the Leavisite enterprise.

For, "human values," "moral force" and "positive values" figure prominently in Kettle's analysis of *Wuthering Heights* as well as his preoccupation with "concreteness." As Kettle claims that this is the factor contributory to the lasting appeal and greatness of the novel, it would be best to examine how it is used and justified in relation to this novel. In order to do this I will examine the interpretations of Kettle and Williams of the celebrated passage when Catherine declares her love for Heathcliff. Kettle quotes:

> My great miseries in the world have been Heathcliff's miseries. . . . My love for Linton is like the foliage in the woods: time will change it. . . . My love for Heathcliff resembles the eternal rocks beneath: a source of little visible delight but necessary. Nelly I *am* Heathcliff. (*WH,* 84)

Commenting on the relationship, Kettle says that this is "not primarily a sexual relationship," nor is it "platonic passion" nor can it be designated "romantic love," but he says that this deep affinity is "forged in rebellion and in order to grasp the concrete and unromantic nature of this book, it is necessary to recall the nature of that rebellion." (*I*, 133) It is crucial here to examine what exactly Kettle means by the term "romantic." Can it refer to the idealistic, the unreal or the sexual? In the "Introductory" entitled "Realism and Romance," Kettle is well aware of the ambiguities of the term. He says:

> Romance is a [n] . . . dangerous word, on the one hand because of its connections with Romance (as opposed to Teutonic or Slav or Celtic) languages, on the other because of all the associations of the Romantic Movement, the fashionable denigrations of which one would not wish to support. (*I*, 27)

Therefore by "romance" and "romantic," he indicates "escapism, wishful thinking, unrealism." (*I*, 26) Therefore, "unromantic" would mean "realistic" or "relevant to real life." (*I*, 26) But by denying the sexual aspect of the Catherine-Heathcliff relationship, he seems also to be endowing the term "unromantic" with the connotation of sexlessness. By stressing "the concrete and unromantic nature of this book," Kettle is limiting his analysis. His hesitation in conceding the sexual nature of the relationship is criticized by Ronald Frankenburg, who further criticizes him in "his search for the hidden asocial essence--a humanity which transcends not only class but also gender."[43] Kettle uses "concrete" here particularly to relate the origin and the genesis of the rebellion to its immediate social context. But in doing so, he goes to the other extreme from romanticism, (to which his statement is meant initially to be a corrective) for example, he talks of how "Heathcliff, the waif from the Liverpool slums, is treated kindly by old Mr. Earnshaw but insulted and degraded by Hindley." (*I*, 133) By analyzing the character of Heathcliff in this manner, by stressing his social connections so emphatically, Kettle is greatly privileging the realistic mode over the other discursive modes within the book.

Further, Kettle looks at Heathcliff and Catherine as comrades-at-arms, and significantly underplays the question of the extraordinary emotional intensity of the relationship (as well as completely ignoring the question of gender differentiation). While they are rebelling conjointly against the tyranny of Hindley, their highly charged emotional relationship cannot be ignored. It appears to be a complete relationship with both Heathcliff and Cathy responding to each other at all levels--ideological, intellectual and physical but above all emotional. Even though Catherine pettishly complains to Heathcliff: "What do you talk about? You might be dumb, or a baby, for anything you say to amuse me," (*WH*, 70) yet this irritable outburst cannot eclipse the complete communication that they share, for instance their childhood rapport, the happiness at their meeting when Heathcliff returns after being "absent and silent for three years" (*WH*, 99) and finally their union in death. It might be suggested that this level of the relationship was maintained by the efforts of the obsessive Heathcliff as opposed to those of the selfish Catherine, yet her speech declaring "My great miseries in this world have been Heathcliff's miseries and I watched and felt each from the beginning: My great thought in living is himself" (*WH*, 84) conclusively silences such doubts. However, if this speech is taken literally, it is evident that Catherine's participation in Heathcliff's miseries has not been "from the beginning" for, at his arrival, her greeting consisted in "spitting on the stupid little thing." (*WH,* 36) However, her subsequent identification with him is complete as will be discussed later. Even though the language of this passage borders on the metaphysical, the basis of this identification is materially explicable as evidenced in the text.

It is significant that Williams also quotes (though not at quite the same length) the same passage. He brushes aside interpretations that name these emotions "mystical" or "romantic." (*TEN,* 66) Taken out of context these words would imply "romantic extravagance" but within the action of the story, "the reality of the relationship is simply there and unbreakable." (*TEN,* 66) For Williams, it is not desire "for" but desire "in" the other. Desire "for" is subject to external conditions and therefore highly variable, whereas desire "in" is a "necessary relationship, in which a self, a world, is at once found and confirmed." (*TEN,* 71) Williams describes it as:

> that kind of relationship which is truly given rather than taken, which is there and absolute before anything else can be said. In its quality as given--here in a childhood, a shared childhood in a place--it is where social and personal, one's self and others, grow from a single root. (*TEN,* 67)

By describing this relationship as given, Williams is covertly reversing his previous position. Here the implication is metaphysical. The other discrepancy in the statement is pointed out by the interviewers in *Politics and Letters,* who confront Williams saying, "What you seem to be pushing towards here is a description of a relationship which is prior to any distinction between social and personal at all."[44] Williams defends himself as follows:

> My own image of the single root was only meant to suggest that the relationship and the most substantial kind of personal identity come from the same experience--not that the experience is pre-social, but that it emerges before the separated categories of social and individual are relevant.[45]

Williams further explains that such relationships do not conform to conventionally accepted norms and therefore are not describable in conventional terms. One may either make use of metaphysical/subjectivist terms, but none is adequate. Analyzing the passage further, Williams says that it contains an affirmation and a denial at the same time – the affirmation being the complete existence and identification of the self in another and the denial is caused by taking this relationship for granted and substituting a more desirable reality in place of it. It is this "false" reality that causes all the disruption as in Catherine's case – her choice of Linton causes a "storm" that is only "calmed" a generation later.

As we have seen, Kettle and Williams read the relationship in different ways following the general drift of their respective arguments. Kettle relates it directly to its social situation stressing its "comrades-at-arms" aspect and while this emphasis is helpful to an understanding of the novel, it overlooks both the fact of gender differentiation and the intensity of the personal, a fact that is stressed by Williams. Williams believes that "the reality of the relationship is simply there and unbreakable" (*TEN,* 66) locating it in a childhood "where social and personal, one's self and others, grow from a single root." This statement, as pointed out earlier, was subsequently substantiated by Williams in *Politics and Letters.* Here again there is no reference to the fact that within the novel of Emily Bronte, feminine/masculine identities are shown to be structured differently.

Gilbert and Gubar comment on this relationship saying that "together they constitute an autonomous and androgynous (or more accurately, gynandrous) whole . . . making up one complete woman."[46] While it is reasonable to agree with the first half of the sentence, it would be preferable to substitute "person" for "woman" in the last phrase. They further explain their compatibility in the following terms:

> [Heathcliff] provides her with an extra body to lessen her female vulnerability, so she fills his need for a soul, a voice, a language with which to address *cultured* men like Edgar.[47] [my italics]

Perhaps the support of a virile figure like Heathcliff can "lessen her female vulnerability" but to "address cultured men like Edgar" was neither Heathcliff's intention nor desire. Besides, Catherine can hardly be designated the typical Victorian "feminine" heroine for she is neither meek nor docile but fiery, full of spirit and aggression and by the logic of Gilbert and Gubar, it would follow that she should be the perfect complement for her opposite Edgar. Rather than being a question of opposites being compatible, it is more a matter of possessing common traits as Catherine tells Nelly: "Whatever our souls are made of, his [Heathcliff's] and mine are the same" (*WH,* 82) and this can be interpreted not in a metaphysical sense but can be traced to the formation of social identity. As Lacan points out:

> Language orders masculinity and femininity, they are positions which shift between and within discourses. . . .The infant is compelled to acknowledge the significance of sexual difference through the presence or absence of the phallus--the primary and privileged sign of sexual difference.[48]

Thus at one level, Catherine's statement "I *am* Heathcliff" might be taken as a projection of this desire for the phallus. At another, it could signify the fact that as a woman she has no position within a patriarchal set-up comprising inheritance and power, and has therefore been reduced to the level of the dispossessed and socially castrated Heathcliff. This realization comes to her as she grows into womanhood. At the predominantly masculine Heights, Catherine is hardly effectively socialized as a girl. As Nelly says "she was hardly six years old, but she could ride any horse in the stable." (*WH,* 35) She is allowed to roam the moors unchecked with Heathcliff and is even allowed to sleep in his bed for "neither little boys nor little girls possess the phallus."[49] It is only during her sojourn at the Grange that her socialization as a girl takes place along stereotypical lines and she returns:

> instead of a wild, hatless little savage jumping into the house . . . there "lighted from a handsome black pony a very dignified person, with brown ringlets . . . the dogs came bounding up . . . she dared hardly touch them lest they should fawn upon her splendid garments. (*WH,* 52)

Catherine has now changed at three levels: she has grown from childhood to adulthood, she had become aware of her femininity and she has been initiated into a consciousness of her class position. It is this education that has inculcated in her the false values that cause a conflict with her primary inclinations and lead to the tragic turn of events. She feels out of her element at the Grange and keeps longing for "home" and the wish that "I were a girl again, half savage and hardy, and free." (*WH,* 130) She rejects the constraints imposed upon her by Victorian society at one level and by civilization as opposed to nature on another. Ellen Moers interprets this desire for a return to "childhood eroticism" much in the manner of Christina Rossetti's *Goblin Market*[50] and states that the relationship carries "the aroma of incest."[51]

The alternative readings of the Catherine-Heathcliff relationship suggest that Kettle's insistence on the "concrete" and socially explicable elements of *Wuthering Heights* produce a narrowing of the novel's possible meanings. A somewhat similar process can be noted in his discussion of the narrative form. According to Kettle, the roles of the two narrators are designed to contribute to the "concreteness" of the novel. Commenting on the subject, Kettle says:

> Their function (they the two most "normal" people in the book) is partly to keep the story close to the earth, to make it believable, partly to comment on it from a common-sense point of view and thereby to reveal in part the inadequacy of such common sense. (*I*, 132)

By using the phrase "close to the earth" Kettle is pointing once again to the novel's realistic aspect. But by questioning the validity of the adequacy of common sense, Kettle is calling the whole realist enterprise into question. Similarly, the reference to narrative method is incompatible with the general drift of *An Introduction to the English Novel* which, as shown in Chapter 3, deals mainly with thematic issues based on the "life-pattern" relationship.

The story filters through the dual perspectives of Lockwood and Nelly continually raising questions as to the possibility of any objective reality existing independent of a subjective reading of it. While Lockwood is relatively disinterested, Nelly cannot be considered as such. Flitting between the Heights and the Grange, and contriving minor strategies, Nelly is as much involved in the dramatic events as the main characters. However, the presence of the two narrators does create a distance between the reader and the characters, "a jolting out of empathy" in Brechtian terms. As Kettle points out, "At critical points in the narrative we are not conscious of their existence at all," (*I*, 132) yet this effect of involvement is frequently dissolved by removing the narrative to a different plane, that is, of immediate conversation between the narrators. For example, there is the reader's total absorption in the intense story which is then alternated by casual comments between the narrators. In simple terms, Lockwood can be seen as the hypothetical reader[52] and Nelly as the author surrogate, both constructing the events that are twice removed from the actual reader's immediate sphere of experience.

While Kettle sees Nelly as down-to-earth and therefore harmless, David Musselwhite does not see her in quite such an innocent role. He says:

> It is this role she performs as insulating mediator that makes Nelly Dean the real villain of the piece for she is the figure of that bland literacy that prevents all reading of the self and all knowledge of the other.[53]

Following Balibar and Macherey, Musselwhite believes that literature is, in fact, an "ideological *operateur*"[54] because it makes use of a standard language which the bourgeoisie has devised as a tool for maintaining its cultural hegemony. He continues:

> The function of this language is to disguise contradictions and it is this language of conciliation which makes the ideological resolutions of conflict in literature possible: literature can do no more than rework and repeat those conciliations at a higher level.[55]

It is true that Nelly does not speak the Yorkshire dialect as Joseph does and only slips into it occasionally. If this seems implausible, Bronte does not forget to make Lockwood remark to Nelly, "Excepting a few provincialisms of slight consequence, you have no marks of the manners which I am habituated to consider as peculiar to your class." (*WH,* 62-63) Nelly's "sensible" narration is designed to lull the reader into accepting all that she says but Lockwood's presence is an effective antidote to such designs. This plus the ambivalent effects generated by the novel prevent one from accepting Musselwhite's thesis *in toto*.

What I wish to reaffirm here is that *Wuthering Heights* is not a "monologic" text but a dialogic one, for it embodies dialogue at three levels. First, it has the dialogue between the two speakers Nelly and Lockwood. At a more abstract level, there is a dialogue between "a fairly coherent set of principles, interests and attitudes."[56] This then is the interaction between opposing categories like "nature" and "civilization," "the head" and the "heart," "calm" and "storm." In fact, "storm" and "calm" represent the two attitudes that are held in dialectic tension throughout the novel. Commenting on this, Traversi says:

> That she felt *both* emotions, that her own creative impulse depended upon the balance, the continual tension set up between them. . . . The impulse to unite these two necessities of her nature is the true source of inspiration of the novel.[57]

Allott also attributes the book's success to Bronte's "attempt to do justice to the conflicting demands of the heart and head"[58] which can be equated with the storm/calm metaphors. Both Traversi and Allott read the novel as trying to resolve the various contradictions and ambivalences that it embodies. This is the typical position of critics trying to trace a Hegelian totality within a realist text. However, there is a sense of ambivalences and pluralism in the novel rather than a neatly resolved structure. Finally, there is the dialogic tension between the various discourses within the text, that is, the Gothic, the Romantic, and the realist as we have seen at length in the previous section.

One consequence of this tension is the text's consistent ability to surprise and shock. Lockwood (as the reader's representative) is the outsider, the Victorian gentleman of leisure, seeking repose in the country. Expecting to find a conventional middle-class set-up, he decides to make a neighbourly call at the Heights, where all his expectations are brutally overturned. Kettle himself produces a persuasive analysis in relation to this point in examination, for example, of the scene when Catherine is dying and "Heathcliff appears out of the night." (*I*, 138)[59]. However, as Kettle points out, the scene could be handled conventionally in two ways--either Catherine would reject Heathcliff and vindicate the claims of the institution of marriage, or the two lovers would be united in adulterous liaison. Bronte accepts neither convention, and the scene that follows is extremely moving in its passionate intensity. Instead of tender words, Heathcliff's response is entirely ruthless and he blames and damns Catherine for her folly in rejecting him. While this reverses normally accepted standards, it is in keeping with the stark character of the relationship.[60]

This element of the shocking, unexpected, the strange does overall then constitute different problems for the approaches of both Kettle and Williams. Their ways of trying to overcome these problems differ. Indeed Williams might seem to contradict Kettle when, in respect of the Catherine-Heathcliff relationship, he says:

> Without the central relationships, the physical and social landscape of *Wuthering Heights* would be a country waiting to be entered, waiting to be understood, for all its careful detail. (*TEN*, 66)

While Williams privileges personal relationships, Kettle stresses the significance of the social situation and its wider symbolic implications. In one of his concluding remarks, Kettle says:

> Its *[Wuthering Heights's]* evocation of nature, of moorland and storm, of the stars and the seasons is an essential part of its revelation of the very movement of life itself. (*I*, 144)

From the specific, Kettle moves to the general. Throughout his analysis, there is a constant attempt to bring out the "literal" and the "symbolic" elements. On the other hand, Williams, while emphasizing that "*Wuthering Heights* is quite central to its time," explains that by this he does not mean its "documentary" element or its "symbolism." (*TEN*, 69) Here again, a direct reversal of Kettle's position is evident. Williams does not see social experience manifesting itself in such direct and unmediated forms as Kettle does. For Williams, social experience "in its very quality as social reality penetrates, is already at the roots of, relationships of every kind." (*TEN*, 65) While realism is the ultimate criterion of value for both critics, they arrive at it through different routes. The final section of this chapter will discuss other facets of their similarities and differences by focusing on the question of fictional tradition and the place of *Wuthering Heights* within it.

III

Williams points out that it has been said that *Wuthering Heights* is a novel without precedents or antecedents. Not willing to accept this absolute and dismissive statement, Williams modifies it:

> Its structure is unique, though in spirit it is in no way isolated; it belongs in an English tradition with Blake and Lawrence and very specifically with Hardy. (*TEN,* 63-64)

The first cause here is fairly straightforward, and can be substantiated in Williams's own words. The "unique" structure can be attributed to:

> The multiple narrative through secondary characters, the complications of the time-scheme, the precision of the complicated plot of inheritance and generations are so deliberate, so measured and the staple of the language so consciously formal. (*TEN,* 64)

The problematic categories here are "spirit" and "English tradition." One dictionary defines "spirit" as "the real meaning, the true intention, underlying principle that binds together different discourses with a single unifying thread."[61] It is in this sense that "spirit" is the connecting link that binds these disparate writers within a tradition. Tradition, as we have seen in Chapter 4, is a process of selection and re-selection (as Williams points out) and therefore changes with each generation. Williams constructs a tradition in opposition to that formulated by Leavis but which does not depart from the limits of the canonical. The tradition (Blake-Lawrence-Hardy) that is suggested here is thus a sort of submerged tradition and it is clear that Williams is not so interested in substantiating this particular connection as he is in establishing the George Eliot-Hardy-Lawrence one, for he does not follow up this connection even in the subsequent chapters on Hardy and Lawrence. Since Williams does not make the links of his sub-tradition clear, I will now examine the binding "spirit" that holds together writers as disparate as Blake, Bronte, Hardy and Lawrence. What is obvious is that Williams takes it for granted that his audience, in the course of his lectures will grasp his intent, needing no further substantiation, which is, perhaps, fair enough.

The reference to Blake might be taken to refer to some element of mysticism. Could this be the common denominator between the different writers? Derek Traversi certainly endows the novel with a mystical significance:

> From a profound sense of the finite and dependent nature of man . . . there arises the desire to make contact with a reality which is beyond the self and by which the self may be completed.[62]

But before we begin to make such links, we must remember Williams's remarks on the famous passage where Catherine likens her love for Heathcliff to the "eternal rocks beneath." Williams says, "These words of Cathy have been called mystical. . . . But I don't know how that can be said." (*TEN,* 66) Similarly, while some critics have picked out metaphysical elements like the "gods" and an unseen all-powerful Fate in Hardy's fiction, Williams does not give much weight to this aspect:

> The complexity of Hardy's fiction . . . he runs the whole gamut . . . difficult humane perception of limitation, which cannot be resolved by nostalgia or charm or an approach to mysticism, but which are lived through by all the characters. . . . (*TEN,* 106)

While Williams, here, dismisses notions of mysticism, it is pertinent to point out that in his own analysis of Lawrence's *The Rainbow,* he does begin to speak in quasi-mystical terms.[63] Describing certain relationships, he says that they are "physical certainly but physical mainly as a discovery of being, of spirit." (*TEN,* 178) However, this is insufficient to make "mysticism" generally applicable to the work of these writers in Williams's reading of them and therefore, it cannot be plausibly included in his use of the term "spirit."

Wuthering Heights and the novels of Hardy and Lawrence could possibly be referred to as "poetic" not in the sense of Leavis's definition of the novel as "dramatic poem"[64] nor in the sense of "poetic" fiction as applicable to, for example, Virginia Woolf's novels, but in a more general linguistic sense. In this broad sense, it would be possible to include most novels rather than just to forge a connection with Blake. Williams himself uses the connecting and opposed categories of "customary" and "educated" language to bind George Eliot, Hardy and Lawrence in a single tradition, but Bronte does not figure in this tradition though Williams does make a passing reference to her use of language, saying that it is "in so many different ways formal, among the roughness, the plainness, of so much of the speech and the life--that we know in reading an extraordinary and intricate tension," (*TEN*, 64) which it seems to me, amounts to much the same thing as the customary/educated dichotomy. However, it is difficult to make any plausible connection with Blake here.

Or can the necessary connection between all these disparate writers be discernible in their handling of particular social themes--perhaps the attention to social relations? In Hardy's case, Williams says:

> Work enters his novels more decisively than in any English novelist of comparable importance. And it is not merely illustrative, it is seen as it is, as a central kind of learning. (*TEN*, 116)

What is more, there is a deep connection between "work and desire," (*TEN*, 117) for example, Tess takes her major decisions while at work. Lawrence brought miners, labourers and the working community into his fictional world and because he feels with them, his language becomes "colloquial and informal" (*TEN*, 173) rather than "abstract and polite." (*TEN*, 173) In *Wuthering Heights,* the inhabitants of the Heights are represented as involved in agricultural labour, but here again, work is not important in itself but as Eagleton points out, "work and human relations are roughly coterminous; work is socialized, personal relations mediated through a context of labour."[65] Blake does refer to the "chimney-sweeper's cry"[66] but he does not describe the work as such. What this implies in Blake is "a new way of seeing the human and social order as a whole,"[67] a method that looks forward to Dickens but Williams does not mention any links with Lawrence or Hardy.

Discussing Hardy's novels, Williams uses words which could very aptly describe the situation in *Wuthering Heights:*

> People choose wrongly but under terrible pressures: under the confusions of class, under its misunderstandings under the calculated rejections of a divided separating world. (*TEN*, 117)

It is under the pressures of social mobility that personal relationships are jeopardized as in the case of Tess and Jude. Correcting the view that Hardy's fiction embodies a sort of timelessness, Williams says that while he does describe the effect of the residual culture on present society and does describe the old landscape of the country, these are not Hardy's primary concerns. What matters is:

> the immediate and actual relationships between people, which occur within existing contemporary pressures and are at most modulated and interpreted by the available continuities. (*TEN*, 113-14)

In this passage, it is the people and their relationships that are of prime importance whereas in the previous one social pressures seem to be paramount. As far as Tess is concerned, her whole life is controlled by past pressures.

In his chapter on Lawrence, Williams spends a great deal of time and space explaining how Lawrence has managed to create a balance between the customary and the educated. Talking about the "experience of community" in *The Rainbow,* Williams remarks:

> a social system, industrialism, has destroyed given reality by forcing people into systematic roles--the new reality, that which in its turn is irreducible and radical, has to be fought for. (*TEN*, 178)

In other words, Williams is repeating what he has already said with regard to Hardy and Bronte. It is ultimately a problem of the "knowable community" which could then encompass most nineteenth century novels.

A further clue can be derived from Williams's comment that though the interests of the Bronte sisters are quite different from those of Dickens or Elizabeth Gaskell, "in experience and in these novels it is not like that." (*TEN,* 60) It is evident that the latter deal more overtly with social problems. Yet the factor common to all is that the experience their novels embody is the penetrating response to the crisis of their period when social mobility was affecting relationships in various ways. It is this stress on the depiction of relationships and finding connections between the social, economic, moral influences, that connects Blake, Bronte, Lawrence and Hardy. Similarly, Bronte, Lawrence and Hardy have reiterated this claim in complex ways, for example, Bronte in the Heathcliff-Cathy relationship, Lawrence on his stress on elemental human passions and Hardy's depiction of rural life and the men working there. Williams describes Blake's world as:

> a world of desire and hunger, of rebellion and of pallid convention: the terms of desire and fulfilment and the terms of oppression and deprivation profoundly connected in a single dimension of experience. (*TEN,* 60)

It is this "connection" that is the unique achievement of Blake and the central factor that binds the work of these writers. Williams's emphasis is on experience. His use of "experience" is different from that of Kettle in relation to *Wuthering Heights,* for according to Kettle the reader is made to "feel" the mists, the moors. This refers to the reader's experience, whereas in the case of Williams, the experience is the general structure of feeling that is put in perspective. The crisis of the time is manifested not in overt political radicalism but in a relationship which is made:

> problematic and dangerous by the increasing pressure, the external and internal and continuing pressure, to reshape, to deform--it is how Blake saw it--this most human, most absolute experience. (*TEN,* 61)

What Williams is referring to, is that the trans-generic connecting link lies in the fact that all of them articulate the general structure of feeling of their period. These writers prioritize "human longing and need" over "the emerging system." (*TEN,* 61) There is thus a gap between the dominant social character of a period and its structure of feeling. Williams defines social character as "a valued system of behaviour and attitudes--is taught, formally and informally; it is both an ideal and a mode."[68] What is finally expressed in art is not the social character, but the structure of feeling. To Williams:

> For here [in the arts], if anywhere, this characteristic is likely to be expressed; often not consciously, but by the fact that here, in the only examples we have of recorded communication that

> outlive its bearers, the actual living sense, the deep community that makes the communication possible, is naturally drawn upon.[69]

It is interesting to note that Kettle also relates *Wuthering Heights* to Blake's poetry. Commenting on the passage when Heathcliff reacts explosively to Nelly's report of how Edgar looked after the ailing Catherine out of "duty" and "humanity," he says:

> The emotion behind his denunciation of Edgar is *moral* emotion. The words "duty" and "humanity," "pity" and "charity" have precisely the kind of force Blake gives such words in poetry. (*I*, 137)

Williams's connections are made primarily on social grounds whereas Kettle relates *Wuthering Heights* to Blake on an ethical basis in a manner reminiscent of Leavis. Kettle is more definitive in his statements, for example, he says, "*Wuthering Heights* is essentially the same kind of novel as *Oliver Twist*." (*I*, 130) Kettle explains the connection saying that both novels are "symbolic" for in both, the writers work "not in ideas but in images."[70]

Williams thus links these writers on the basis of an essentially Romantic structure of feeling which is "an intense affirmation of love and desire and an intense often desperate apprehension of isolation and loss." (*TEN*, 61) This kind of feeling is found in Blake and Williams considers it an achievement of the Bronte sisters that they "remade the novel so that this kind of passion could be directly communicated." (*TEN*, 61) But the difference between Charlotte and Emily Bronte lies in the fact that in the former this disparity between "desire" and "loss" is resolved, in Emily it is irreconcilable in the manner of tragic dilemmas. In Hardy, there is a sense of loss but finally there is a note of affirmation as in *Tess of the d'Urbervilles*. Hardy is different from Lawrence because he does not "celebrate isolation and separation" (*TEN*, 117), although he does register it in the later novels.

In Williams's opening statement, the problematic category "spirit" is finally undefinable, for it has connotations of intangibility just as the word experience has. For Williams all experience is a process, and it is the ability to articulate the structure of feeling of their time that places these writers in a tradition. The thread that finally links these writers is the expression of unfulfilled social desire and the situation is somewhat akin to Goldmann's problematic hero who looks for fulfilment in a society that denies it or the "degraded . . . search for authentic values in a world itself degraded."[71] In Emily Bronte, Heathcliff and Catherine, in Hardy, Tess and Jude, in Lawrence, Paul Morel are all characters struggling against implacable social forces.

To place *Wuthering Heights* in a more familiar tradition would mean including "the fire and madness of romance; the apparitions and dreams of the Gothic." (*TEN,* 62) Williams does not follow these connections beyond this preliminary reference. As discussed in Section I, neither does Kettle, for in the case of both critics the emphasis is on realism. The articulation of the structure of feeling of a particular period is a strategy of realism. Williams places *Wuthering Heights* with the works of Blake, Lawrence and Hardy without reference to any specific work. On the other hand, Kettle relates it to *Oliver Twist* just as Leavis brackets it with *The House with the Green Shutters.* By drawing the links on the basis of the symbolic, Kettle is not losing sight of his basic argument in favour of realism. On the contrary, it is particular instances that point to larger issues, for Bronte's novel is "not abstract but concrete, not vague but particular"(*I,* 144) and therefore she is able to present not only the "life of Victorian England" but a "statement about life as such." Similarly, when Oliver Twist asks for more gruel in the workhouse, Kettle explains the power and appeal of the scene to millions of readers all over the world:

> We care, we are involved, not because it is Oliver we are close to . . . but because every starved orphan in the world is involved, and the master of the workhouse . . . is not anyone in particular but every agent of an oppressive system everywhere. (*I*, 117)

While in the case of Williams the connection is made at a thematic level Kettle works on the basis of technique. Williams believes that tradition is a highly selective process and must be constantly structured and restructured in the manner of Goldmann's theory of world-views. Hence his construction of the alternate traditions.

This then raises the question of the validity and the working of "tradition." How far is it an ideological construct and to what extent is it arbitrary, are issues closely related to the above discussion.

According to Frank Kermode, "tradition" is the word for the continuum, "talent" is the historical agent of renovation.[72] Tradition is not a simple process of handing down from past to present but a dynamic one of renewal and replenishment. Taken in its widest connotation, it involves a historical sense which

> compels a man to write not merely with his own generation in his bones, but with a feeling that the whole of the literature of Europe from Homer and within it the whole of the literature of his own country has a simultaneous existence and composes a simultaneous order.[73]

It is presumed that "man" here would include the writing of women as well. As we have seen, traditions and sub-traditions are formed on the basis of the preoccupations of those who "map the field." Leavis frames his "great tradition" on an ethical basis. Williams's tradition is a corrective to this followed by Eagleton's modifications, thus resulting in a "critical" tradition. Kettle's "tradition" is framed on a progressive outlook, not in the sense of dealing with working-class writers or those with a strictly progressive world-view, but in the sense of extending and secularizing it. It is evident that all these are, what can be termed primary traditions as opposed to sub-traditions which take into account minority projects like women's writing.

Gilbert and Gubar in *The Madwoman in the Attic* trace a tradition of women's writing, beginning with an account of Jane Austen, to Mary Shelley, to Emily and Charlotte Bronte, George Eliot and the writings of women poetesses in the nineteenth century, Emily Dickinson in particular. It is clear that the established women writers alone find a place in this tradition. John Gross attributes the reason for a partial discussion of women writers to the fact of "residual Great Traditionalism."[74] This once again points to male domination within the field of literature and academia. Ellen Moers extends the tradition to an international level starting from the eighteenth century to the present and believes that women's writing may be "apart from, but hardly subordinate to the mainstream."[75]

This leads to the question of Bronte's position as a woman writer. At roughly the same time that she was writing, "Both women and the working class emerged in the 1840s, two universal social and political categories which demanded universal rights and liberties."[76] It is questionable whether Bronte was aware of these emerging trends and how far these determined her writing. For novel writing was a predominantly male domain even though the activity may be considered "feminine"[77] as it is restricted to the home which is considered a female preserve. The nineteenth century is regarded as an "age of women writers"[78] though Richard Altick estimates that from 1800 to 1935, the percentage of female to male novelists was only about 20 percent.[79]

Showalter distinguishes three major phases in women's writing. The first phase, the Feminine is characterized by the adoption of male pseudonyms and a process of "*imitation* of the prevailing modes of their dominant tradition, and *internalization* of its standards of art."[80] This phase extended from 1840 to 1880, the time of George Eliot's death. Bronte clearly belongs to this category but how far she imitated the dominant tradition or modified it, will be assessed in the next section.[81] Ellen Moers believes that some women writers, especially Jane Austen, were influenced by women's writing, whereas Emily Bronte was "hardly at all."[82] This inevitably leads to the issue of whether various modes of writing can be termed gender-specific. Terry Lovell agrees that men and women have different social experiences and "This experience plus their socialization into 'feminine' identities generates a feminine sensibility more often in women than in men" and that certain genres do attract women writers, but "writing *per se* is gender ambiguous" and that "the sexual identities of authors cannot be inferred from his/her skill in utilizing different conventions"[83] for not only can conventions be learnt but they are also subject to change.

The point in referring to these traditions is to highlight the fact that "traditions" cannot be taken as either objective or as authoritative. For example, it is possible to make cross-cultural connections between *Wuthering Heights* and Faulkner's *Absalom, Absalom* ! Not only is the structure of the novel convoluted, it even employs the multiple narrator technique and a deliberate distortion of chronological sequence which demands active reader participation in order to piece together the various relationships that the novel depicts. Traditions, as we have seen, can be constructed on the basis of thematic, technical, linguistic considerations, but ultimately these considerations are ideological.

However, that is not to dismiss the need or value of traditions. Williams, by pointing in the rather unusual direction of Blake and in tracing links with Hardy and Lawrence has highlighted aspects that have been hitherto ignored. By referring to *Oliver Twist* and *Wuthering Heights,* Kettle has explained both to advantage. Traditions, therefore, are useful only in so far as they structure and highlight fresh links.

IV

Wuthering Heights then is far from the model classic realist text and poses quite severe problems when viewed from this perspective. While it is true that, in general, the Marxist position has rescued Emily Bronte's novel from the "transcendentalists" (as Kettle points out in a more specific context, (*I*, 143) who view it in mystical terms, and placed it on a firmer material footing, yet its tendency has been to take the realist standpoint which has led to an inadequate reading of it. For example, as we have seen there is a strong element of the Gothic in *Wuthering Heights,* whereas in the majority of the prominent nineteenth century novels (that is, in those of Eliot, Thackeray, Mrs. Gaskell and Hardy) this element is absent. To base a model of analysis on these texts and to apply it to "deviant" ones like *Wuthering Heights,* is unhelpful. Lockwood's ghastly dream which triggers off his curiosity, Heathcliff's ghoulish grave-digging, the shepherd's vision of the ghostly figures, are some major instances which cannot be ignored. These "non-realistic" elements are constantly pulling the text away from the solely representational. Yet the Gothic is one aspect that neither Kettle nor Williams emphasize.

Their focus is on realism, a highly problematic category, for even within a Marxist framework, varying definitions coexist, as we have already seen. While Kettle and Williams could be broadly placed within a classic realist position, their stance differs. Kettle's position alternates between that of the socialist realists on the one hand and the Leavisites on the other as exemplified by his reference to Heathcliff as representing the working classes[84] and in looking for the "concrete" in terms of textual experience. Williams looks for social experience in more mediated forms, that is, in terms of personal relationships. However, neither analysis covers all the dimensions of the Catherine-Heathcliff relationship, which again is neither a crisis of social identity nor is it simply a question of the individual psyche, but a complex of both. Nor does their reading adequately account for the character of Heathcliff.

Wuthering Heights, does not have a single authoritative narrator mediating, directing and controlling the reader's responses. On the other hand, the text is de-centred by the narration being placed in the hands of secondary characters. Thus the "monologism" is dispersed and the "dialogism" between the narrative voices produces a "polyphonic" effect. As Bakhtin says of Dostoevsky:

> What unfolds in his works is not a multitude of characters and fates in a single objective world, illuminated by a single authorial consciousness; rather a *plurality of consciousness, with equal rights and each with its own world,* combine but are not merged in the unity of the event.[85]

It is in this sense of the "unfinal," that Bronte's novel approximates to Dostoevsky's *The Brothers Karmazov.* This plurality and ambivalence can, to some extent, be seen as constitutive of the powerful effect of the novel. No doubt, the dominant mode of the Victorian novel is "realism," yet *Wuthering Heights* is also pre-Victorian in that it incorporates earlier modes like the Romantic and the Gothic. Heathcliff cannot be seen simply in realist, Gothic or romantic terms. None of these labels is exhaustive or characteristic, and the term that covers various aspects then is that of the "other," again a term that neither Williams nor Kettle touches upon.[86]

By placing *Wuthering Heights* in a tradition with Blake, Hardy and Lawrence, Williams substantiates his own thesis that traditions are a process of constant selection and re-selection. The binding "spirit" can be either a moral preoccupation (in the case of Leavis) or an articulation of a specific structure of feeling or even simply a case of gender. By virtue of being a woman writer, Bronte can also be placed within a tradition of women's writing, as opposed to the mainstream tradition. However, Williams acknowledges the difficulties involved for women writers:

> But at least we must say that the Bronte sisters knew directly a whole structure of repression in their time; knew it and in their

> own ways broke it with a strength and courage that puts us all in their debt. (*TEN*, 63)

Beyond this preliminary observation, Williams leaves the question of women's writing unattended. Similarly, Kettle ignores this area. Williams does not relate Charlotte and Emily Bronte within the same tradition on account of the different modes that they employ. On the other hand, they can be linked together because of their "emphasis on intense feeling, a commitment to what we must directly call passion, that is itself very new in the English novel." (*TEN*, 60) But this then is not a characteristic of women's writing, for it is this way of depicting human experience that links Bronte to Blake, Lawrence and Hardy.

Having read *Wuthering Heights* primarily from the standpoint of Kettle and Williams, the question that now arises is how flexible or rigid their models are. In the case of Kettle, the framework of *An Introduction to the English Novel* is based on primary concepts of the "life-pattern" relationship, on realism and romance and the allied concepts of "moral fable," "the symbolic" the "concrete," and "positive values." Kettle's analysis does follow these broad limits, for example, he praises *Wuthering Heights* because it is "concrete" (*I*, 130) and is not "a romance," (*I*, 131) nor is it a "moral fable." (*I*, 131) Heathcliff embodies "positive values" (*I*, 135) and the novel is a "symbolic" protest against "oppression" (*I*, 144) and thus embodies a "revolutionary force." (*I*, 137) It would thus seem that Kettle operates within the methodology that he had proposed at the outset.

The binding thread in *The English Novel from Dickens to Lawrence* is Williams's concept of the "knowable community," but as far as his analysis of *Wuthering Heights* is concerned, he does not mention it. Nor does he mention the "structure of feeling" as a concept, but as we have seen, he bases his tradition upon it. Thus while Williams does not hold rigidly to the concepts that he has formulated, his basic technique is geared towards analysis rather than evaluation.

Both Kettle and Williams deal with the novel in realist terms but their reading is inadequate in dealing with non-realist modes like the Gothic, or notions of "polyphony" or even the "other." However, it is evident that *Wuthering Heights* not only incorporates the residual modes (that is, the Gothic and the Romantic) to the dominant one (that is, realism) but also reveals elements of the emergent (that is, modernism) and it is this trait that makes it a prominent, though not characteristic, paradigm of the Victorian novel. On the other hand, *Middlemarch* is considered the model classic realist text and in the following chapter, I will try to determine how far the models proposed by Kettle and Williams work in relation to it.

NOTES

1. David Musselwhite, "*Wuthering Heights*: The Unacceptable Text," *Literature, Society and the Sociology of Literature,* Francis Barker et al, eds. (University of Essex Conference, July 1976), p. 159.
2. In Ronald Frankenburg, "Styles of Marxism; Styles of Criticism; *Wuthering Heights:* A Case Study," *The Sociology of Literature: Applied Studies,* Diana Laurenson, ed. (Univ. of Keele 1978), p. 115.
3. Balibar and Macherey referred to by Musselwhite, p. 155.
4. *Politics and Letters* (London: Verso, 1981), p. 255.
5. *Modern Quarterly Miscellany,* No. 1, London, 1947, quoted in Ronald Frankenberg, p. 115.
6. "Theme and Conventions in *Wuthering Heights," The Critic,* Vol. I, No. 2, Autumn 1947, p. 43.
7. *Aspects of the Novel* (London: Edward Arnold), p. 12.
8. *Wuthering Heights* and *Agnes Grey* (London: Smith, Elder, 1910), p. 50. Hereafter cited as *WH.*
9. This dialectic process has been a continuing one and what I wish to point out is that this reference to the social transformation does not mean a reference to a precise historical fact but only to a general evident pattern.
10. The gipsy-ploughboy equation further reveals the trends of rural relations wherein the lowermost rungs of society are equated with the social "undesirables."
11. R. Williams, *Keywords* (London: Fontana, 1983), p. 62.
12. "Class and Class-Consciousness in early Nineteenth Century England, 3 Classes or 5?," *Victorian Studies,* Vol. XII, No. 1, Sept. 1968.
13. *Ibid.*, p. 23.
14. *Loc. cit.*
15. *Ibid.*, p. 11.
16. *Politics and Letters,* p. 255.
17. Rosemary Jackson interprets Heathcliff thus: "He is self become other. He and Cathy are two non-identical doubles, reflections of a unified self. Each regards the other as the self transformed. Cathy declares 'I *am* Heathcliff,'

and their quest is to regain their essential unity. *Fantasy and the Literature of Subversion* (London, 1981), pp. 128-29.

18. *The Madwoman in the Attic* (New Haven: Yale Univ. Press, 1979), p. 276.
19. Frankenburg, p. 115.
20. *A Reader's Guide to the Nineteenth Century British Novel* (New York: Octagon Books, 1980), p. 77.
21. *Ibid.*, p. 141.
22. *Criticism and Ideology*, p. 100.
23. Winifred Gerin, *Emily Bronte: A Biography* (Oxford: Clarendon, 1971), p. 219.
24. Q.D. Leavis in her essay "A Fresh Approach to *WH*," also follows this connection at length.
25. "Literary Influences on *Wuthering Heights*," (1958) *Wuthering Heights*, ed. M. Allott (London: Macmillan, 1970), p. 232.
26. David Punter, *The Literature of Terror* (London: Longmans, 1980), p. 407.
27. *Ibid.*, pp. 408-9.
28. *Ibid.*, p. 417.
29. Rosemary Jackson, p. 124.
30. Celia Britton, "The Dialogic Text and The Texte Pluriel" King's College, London, Univ. of Essex, *Occasional Papers in Poetics*, 14 Aug. 1974, p. 55.
31. *Ibid.*, p. 57.
32. "The Other Question," H.K. Bhabha, *Screen*, Vol. 24, No. 6, Nov.-Dec. 1983, p. 30.
33. "The Domestic Impact of Imperialism in Britain: 1880-19 0," Keith Burgess, *Literature and Imperialism*, A Conference Organized by the Eng. Dept. of the Roehampton Institute in Feb. 1983, Bart Moore-Gilbert D.Phil, ed., 1983, p. 49.
34. *Orientalism* (London: Routledge and Kegan Paul, 1978), p. 207.
35. Bhabha, p. 24.
36. " 'This Thing of Darkness I acknowledge mine,': *The Tempest* and the discourse of colonialism" in *Political Shakespeare*, eds. J. Dollimore and A. Sinfield (Manchester: Manchester Univ. Press, 1985), p. 68.
37. Kettle points out that names are particularly important in symbolic fiction.
38. Collins, p. 45.
39. *The Great Tradition* (London: Chatto and Windus, 1960), p. 196. Leavis's use of concrete is discussed more fully in an earlier chapter.
40. Elsewhere in *An Intro*, Kettle bases his analysis on "types" in the sense used by Lukacs, and there is an attempt to blend the Lukacsian with the Leavisite, yet here the analysis is Leavisite.

41. While this seems dismissive of the use of ideas and indirectly of the *roman a these,* the claim for the *roman a these* is subsequently vindicated in Kettle's recognition of the fact that *Tess of the d'Urbervilles* is in this category and that this does not stand in the way of its greatness.

42. "A Fresh Approach to *Wuthering Heights," Collected Essays, Vol. I, The Englishness of the English Novel* (Cambridge Univ. Press, 1983), p. 237.

43. Frankenburg, p. 119.

44. *Politics and Letters,* p. 254.

45. *Ibid.*, p. 295.

46. *The Madwoman in the Attic,* p. 295.

47. *Ibid.*, p. 295.

48. Sally Alexander, "Women, Class and Sexual Differences in the 1830s and 1840s: Some Reflections on the Writing of a Feminist History," *History Workshop Journal,* Issue 17, Spring 1984, p. 132.

49. Lacan, quoted in S. Alexander, p. 132.

50. *Literary Women* (London: The Women's Press, 1980), p. 106.

51. *Ibid.*, p. 100.

52. As Eagleton points out in *Myths of Power* (London: Macmillan, 1975).

53. "Wuthering Heights: The Unacceptable Text," pp. 156-57.

54. *Ibid.*, p. 157.

55. *Loc. cit.*

56. Celia Britton, "The Dialogic Text and the Texte Pluriel." As Belsey points out, Bakhtin "is concerned only with the aesthetic implications of polyphony and not with meaning. Since he is interested in the author's position rather than the reader's, he does not pursue the effect of the form he identifies. . . . [B] seems to work on the basis that the main consequences of polyphony are a profound respect for and analysis of 'the man in man,' subjectivity, point of view." *Critical Practice,* p. 150.

57. "*Wuthering Heights* After a 100 years," *Wuthering Heights,* Miriam Allott, ed., p. 173.

58. Allott, "The Rejection of Heathcliff," *Wuthering Heights,* Allott, ed., p. 186.

59. Though unimportant, it must be pointed out there is a slight temporal mix-up here for Heathcliff does not make a nocturnal visit but arrives on a Sunday afternoon when the family were away at church.

60. Like Kettle, Derek Traversi, in his essay, "*Wuthering Heights* After a Hundred Years," (1949) uses the criteria of "concreteness" and "precision" to evaluate the novel. His argument is that it is precision and concreteness that saves the novel from being purely romantic in tone and accounts for its greatness. For example, even in the most melodramatic situation of Lockwood's nightmare at the Heights, the illusion of reality is maintained.

(Traversi, p. 160) The reason for pointing out the links with Traversi are to reinforce the connection with the Leavisites, for Traversi is closely associated with *Scrutiny.*

61. *The Universal Dictionary of the English Language* (London: Routledge and Kegan Paul, ND).

62. "*Wuthering Heights* After a 100 Years," p. 163

63. In his reading of the Catherine-Heathcliff relationship, Williams uses similar terminology.

64. Discussed earlier.

65. *Myths of Power,* p. 106.

66. *The Country and The City* (London: Chatto and Wincus, 1973), p. 143.

67. *Loc. cit.*

68. *The Long Revolution,* p. 47.

69. *Ibid.,* p. 48.

70. Williams finds references to the symbolic, reductive. He says: "My quarrel with a whole tradition of criticism of fiction is about just this kind of endless reduction of deliberately created realities to analogues, symbolic circumstances, abstract situations." (*TEN,* p. 145)

71. Goldmann, *Towards A Sociology of the Novel,* trans. Alan Sheridan (London: Tavistock, 1975), p. 1.

72. *The Classic,* The T.S. Eliot Memorial Lectures, Delivered at Eliot College, Univ. of Kent, Canterbury, 1973 (London: Faber and Faber, 1975), p. 21.

73. T.S. Eliot, "Tradition and Individual Talent," *Selected Prose,* ed. John Hayward (Harmondsworth: Penguin, 1953), p. 23. This definition is not only sexist but imperialist as well.

74. Showalter, *A Literature of Their Own,* p. 7.

75. *Ibid.,* p. 10.

76. S. Alexander, p. 146.

77. Lovell, p. 16.

78. Showalter, p. 3.

79. Lovell, p. 16.

80. Showalter, p. 13.

81. Showalter's Feminist phase concedes with the winning of the vote, lasting from 1880-1920, and marking a period of "*protest against these standards and values,* and *advocacy* of minority rights . . . a demand for autonomy." (13) The Female phase extends to the present, its characteristic trait being "*self-discovery,* a turning inward freed from some of the dependency of opposition, a search for identity." (p. 13)

82. *Literary Women,* p. 45.

83. "Writing Like a Woman: A Question of Politics," *The Politics of Theory*," Univ. of Essex, April 1983, p. 22.

84. Kettle has since changed his position as he states in the Interview.

85. Bakhtin, *Problems of Dostoevsky's Poetics*, ed. and trans. Caryl Emerson, Intro, Wayne C. Booth (Manchester: Univ. Press, 1984), p. 6.

86. For the simple reason perhaps that this term has only recently been popularized with the heightened interest and awareness of the imperialist and colonial discourses in literature.

Middlemarch

It might now seem as if nothing more could be added to what has already been said about *Middlemarch,* yet as Eliot once remarked:

> it is often good to consider an old subject as if nothing has yet been said about it, to suspend one's attention even to revered authorities.[1]

However, my intention is to take specifically two "revered authorities," that is, Kettle and Williams, and to propose a fresh look at the text. Whereas *Wuthering Heights* is characteristically taken as the work of "idiosyncratic" genius as pointed out earlier, *Middlemarch* is more often seen as embodying a more studied and mature genuis.[2] According to Lerner, "Everyone now agrees that *Middlemarch* is George Eliot's masterpiece, and perhaps the greatest of all English novels."[3] It is taken as the primary example of the classic realist text, defined by Colin McCabe as:

> one in which there is a hierarchy amongst the discourses which compose the text and this hierarchy is defined in terms of an empirical notion of truth.[4]

The narrative voice is the metalanguage that is firmly at the helm of the narrative, directing, negotiating and controlling reader responses.

In this chapter, the discussion will centre on four selected statements--three from Kettle and one from Williams. Kettle in *An Introduction to the English Novel, Vol. I*, ends with the chapter entitled *George Eliot: Middlemarch.* The reason he assigns for this choice is the fact that "George Eliot's great novel is in a number of respects the culminating point of Victorian fiction." (*I*, 8) Williams, on the other hand, deals with "George Eliot" in general, commenting briefly upon various novels *The Mill on the Floss, Adam Bede, Felix Holt, Daniel*

Deronda and finally *Middlemarch.* The four statements will constitute the sub-sections of this chapter.

The first section will focus on the long-standing critical controversy as to whether or not Ladislaw is a successfully realized character. According to Henry James, Ladislaw is Eliot's "eminent failure"[5] while Leavis simply feels that he is "not substantially . . . there"[6] and Walter Allen designates him a product of his author's "dream fantasies."[7] Kettle falls in line with this "school" of thought and what is then called into question is this general consensus. However, it is only Kettle's position that will be discussed in detail and the extent to which it is justified in relation to the text. Can Ladislaw be judged as a conventional hero of Victorian fiction in terms of class, birth and money or is he produced in opposition to accepted standards and values? How far do the sample evaluations listed above adequately represent him positively or to what extent can he be taken as a proto-modernist hero? Williams, in fact, takes a positive view of Ladislaw's presentation, seeing Eliot "as trying to pull free, trying to reach beyond that connecting, interlocking threaded consciousness" towards the future which leads to an examination of Williams's position and its essential differences from that of Kettle. This again focuses on the issue of Ladislaw as a socially and textually marginal figure and suggests a possible role as part of a strategy of subversion. McCabe has referred to:

> the possibility of *moments* within a classic realist text which subvert it. . . . These *moments* are those elements which escape the control of the dominant discourse in the same way as a neurotic symptom or a verbal slip attest to the lack of control of the conscious subject. They open up another area than that of representation of subject and object caught in an eternal paralysed fixity–in order to investigate the very movement of articulation and difference–the movement of desire.[8]

However, in the case of Eliot, I will suggest that such *moments* are neither mere slippages nor can they be taken as conscious statements of the author's intentions, but appear as an articulation of the world-view of a particular moment in history which may be in opposition to the dominant ideology.

Section II deals with an allied issue, that is, the presentation of Dorothea's character. Here again, critical opinions differ, for example, Leavis sees her as an idealized version of her author,[9] "Dorothea, to put it another way, is a product of George Eliot's own 'soul-hunger'--another day-dream ideal self." Kettle, however, praises her, among other qualities, for the "positive force" she embodies. (*I*, 175) How does this notion relate to Leavis's "positive values" and how does it approximate to Kettle's own use of it in relation to Heathcliff? Williams, on the other hand, passes no value judgement on the issue, viewing Dorothea's presentation as another development in Eliot's art, leading from Maggie Tulliver, and he terms this in Eliot's words as "the double change in self and beholder." (*TEN*, 90) It will be possible here to look into the question of how far George Eliot can be viewed as a "feminine" writer and *Middlemarch* as a proto-feminist text.

The discussion in the third section will be initiated by Williams's concept of the "knowable community." In Chapter 4, we have dealt with this concept in its theoretical dimension, and here, for the first time, it will be examined in its practical aspect. It is thus pertinent to analyze how far it is helpful in assessing *Middlemarch* and its efficacy, in general, as a tool of critical analysis in relation to specific novels. This will generate a discussion of the relation of the individual to society, the defining consciousness of the writer and the problem of "realistic" representation in art.

The fourth section hinges on Kettle's assertion that *Middlemarch* "as a whole is not a deeply moving book." (*I*, 168) Apart from an analysis of Kettle's reasons, general technical issues regarding the role of the omniscient narrator, the notion of "unity" and what constitutes this "unity," will be discussed along with an examination of their underlying ideological assumptions.

In the final section, I will sum up the advantages and limitations of the models proposed by Kettle and Williams and their efficacy or otherwise in dealing with "classic realist" texts like *Middlemarch.*

I

> The artistic failure of George Eliot with Ladislaw, her failure to make him a figure realized on the artistic level of the other characters of the novel, is inseparable from the social unrealism

> in his conception. Artistically, he is not "there," not concrete because socially he is not concrete but idealized. (*I*, 176)

There are certain key terms in this passage that immediately indicate Kettle's critical stance. First, there is the reference to "social unrealism" and second, there is the touchstone of the "concrete" involved in this value-judgement. As pointed out in the last chapter, the term "concrete" is strongly reminiscent of Leavis. For Leavis, "concrete" is representational, true-to-life, *vraisemblable*, a dramatization of moral values. In his reading of *Wuthering Heights,* Kettle uses "concrete" in this sense. Here, he relates "concrete" directly to the writer's "social awareness" and assigns to it political connotations, as will be discussed later. However, to trace the Leavis connection further, Kettle's observation that he is not "there" is an echo of Leavis who also believes, "He is not substantially *(everyone agrees)* 'there' but we can see well enough what qualities and attractions are intended."[10] [my emphasis] Leavis's statement that "everyone agrees" seems a typical device of his coercively consensual ideology designed to regiment and control opinion, implicitly endorsing the fact that "everyone-agrees-and-so-must you" thereby quelling opposition of any kind. Having enlisted the reader-as-consumer's support, it is easy to make subjective judgements and pass them off as universal and objective facts. The keynote of such criticism is "universality." The influence of this strategy is evident not only in Leavis's "This is so, is it not?" but also in Kettle's critical practice. The general agreement implied leads one to the question of power relations involved in the field of critical practice and the compatibility of this position with Kettle's progressive outlook. The critic thus asks the reader to recognize what he already knows rather than opening any further vistas. Belsey interprets the process:

> The *critic's* voice now takes over from the author's and appropriates a corresponding authority. The critical text pronounces the judgements which the narrative voice fails to supply, and thus constructs a shadowy alternative text which does not conform to the evident laws of a natural order. It "places" the experience correctly and so restores the order from which the novel has deviated. Bourgeois mythology is saved.[11]

While Kettle certainly does not profess to be the saviour of such "bourgeois mythology," he is still operating from within its framework. His analysis of Ladislaw thus incorporates notions of "social realism" and Leavisite criteria. Ladislaw is rebelling against a frustrating society, though Kettle terms this rebellion "ineffectual." Kettle feels that Ladislaw lacks the positive force to change society and attributes this flaw to George Eliot's "mechanistic philosophy, its failure to incorporate a dialectical sense of contradiction and motion." (*I*, 177) By seeking a one-to-one and unmediated relation between a writer's conscious philosophy and its manifestation in a work of art, Kettle is taking the stance of the socialist realists of the 1930s.

Kettle also believes that Ladislaw "is saved from degeneracy implicit in his way of life only by the convenient financial support of Casaubon, Mr. Brooke and finally Dorothea herself." (*I*, 177) It is, however, difficult to square this with the manifest evidence of the text. For, in order to escape being a parasite, Ladislaw rejects Casaubon's support from his own sense of integrity and is not supported by Brooke but is paid by him for services rendered. He also refuses to accept the financial support that Bulstrode offers him, on a matter of principle. Unlike Lydgate, who continues to submit to Rosamond's will, Ladislaw defies Casaubon's unfair demands to leave Middlemarch and manages to find a respectable occupation for himself. Kettle is rejecting Ladislaw on moral grounds; his position here is not unlike that of the Middlemarchers who reject Ladislaw for very similar reasons.

To the charge that Ladislaw is unconvincing as a character, Williams counters with the query:

> but what is it, in a character, that "convinces"; it depends on general experience quite as much as on what is actually done with fiction. (*TEN*, 92)

Williams does not specify further, leaving the issue open-ended. He defends Ladislaw because of his freedom from (not lack of) "good birth," inherited property and fixed emotions:

> Coming from "nowhere," belonging "nowhere," he is able to move, to relate and so to grow in ways that the others are not. And it is to this after all, that Dorothea responds. (*TEN*, 93)

Unlike Rosamond, to whom "It always makes a difference . . . to be of good family," (*II*, 128) Dorothea, who yearns for the higher life, is not interested in the antecedents of Ladislaw. Ladislaw is similar to Birkin in Lawrence's *Women in Love,* for like Ladislaw, Birkin, unlike Crich, has no family connections, and so is able to operate and develop in an independent manner. In fact, Williams sees the character of Ladislaw as a great achievement, for in him, Eliot is able to go beyond the restricting social norms of her own day and age and to embody the social forces of the future. This perhaps is the reason why some twentieth century readers find it easier to relate to Ladislaw's character than did those of the 1870s, when the readership was conditioned to accepting different values in leading characters. According to contemporary reviews, Lydgate was the most acceptable candidate for Dorothea's hand. One contemporary review in *The Examiner,* 7 Dec. 1872, states:

> It is not easy to like young Ladislaw; one is tempted to think that, in marrying him, Dorothea makes nearly as great a blunder as she did in marrying Mr. Casaubon. How much pleasanter it would have been for Lydgate to be her husband? But, unfortunately, things do not always go pleasantly in real life, and the fate that befalls Dorothea is very natural though not very welcome.[12]

Frederick Napier Broome, in *The Times,* 7 March 1873, says:

> though in time Ladislaw is successful and gets into Parliament, we feel to the last "to love what is great, to try to reach it, and then to fail," has been Dorothea's lot. (110) Lydgate, who, had the author consulted the properties of romance and the fitness of things, should have married Dorothea.[13]

This kind of moralistic judgement prevents a positive interpretation of Ladislaw. There is much in *Middlemarch* to recommend him. He makes genuine efforts to befriend everyone, even the unimportant like Miss Noble. "He had a fondness . . for little children . . . he was given to ramble about among the poor people."[14] Yet Middlemarch society never takes to him because he was a man without connections and connections are the crucial credentials which are the necessary precondition of acceptance in English society. He had neither birth nor rank nor money to recommend him. It is evident that to be socially acceptable one would either have to be county gentry like the Brookes or the Chethams or Casaubon, or have money like Bulstrode or power like Mayor Vincy. Ladislaw had none of these, with the added liability of having Polish blood in his veins. He is referred to as being of "foreign extraction" and is likened to an "Italian with white mice." Whatever his personal qualities, he is rejected on these grounds. From an Anglocentric perspective, he is regarded as the other. And the "other" is always mythicized and placed into knowable categories--the sly Oriental, the passionate Mediterranean. Thus we hear, "Oh he's a dangerous young sprig, that Mr. Ladislaw, with his opera songs and his ready tongue. A sort of Byronic hero, an amorous conspirator" (*MM,* 365)--traits attributable to flighty foreigners rather than to sensible Englishmen. What the Middlemarchers misinterpret and what Dorothea can perceive, is the rationale underlying his hedonism:

> The best piety is to enjoy--when you can. . . . And enjoyment radiates. It is no use to try and take care of all the world; that is being taken care of when you feel delight--in art or in anything else. (*MM,* 213)

W.J. Harvey attributes Will's weakness to the fact that he "has no real relation to the provincial society depicted in the novel."[15] But as pointed out above, because of these prevalent attitudes, he could only remain at the periphery of the social set up. And his importance lies in precisely the fact that he is the outsider and not part of the immediate community of Middlemarch and it is for this reason that his attitudes are different. Within Eliot's fictional world, Daniel Deronda is the character who comes closest to Will. A Jew in search of his identity, Deronda must reject English society if he is to fulfil his aspirations in his chosen cause of Zionism. Aware of this imperialist racial contempt, Eliot states her position in a letter to Mrs. Harriet Beecher Stowe:

> not only towards the Jews, but towards all oriental people with whom we English come in contact, a spirit of arrogance and contemptuous dictatorialness is observable which has become a national disgrace to us. There is nothing I should care more to do, if it were possible, than to rouse the imagination of men and

> women to a vision of human claims in those races of their fellow-men who most differ from them in customs and beliefs.[16]

The racial prejudice extends to women characters (in fiction) as well. A foreign woman is usually seen as a mistress or whore rather than a wife. For example, Lydgate recoils from the exotic Laure who had murdered her husband and marrying the beautiful Englishwoman, realizes too late that he must face a fate worse than death--spiritual castration. Similarly, Harold Transome and Rochester are allowed foreign mistresses.

Many critics have reacted negatively to Will's "outsider" image. Quentin Anderson, however, is able to appreciate the fact that he provides a link between insular Middlemarch and the outside world:

> Throughout the book Ladislaw speaks authoritatively about the world outside the town's awareness. It is he who tells Dorothea that Casaubon's work is useless because he has not read the German scholars, it is he who demands fidelity to a standard of artistic accomplishment, he alone has some sense of national politics.[17]

Kettle does not take this aspect of Will's character into account. Williams, however, is able to recognize the essential difference in his identity from that of the other characters. According to Williams:

> For this is George Eliot thinking beyond, feeling beyond, the restrictions and the limitations she has so finely recorded; thinking into mobility not as dislocating but as liberating; with some anxiety, certainly--some registered qualified anxiety but following a thread to the future. (*TEN*, 93)

Eliot is not making a mystical prophecy but only revealing her understanding of social processes at work in the shaping of human destinies. Her remark about the inter-relatedness of the public and the private in *Felix Holt* confirms this. And Williams seems to be in total agreement with this positivist belief:

> Every aspect of personal life is radically affected by the quality of the general life, yet the general life is seen at its most important in completely personal terms.[18]

In *Middlemarch,* it is obvious that Ladislaw is born too soon. The society based on birth and financial considerations cannot fulfil the aspirations for scientific excellence as in the case of Lydgate or for artistic achievement for people like Ladislaw. It is in this sense that *Middlemarch* can be read as a historical novel. Ladislaw was perhaps more suited to the 1870s than the 1830s society, in which success was gauged more in terms of individual achievement rather than hitherto traditional considerations. Thus there is a perspective on the nature of English social development.

Williams's useful distinction of the residual, the dominant and the emergent[19] can be roughly equated with the three levels of interaction within the structure of feeling of a particular time. These three strands can be found in the character of Ladislaw. The residual convention of the Romantic hero is foregrounded in the references to his Byronic image. Though not financially, he is in experience superior to Dorothea as he is able to tell her, "I suspect that you have some false belief in the virtues of misery, and want to make your life a martyrdom." (*MM,* 213) This observation can somewhat exempt Ladislaw from the charge of idealizing Dorothea. It may be pointed out that the residual, emergent and the dominant do not always exist in consonance but the former two can be in opposition to the dominant. The dominant Victorian ethic of honour, self-help, high moral principles and courage are also present in him, for instance he is able to reject Bulstrode's ill-gotten money in a bid to maintain his "unblemished honour." By divesting him of money and title but not worth, Eliot is looking forward to a truly progressive society where human worth is gauged on merit rather than on birth or money.

It is significant that both Kettle and Williams go back from the text to the author--Kettle assigning the blame to Eliot's unsound philosophy while Williams praises her for visualizing the possibilities that lie on the other side of a "frustrating world." Kettle's search is for "social realism," "concreteness" and "positive forces" while Williams apart from presenting an analysis of the "knowable community," bases his reading on the epistemological problem of "what is it that convinces?" These readings are author-oriented and diachronic as opposed to Barthes's call for "the death of the author."[20] This strategy can be summed up in Homi Bhabha's words (taken from a different context):

> The "image" must be measured against the "essential" or "original" in order to establish its degree of *representativeness,* the "concreteness" of the image. The text is not seen as *productive* of meaning but essentially reflective or expressive--as Hirst says of ideology in a functionalist context, neither a discourse nor a practice, but a form of recognition. Such analysis is largely content-oriented.[21]

This then sums up the strategy of the classic realist text. Ladislaw, however, is not formally introduced in the accepted convention of the nineteenth century classic realist text. For as G.S. Haight points out, "George Eliot describes him indirectly, dropping details here and there."[22] When Celia first catches a glimpse of him, she describes him as "a gentleman with a sketchbook . . . light brown curls. I only saw his back. But he was quite young," (*MM,* 102) thus generating a general interest in his identity. While his identity is a source of constant speculation to the Middlemarchers, it is quite clear to the reader who he is, what he looks like, what his prospects are (whether the reader approves of him, is a different question), and hence the question of his "vagueness" or "impalpability"[23] does not arise. However, Eliot achieves this, not by direct presentation but by subtle hints cleverly inserted in the narrative. As for his *dilettantism,* he does take an amateur's interest in sketching and painting, and the reason why he does not wish to adopt it as a profession is that it would be "too one-sided a life" for him. He seems to be aspiring to the Aristotelian "golden mean," unlike Casaubon, whose fanatic devotion to the "Key to All Mythologies" has left him dry and impotent. While Casaubon stands for darkness and futility, Will is representative of light and endless possibility. Therefore, it is not difficult to understand why Dorothea gravitates towards him after her shattering experience with Casaubon. As Williams points out, "he understands art and learning better than Casaubon and reforms much better than Brooke." (*TEN,* 93) He would have kept to his career as political journalist had circumstances been more stable. This is not to say that he submitted meekly to circumstances, but at the end of the book, we are told that he is planning to study law to prepare himself for his career as a public man. In fact, his image as a respectably married man supersedes the earlier one of the *dilettante*.

Leavis's criticism of Ladislaw is devastating. For Leavis, "he has no independent status of his own—he can't be said to exist." (*TGT,* 75) Yet no character in life, and even more so in literature, can be said to be independent, for each character like each word is significant only relationally. In Belsey's words:

> The plausibility of the individual signifieds is far less important to the reading process than the familiarity of the connections between the signifiers. It is the set of relationships between characters or events, or between characters and events which make [even] fantasy plausible.[24]

As far as the question of Ladislaw being a "woman's man" is concerned, Gilbert and Gubar point out:

> While critics like Henry James have castigated Will Ladislaw as a lady's man, Will is Eliot's radically anti-patriarchal attempt to create an image of masculinity attractive to women.[25]

These sexist categories are socially constructed to preserve male dominance from the beginning of history, regardless of class, culture or nationality. James's criticism, in this instance, tends to be subjective and intuitive rather than factual. In fact, Ladislaw can be seen as Eliot's attempt to present an alternate hero, an androgynous person rather than the typical "male." He is represented as having "light-brown curls and slim figure," (*MM,* 102) characteristics generally associated with "feminine" qualities. There are references to his delightful smile "illuminating the transparent skin," (*MM,* 237) and he has this "girlish" habit of colouring under intense emotion. During his meeting with Dorothea in Rome, he is described in the following words:

> He was the elder by several years, but at that moment he looked much the younger, for his transparent complexion flushed suddenly and he spoke with a shyness. (*MM,* 236)

This is quite contrary to the accepted dominant notions of what constitutes the "masculine"—toughness, self-assurance and a dominating manner. Raffles gets the impression that "The slim young fellow with his girl's complexion looked like a tiger-cat ready to spring on him." (*MM,* 657) The epicene element is further stressed here. Similarly, Dorothea is not depicted as the typical "feminine" heroine, with qualities of meekness and submission but one who knows her mind and expresses it. For example, when she refuses Sir James's offer of a horse, she says, "I have made up my mind that I ought not to be a perfect horsewoman, and so I should never correspond to your pattern of a lady. Dorothea looked straight before her . . . very much with the air of a handsome boy." (*MM*, 44) Thus both Ladislaw and Dorothea can be said to be complementary, both being androgynous.

Most critics have found the Will-Dorothea relationship unsatisfactory. Leavis objects to "those impossibly 'high-falutin' *tete-a-tete*--or soul to soul--exchanges between Dorothea and Will which is utterly without irony or criticism."[26] Harvey finds the relationship unsatisfactory because he feels that Eliot was unable to treat "romantic or passionate love between two adults."[27]

Gilbert and Gubar say that as opposed to the father-daughter relationship between Casaubon and Dorothea, there is this "erotic sibling relationship which is here (as elsewhere in Eliot's fiction) made to function as an alternative to the power struggles of heterosexuality."[28] While there is evidence of erotic sibling relationships in Jane Austen's *Mansfield Park, David Copperfield* and *Wuthering Heights,* such a generalization is impossible in this case. The attraction between Will and Dorothea on the one hand, and Maggie and Stephen Guest on the other, is primarily sexual. In the scene when Dorothea and Will come together, there is thunder and lightning, a favourite conventional device used to underscore passion. As for the power relations involved in a heterosexual relationship, the conventional roles are reversed, for here, Dorothea is in a superior position socially and financially and in order to achieve a balance, she gives up money and position to lead a liberated life with the man she loves. Not even her maid Tantripp is willing to believe that Dorothea would marry Ladislaw for, "Madam would look higher than Mr. Ladislaw, else I don't know her." (*MM,* 585) The very fact that she breaks class barriers can be taken as evidence of her successful rebellion.

For Kettle, Dorothea's "aspiration to a life nobler than the Middlemarch way of life" is the "positive force" in the novel, yet Kettle says that when she becomes involved with Ladislaw, "we become seriously uneasy about Dorothea." (*I*, 175-76) Kettle's "uneasiness" is slightly contradictory, for Dorothea carries off her coup against Middlemarch values only in conjunction with Will. Williams comments briefly on the suitability of the relationship. (*TEN,* 4-5) By looking for social realism in the character of Ladislaw, Kettle is aligning himself to a content-oriented reflectionist mode of analysis, equating the representation of a particular world-view with artistic excellence. This then restricts his reading to established conventional standards. Kettle condemns Ladislaw for his unconventional lifestyle, whereas Williams praises him on that very account. Hence the plurality of interpretation exists on the basis of personal perspective rather than on ideological grounds. Kettle's model has close parallels with the structure of the classic realist text itself and is inflexible to the extent that it only deals with broad areas that conform to it, ignoring other issues that fall outside its scope. Williams, on the other hand, does not limit himself, in this case, with a rigid definition of realism and is thus able to perceive Ladislaw from the standpoint of Eliot and Dorothea. Though he does not follow the connection through, Williams is able to point out that with Ladislaw, George Eliot is trying to subvert the dominant ideological discourse of her society. She achieves this within a classic realist framework, for as McCabe points out:

> The contradictions between the dominant discourse in a classic realist text and the dominant ideological discourses at work in a society are what provide the criteria for discriminating within a classic realist text. And these criteria will often resolve themselves into questions of subject-matter.[29]

For George Eliot is a woman writing within a patriarchal society and while representing the dominant values, she is also subverting them. In order to examine her strategy further, I will now take up the issue of Dorothea's characterization, and the position that Kettle and Williams take in relation to it.

II

Like Ladislaw, Dorothea has been the subject of a wide-ranging critical controversy though unlike Ladislaw she has had an almost equal share of praise and blame. Henry James calls her "a genuine creation"[30] while Leavis sees her as the product of Eliot's "soul-hunger--another day-dream ideal self."[31] A few pages earlier, he says that, "The weakness of the book . . . is in Dorothea."[32] Explaining the nature of the weakness, Leavis wonders: "Isn't there something dangerous in the way the irony seems to be reserved for the provincial background and circumstances, leaving the heroine immune?"[33]

While in the case of Ladislaw, Kettle is in agreement with Leavis, here he holds a different viewpoint, while retaining the general Leavisite methodological terms:

> For although there is this weakness (which increases as the book goes on) it is also true that the strength of the book is in Dorothea. In spite of all our reservations it is Dorothea who, of all the characters of the novel, most deeply captures our imagination. It is her aspiration to a life nobler than the Middlemarch way of life that is the great positive force within the novel and the force which, above all, counteracts the tendency to present society as a static, invincible force outside the characters themselves. (*I*, 175)

First, the connection with Leavis is evident in the general tone of the passage. The phrases "our reservations," "captures our imagination," presuppose the existence of a system of shared assumptions and are part of the authoritarian discourse that seeks to retail subjective opinions in objective and universal terms. This then seems to be a legacy of intuitive critical practice where judgements are primarily a matter of personal taste. Secondly, "positive force" is a category that Kettle shares with Leavis.[34] Dorothea's strength lies in her "positive" force, an evaluative term that is also used in connection with Heathcliff. However, Heathcliff's aspirations to rebel against his society are conditioned by a deep sense of deprivation and social injustice. Eliot does not specify the origins of Dorothea's noble inclinations though she vaguely puts it down to her confession: "I have always been finding out my religion since I was a little girl." Is Eliot then associating religiosity and passion for goodness with the female principle? Is this the writer's position or is she simply recording the dominant social character of her time? These questions will be dealt with later. However, it is sufficient here to refer to Williams's observation that in Eliot's vision, the "fallen woman" has no place, for example Hetty Sorrel is abandoned after her "sin." Dorothea appears in the tradition of Virgin Mary and Saint Theresa.

What, then, according to Kettle is this weakness that he attributes to her character ? He refers to Leavis's analysis which sees her character as "self-indulgence" and "soul-hunger" on the part of her author. While Leavis puts down the excessive emotionalism in Dorothea's conception to "immaturity" on the part of Eliot, Kettle attributes it to her dilemma which results from the fact that "she hates the values of the society she depicts and has a faith in men and women which her mechanistic philosophy cannot destroy." (*I*, 175) Thus Kettle relates the weakness to Eliot's conscious mechanistic philosophy and because there is this opposing tendency of "noble humanity" (*I*, 175) also present in her, the weakness finally gives way to strength. Kettle's statement is important on the grounds that it implies a form of opposition which cannot, however, be termed "dialogic" for it refers to resolution as opposed to the ambivalences that "dialogism" generates. Leavis only sees the weakness in Dorothea, while Kettle lays greater emphasis on the strength. But in both cases it is clear that the author's attitudes are the decisive factor. Kettle continues:

> Dorothea is the force she is in the novel precisely because she encompasses this vital motive force in human life; and she fails ultimately to convince us because in George Eliot's conscious philosophy she has no place. (*I*, 176)

Here Kettle sees Dorothea as representative of the "vital motive force" which appears to be synonymous with "positive force." As pointed out earlier, "positive force" as an evaluative term has been used with equal success in the cases of Heathcliff and Dorothea. But even the presence of this force cannot prevent Dorothea from failing as a convincing character. How far this criticism is justified will be examined in the light of textual evidence. By relating the world-view in the novel to the author's conscious philosophy, Kettle is substantiating his earlier statement:

> The history of the novel is, in this sense, the history of the novelist's search for an adequate philosophy of life . . . and it is his view of life which will determine the nature and profundity of the pattern of his book. (*I*, 24)

This view is similar to that of Lukacs who says that "the novelist's ethic becomes an aesthetic problem of the work."[35]

Both Leavis and Kettle trace Dorothea's weakness to Eliot herself--Leavis to her "emotional immaturity" and Kettle to her unsound ideology. Kettle's views are similar to those of Engels, as pointed out earlier:

> A writer may hold a very profound conscious philosophy and yet be no artist (though the chances are that if his philosophy is truly profound in its human understanding his writing will achieve something of the quality of art); and a great artist may not be able to formulate his view of life satisfactorily in philosophical terms. (*I*, 24)

This relation between the writer's conscious philosophy and his/her achievement is simplistic to the extent that it ignores the whole range of discourses which constitute the complexity that is a literary text. This locates artistic value in content alone. For example, some progressive thirties novelists may depict sound ideological themes but their work may ultimately have no more than historical value. What is evident from the discussion so far is that by attributing the strength and weakness of the novel to Dorothea, Kettle is making a paradoxical[36] and weak statement, (for Dorothea is not synonymous with *Middlemarch*) a statement that purports to assume authority simply by enlisting the reader's assent.

Williams, on the other hand, does not enter the debate on Dorothea in these terms. His interest lies in tracing the development of Eliot's mode of characterization. He assesses Dorothea in the following words:

> Dorothea has elements of Maggie Tulliver, but she is now at arm's length being looked at. Virtually all the other characters and indeed the society are looked at, examined in this public way: "the double change in self and beholder." (*TEN*, 90)

In Maggie's case, Eliot is still conforming to the Romantic tradition while in *Middlemarch,* the personal is examined in impersonal terms. Williams attributes this mode to "an anxious class preoccupied with placing, grading, defining." (*TEN,* 91) Maggie and Dorothea share similar aspirations to a nobler life, though their final destinies differ. Maggie rebels only to conform to the social values of St. Oggs, while Dorothea's success may be somewhat tied up with her class position.

According to Henry James, "Dorothea was altogether too superb a heroine to be wasted yet she plays a narrower part than the imagination of the reader demands."[37] The repeated reference to the reader's imagination (here as in the case of Kettle) seems to assume that this was a universal phenomenon. However, it may seem as if the parallel Lydgate story was being assigned more importance, yet it is Dorothea who exemplifies the St. Theresa theme with which the book opens and ends. But the book is not called Dorothea and Kettle explains:

> So finally is the story of Dorothea in those early chapters "set" in the society of which she is a part, that it seems almost inevitable that an adequate examination of Dorothea must involve an examination of the Middlemarch world more thorough than that so far contemplated and there is no doubt that it was under a sense of this compulsion that George Eliot altered the plan of the book and called it *Middlemarch.* (*I,* 168)

This confirms Kettle's method of moving back from the individual to an analysis of society. By calling the novel *Middlemarch,* Eliot is asserting the primacy of society over the individual. This rootedness in her social milieu saves Dorothea from becoming a mythical figure like Saint Theresa, operating *in illo tempore,* to borrow a phrase from Mircea Iliade. There is thus a tension between her Saint Theresa aspect on the one hand and the limitations imposed by the social set-up on the other. Middlemarch society may have proved a destructive force in the careers of Lydgate and Bulstrode but because it fails to thwart Dorothea's rebellion, Eliot's presentation of it as a "static, invincible force" is somewhat redeemed. Walter Allen refers to the theme at the macrocosmic level:

> For in *Middlemarch,* George Eliot is investigating human aspiration to serve and to be good, under two aspects, there is the part played by the individual human being himself, with all his frailties, his imperfect self-knowledge and his will-power and there are the limits set by the society in which he is born.[38]

It is these "limits" that Dorothea transcends in order to marry Ladislaw. But:

> Many who knew her, thought it a pity that so substantive and rare a creature should have been absorbed into the life of another, and be only known in a certain circle as a wife and mother. But no one stated exactly what else that was in her power she ought rather to have done. (*MM,* 793)

However, Kettle defends Dorothea's position based on her:

> dissatisfactions with the fatuous, genteel life of the women of her class, seeking something beyond the narrow "selfishness" of her acquaintances and turning towards a religious Puritanism . . . to satisfy her unfulfilled potentialities. (*I,* 166)

This then is a key description of Dorothea's position and one that might inspire a feminist reading. Such a reading would point to whole avenues in the text that remain unexplored by Kettle and Williams. To follow this line will thereby indicate some of the limiations of the approaches under discussion.

It is evident that very few options were plausibly open to women in Dorothea's position. As Gilbert and Gubar have pointed out, Dorothea did not for a moment think of herself as Milton but only as one of his dutiful daughters, ever-willing to serve. In fact, Dorothea lives out:

> the classic role of women who are denied the status of artist because they are supposed somehow to become works of art themselves . . . or because they are destined to remain merely artistic, channelling their capabilities into socially acceptable accomplishments.[39]

For example, Will informs Dorothea, "You are a poem." (*MM,* 217) A female subject, like the work of art depends for its existence upon external agencies like the poet and is thus ultimately an object in the sense of having secondary and relational status. Gilbert and Gubar castigate Eliot for internalizing the values of a patriarchal society and point out:

> Eliot's punishment of her heroines, her frequent bouts of illness, her often censorious avuncular tone, and her masculine pseudonym all suggest the depth of her need to evade identification with her own sex.[40]

What Eliot was possibly evading was not identification with her sex but with the stereotypes associated with her sex. For example, "censorious avuncular tone" is itself a stereotypical generalization and according to Gilbert and Gubar a more feminine tone would be more appropriate in the interest of identification. For Eliot there was a pull in two directions--maintenance of her female identity, and the need to succeed in a male domain. The latter desire prompted the need for the adoption of the male pseudonym whereas the former is encoded within the text as we shall see.

It might seem as if Eliot's essay "Silly Novels by Lady Novelists"[41] did indicate a compromise with patriarchal values. However, it is not an adverse comment on women's writing, but is only derisive of "feminine fatuity" which results in the novels of the "*mind-and-millinery* species." It is also significant to remember that her title specifies novels by "lady" novelists which obviously has a class connotation, for these particular novelists 'have no notion of the working-classes except as 'dependents.'[42] She believes that women are capable of producing:

> novels not only fine, but among the very finest;--novels, too, that have a precious speciality, lying quite apart from masculine aptitudes and experience. No educational restrictions can shut women out from the materials of fiction, and there is no species of art which is so free from rigid requirements.[43]

That Eliot is a woman speaking for women, to whatever extent, is a fact largely ignored by both Kettle and Williams. Williams makes a passing reference:

> And in this tightening world it's then significant, surely, how much was kept alive, how much was newly affirmed, by a group of women novelis s–by Elizabeth Gaskell, by Charlotte and Emily and Anne Bronte, and by–but see how the convention bore down–by Currer and Ellis and Acton Bell, by Marian Evans becoming George Eliot. That tension, I think, can never be forgotten. (*TEN,* 62)

However, there is no further investigation of this tension. Nevertheless, it is significant here that even when her identity was undisclosed, Charles Dickens was able to perceive Eliot's gender upon reading *Scenes from Clerical Life.* In a letter to "George Eliot" written on Monday 17 Jan. 1858, he says:

> I am . . . bound to adopt the name that it pleases that excellent writer to assume. I can suggest no better one: but I should have been strongly disposed, if I had been left to my own devices, to address the said writer as a woman. I have observed what seemed to me such womanly touches in those moving fictions, that the assurance on the title-page is insufficient to satisfy me even now.[44]

In the light of this it is worth asking whether as a woman, Eliot was writing a different discourse. In fact, some feminist critics cannot forgive Eliot for what they see as a compromise to patriarchal values. The general objection here is based on what Eliot *should have* depicted as opposed to what she *has* depicted, working as she does within a realist framework. another feminist critic Ellen Moers sees Dorothea's character as conventional and unfeminist, calling her:

> an arrogant, selfish, spoiled rich beauty, she does little but harm in the novel. Ignorant in the extreme and mentally idle . . . Dorothea has little of interest to say, but a magnificent voice to say it in.[45]

Indeed, Will comments on its "Aeolian harp" quality and Caleb Garth admits that it reminds him of "bits in the Messiah." (*MM,* 526)

Turning to the text, it is clear that even as a woman, Dorothea may be viewed from different angles. Closely tied to this is her class position. For even though, she is presented as the Saint Theresa surrogate, her desire for doing good is initially inseparable from the bourgeois ethic of generalized charity. For instance, on her visit to Lowick when she finds that there was nothing she could do for there were no poor to help, the narrator describes the situation a trifle ironically:

> her mind had glanced over the possibility, which she would have preferred, of finding that her home would be in a parish which had a larger share of the world's misery, so that she might have had more active duties in it. (*MM,* 77)

Dorothea has thus initially fully internalized the dominant social values of her time, though she realizes a little later that her wish is "perhaps foolish and wrong." (*MM,* 77) Mr. Casaubon consoles her saying, "Each position has its corresponding duties" thereby reinforcing the dominant social norms.[46]

There are also frequent references to Dorothea being like a "queen." To quote just one example, Celia tells Dorothea that "James always said you ought to be a queen." (*MM,* 879) This, instead of an idealization, can be taken as closely related to her class position that in turn is tied up with her androgynous quality, to which I have referred earlier. For by virtue of the power invested in her, the queen, with her sceptre, transgresses into the male domain and is thus set apart from her own sex. Dorothea, though not a queen, is powerful by virtue of her rank, class and money and is looked up to by various men from Lydgate to Garth to Chettam, whereas as a woman she is patronized.

The general critical consensus against Dorothea seems to be that she is idealized. How might this charge then be countered? W.J. Harvey tabulates a set of codes by which an "idealized" character may be recognized:

> 1. when a character is too static or is insufficiently elaborated 2. when a character is too isolated 3. when a character remains theoretic 4. when a character cannot bear the weight of the value or significance attached to him 5. when the author is too emotionally involved in his characters 6. when the author evades certain problems or areas of experience necessary to the full realization of a character.[47]

None of these propositions holds true when tested against the character of Dorothea. Dorothea's character is "sufficiently elaborated" and she grows and develops. For example, in the earlier chapters, she is perversely insistent upon renouncing horse-riding and arrogant in her attitude to Celia's delight in her mother's jewels, but this is a different Dorothea, who in her night of suffering, is able to visualize a larger world than the one perceived from within the egoistic limits of the self. Dorothea is hardly isolated and is not only active within the social set-up of the landed gentry, but is equally involved in Middlemarch affairs, that is, her interest in the hospital. Nor can Dorothea herself be taken as "theoretic" even though she yearns for the "theoretic life" which can be seen as her earlier perversity though later, on account of her shattering experience with Casaubon, she becomes more "human." If in certain instances it might seem that Dorothea is unduly idealized and praised, there are comments within the text that set the balance right. Mrs. Cadwallader, for instance, is cynical about Miss Brooke's alleged cleverness and tells Chettam that he was well rid of her, for she "would have been requiring you to see the stars by day." (*MM,* 58) Celia likewise, refuses to encourage any high-falutin notions in her sister and accuses Dorothea of impatience "when people don't do and say just what you like." (*MM,* 81) Dorothea is thus seen through various prisms. While examining her relationships with the other characters in the book, it will be found that their opinions and impressions of her transmit a polyphonic effect, which is then orchestrated by the androgynous narrator's voice.

In *Middlemarch,* Eliot is articulating not only the dominant social values of her time, but is also verbalizing an alternative standpoint. For example, Brooke is the typical example of chauvinistic attitudes--patronizing, dismissive and indulgent as is obvious from his comment, "there is a lightness about the feminine mind." (*MM,* 73) For Lydgate,"The shallowness of a water-nixie's soul may have a charm till she becomes didactic," (*MM,* 700) thus showing that the male may often appreciate the female for frivolous reasons. On the other hand, proto-feminist comments, laced with irony, are strategically placed within the text:

> A man's mind--what there is of it--has always the advantage of being masculine--as the smallest birch-tree is of a higher kind than

> the most soaring palm--and even his ignorance is of a sounder quality. (*MM,* 44)

The narrator thus makes a devious dig at male pomposity. The dictates of patriarchal society affirmed:

> A wife, a modest young lady, with the purely appreciative, unambitious abilities of her sex, is sure to think her husband's mind powerful. Whether Providence had taken equal care of Miss Brooke in presenting her with Mr. Casaubon was an idea which could hardly occur to him. Society never made the preposterous demand that a man should think as much about his own qualifications for making a charming girl happy as he thinks of hers for making himself happy. (*MM,* 313)

This is an oblique comment on the place assigned to women in Victorian society. However, neither Dorothea nor Rosamond are typical submissive women and the latter reverses Lydgate's notion of:

> the psychological difference between what for the sake of variety I will call goose and gander: especially on the innate submissiveness of the goose as beautifully corresponding to the strength of the gander. (*MM,* 391)

Dorothea refuses to be cowed down by Casaubon's insistence on giving him an unspecified pledge. Even Celia, the typical "feminine" character, unwittingly makes an apt remark, telling Dorothea that "of course men know best about everything, except what women know better." (*MM,* 792) These examples thus prove the coexistence of the different discourses within the text.

By viewing Dorothea from a feminist perspective, it is clear that Kettle's objections (and those of other critics following the same line) can be refuted by textual evidence. Also, taking into consideration the fact that Eliot is writing in and against the patriarchal social set-up, it is difficult to characterize her philosophy in clear-cut terms. Hence the weakness referred to in Kettle's argument is invalidated at a fundamental level. Since neither Kettle nor Williams refers to the feminist aspect of the novel, it is clear that the general nature of their critical enterprise is androcentric and therefore the models proposed cannot deal with the plurality of the discourses embodied in the text. Kettle and the critics before him assume a moralistic stand in relation to the characters whereas Williams relates the effect to the author's method and the social conditions that contribute to it. These two strands are amalgamated in Williams's concept of the "knowable community." How useful this model is in relation to *Middlemarch* will be analyzed in the following section.

III

> What is found in *Middlemarch* is a knowable community, but knowable in a new sense. Socially it is in some ways contracted. The country labourers . . . are a brief chorus . . . talking sharply but instrumentally about their social superiors, the main characters of the novel. (*TEN,* 89)

What is crucial here is the concept of the knowable community. Earlier, we have already discussed it in its theoretical aspect. Now the focus will be on how far it succeeds in practical terms and to what extent it furthers our understanding of the novel. This term can be seen as the unifying factor in *The English Novel from Dickens to Lawrence* although this socio-historical, literary-textual category is defined theoretically for the first time in *Politics and Letters:*

> Those novels which can attain an effective range of social experience by sufficiently manifest immediate relations possess a knowable community.[48]

It involves the examination of relationships in a particular society at a specific point in time, and in seeing how these relationships are manifested in concrete terms in fiction. However, the "knowable community" is not an objective fact alone, in the sense that it is not only "what is there to be known," (*TEN,* 17) but also what the observers desire and need to know. Thus it incorporates both social fact on the one hand and the consciousness of the author on the other.[49] For "novelists did not simply react to the conformations of the social crisis, but subjected them to intricate processes of redefinition."[50] Referring to George Eliot, Williams differentiates between the "knowable" and the "known" communities:

> The knowable community is the common life, which she is pleased to record with a necessary emphasis. But the known is something else again--an uneasy contract, in language with another interest and another sensibility. (*TEN,* 82)

This "uneasy contract" is the tension between the "narrative idiom of the novelist and the recorded language of her characters." (*TEN,* 79-80) It is on the basis of this continuous conflict between "customary" and "educated" language that Williams traces connections with Hardy and Lawrence, a point I will discuss later.

To return to the statement that the community of Middlemarch is "socially contracted." This is relative, for when compared with the community of Jane Austen, in which only the propertied class is "knowable," as Williams points out, (*TEN,* 24) Eliot extends her world to include farmers, craftsmen and other inhabitants of provincial England. Yet as Williams says:

> though George Eliot restored the real inhabitants of rural England to their places in what had been a socially selective landscape, she does not get much further than restoring them as a *landscape*. (*TEN,* 77)

For while Eliot offers to "know" them, she cannot finally individuate them because of her own class-position. However, Eliot's inattention to individuating working people can be taken as a collective blind-spot rather than an individual one and the simple structural reason that she did not wish to individuate them is that they fell outside the scope of her book. Though not belonging to the upper class, Eliot belongs to the educated section of society that was restructuring class and gender barriers. It was by virtue of her education that Eliot was able to infiltrate the male preserve of the editorship of the *Westminster Review.* In *Middlemarch,* for example, Fred Vincy, grandson of an inn-keeper, son of a tradesman, by virtue of his university education, had managed to step outside his own class. Eliot is addressing herself to this kind of educated readership and even though she feels for the working people, she does not ultimately feel *one* with them. Williams illustrates this by quoting from *Adam Bede,* "I am not ashamed of commemorating old Kester: You and I are indebted to the hard hands of such men." (*TEN,*

81) While Eliot's consciousness encompassed the lives of even the socially "unknowable" she did not overtly transcend her class ideology.

In *Middlemarch*, we are introduced to Solomon, Mrs. Waule, Brother Jonah, Mr. Borthrop Trumbull and at once the reader can place them in the fraternity of the Pumblechooks in Dickens or the Dodsons in Eliot herself. This sense of *deja vu* is also experienced in relation to Hardy whose rural characters are also presented as a "chorus." Yet there is a difference, for example we are *told* about The Tankard, where many a reputation is made or marred, the particular instance being the condemnation of Lydgate and his new-fangled medical practices. In Hardy, a similar scene is handled dramatically for example, in Chapter 36 of *The Mayor of Casterbridge* (1886), when the skimmity ride is being planned by the inhabitants of Mixen Lane at the Peter's Finger, we are *shown* the lively scene in all its complexity. This is, to some extent, an indication of the changing and extending consciousness of writers from Austen to Hardy.

In Jane Austen, there is no tension between her personal idiom and that of her characters and this accounts for the "cool" balanced tone of observation. Eliot finds herself caught between two worlds, "one dead, the other powerless to be born," one in which "the old confidence of individual liberation has gone and the new commitment to social liberation has not yet been made." (*TEN,* 88) With Hardy, the process is furthered in the sense that now there is a greater emphasis on the lives of rural people even though Hardy's reproduction of their dialect could be taken as a concession to the expectation of his readers. However:

> Work enters his novels more decisively than in any English novelist of comparable importance. And it is not merely illustrative, it is seen as it is, a central kind of learning. (*TEN,* 116)

Yet the disparity between the "customary" and the "educated" remains. It is only in Lawrence that a balance is attained, though not for technical reasons:

> He is writing like that because he is feeling with his people, not of them or about them, but within a particular flow--what he once called sympathy but isn't that formal, he is simply writing where he lived. (*TEN,* 173)

Earlier, the novelist would depict people and their relationships on the assumption that the author and the reader shared a common knowledge and that social relationships are a reliable index through which persons can be known. But, as a result of the rapid changes taking place in nineteenth century society, this confidence gave way to the uncertainty that people are only partially knowable. It became increasingly difficult to apprehend the complex urban society that was causing the fragmentation within communities. Thus "an important split takes place between knowable relationships and an unknown, unknowable, overwhelming society." (*TEN,* 15) Society is no longer seen as a passive background against which the drama of lives unfolded itself, but is seen as "an agency, even an actor, a character . . . a process that entered lives to shape or to deform." (*TEN,* 13) And "society" does not admit of distinctions into country/city dichotomies, for while this contrast is "dramatic and important," it is wrong to say that city writing is complex whereas country writing is "an epitome of direct relationships."[51] As Williams explains, "But a knowable community, within country life as anywhere else, is still a matter of consciousness, and of continuing as well as day-to-day experience."[52] And this day-to-day experience may not necessarily be depicted on a Tolstoyan grand scale, just as it was not essential for Jane Austen to depict the Napoleonic wars. The exact nuances of Eliot's position in *Middlemarch* have been adequately re-phrased in Leavis's words:

> The sheer informedness about society, its mechanism, the ways in which people of different classes live and (if they have to) earn their livelihoods, impresses us with its range, and it is real knowledge, that is, knowledge alive with understanding.[53]

What is significant here is that "knowledge" is not used in the sense Casaubon understands the term but knowledge, as Ladislaw knows it, "knowledge pass[ing] instantaneously into feeling, and feeling flashes back as a new organ of knowledge." (*MM,* 217) In this debate about the nature of knowledge, Eliot's own epistemological position is evident.

Eliot was greatly influenced by Spencer's evolutionary theory which was developed on the analogy between society and living organisms. To quote Spencer:

> In low aggregates, both individual and social, the actions of the parts are but little dependent on one another, whereas in developed aggregates of both kinds, that combination of actions which constitutes the life of the whole makes possible the component actions which constitute the lives of the parts.[54]

This sense of interrelatedness of the part to the whole and the private to the public, is what informs the structure of Eliot's novels. It is also the basis of Williams's definition of realism. According to the narrator in *Middlemarch:*

> I at least have so much to do in unravelling certain human lots and seeing how they were woven and interwoven, that all light I can command must be concentrated on this particular web, and not dispersed over that tempting range of relevancies called the universe. (*MM,* 137)

This concentration on the "web" instead of on the "universe" reinforces the point I made earlier regarding the distinction between a "regional" and a "universal" novel. The web metaphor has been widely commented upon. Williams points out its positive as well as negative connotations in *Culture and Society.* Its positive aspect lies in its "indication of complexity" whereas its negativity in the fact that "it tends to represent social–and indeed directly personal–relationships as passive."[55] Similarly, the metaphor of the world as an udder suggests a passive and thereby determinist image of the working of society as Kettle points out. (*I*, 172) Williams also castigates Eliot for merely touching upon the lives of the working people and thus surrendering:

> virtually without a fight, to the general structure of feeling about these matters . . . which she was at once too hesitant to transcend, and too intelligent to raise into any lively embodiment.[56]

Later, however, in *The English Novel from Dickens to Lawrence* (77) and in *The Country and the City* (206), he says, "I would not make the point bitterly, for the difficulty is acute." The difficulty that Eliot faces is the problem of trying to "reach beyond" the web (*TEN,* 92) and according to Williams she does this in Ladislaw's character, a pointer to the emerging modern consciousness in Eliot.

The "web" cannot be seen as passive for no thread can be moved in isolation as "Every act of man has an incalculably diffusive act on that tangled whole."[57] In fact, to quote just one example, when Dorothea looks out of her window after a night of sleeplessness and suffering, she recognizes that "She was a part of that involuntary, palpitating life, and could neither look out on it from her luxurious shelter as a mere spectator, nor hide her eyes in selfish complaining." (*MM,* 750) And it is this quasi-mystical realization that prompts her to visit Rosamond in a gesture of affection and sympathy. Eagleton interprets the use of nature imagery as an attempt to "signify how a fulfilling relation to the social totality can be achieved, not by ideological abstraction, but by pragmatic, apparently peripheral work."[58] Williams's method takes into account the author's intentions as well as the social constraints involved in carrying them out so that the "web" of *Middlemarch* can be seen as the "limiting" web of Eliot's own society while Eagleton, on the other hand, is interpreting a "text."

Williams believes that art must be viewed as a practice and says:

> we have to break from the common procedure of isolating the object and discovering its components. On the contrary, we have to discover the nature of a practice and then its conditions.[59]

Instead of simply explaining texts, Williams attempts to discover the writer's method and form of consciousness so that the connections can be made not within genres alone but across them as well. Kettle, on the other hand, views the text in the light of the writer's philosophy. It is because he considers the society presented in *Middlemarch* as static that he regards the novel as falling short of an impelling final effect:

> Nor is this simply because provincial society in the Midlands about 1832 was indeed comparatively unchanging (no society is really static when an artist looks at it) . . . what is more important is the failure of the attempts to give "historical colour" (like the surveying of the railroad and the election scenes) which are conscientious but not--on the artistic level--convincing, not integral to the novel's pattern. (*I*, 171)

These views are corroborated by Eagleton, who believes that the era of *Middlemarch* constitutes a "historical vacuum." As for the notion of society being static, the narrative voice in Chapter 11 seems to suggest otherwise:

> Old provincial society had its share of this subtle movement:had not only its striking downfalls . . . but also those less marked vicissitudes which are constantly shifting the boundaries of social intercourse, and begetting new consciousness of interdependence. Some slipped a little downward, some got higher footing. . . . Municipal town and rural parish gradually made fresh threads of connection. (*MM,* 94)

This generalization is amply substantiated in the course of the narrative. As for its historical dimension, Eliot goes to a deeper level of society than historical or political events can indicate. The action of the novel begins in September 1829, concluding in May 1832, and because Eliot:

> skillfully uses indirection, few readers realize they are reading a novel full of documented, accurate, historical information, none feels history obtrudes inorganically upon the fiction.[60]

Though set in the 1830s, Eliot writes from the perspective of the 1870 s and her method can be described as "the establishment of a position in human experience which was capable of judging--not incidentally but totally--the very society that was forming and changing it." (*TEN,* 13) This sense of history, of not going too far back into the past for it to become spectacle as in Scott, but "going back to the decisive origins of their own epoch" (*TEN,* 14) that the real growth took place. And it is in these ways that novelists learnt to look historically at the crises of their own immediate time: "at Chartism, at the industrial struggle, at debt and speculation, at the complicated inheritance of values and of property." (*TEN,* 14) The problems of the individuals are peculiar to the social context of Reform England and thus there is no question of "timelessness" or "vacuum" e.g. Dorothea's problems would not exist in the same form in either the 1930s or indeed in the 1730s.

The action of the novel takes place within a specific historical setting and it would be relevant to see how far Williams's concept of the "knowable community" is useful towards understanding the complex narrative structure of the whole. For what is important, according to Williams, is not only what is "knowable," but also what is "known" or "to-be-known." *Middlemarch* is *A Study of Provincial Life* and is neither a story about Dorothea nor Lydgate, the main characters, but is a complex structure of five stories, each of them organized into a balanced whole.[61] The focus is thus dispersed over a wider range of personal relationships. Many critics, taking organic unity as the central evaluative criterion, see this as a limitation. For example, Kettle observes, "Many of the chief characters are related by blood, but their artistic relationship within the pattern of the novel is not fully realized." (*I*, 172) Williams, on the other hand, proposes the concept of the knowable community which will now entail an examination of how society is structured in *Middlemarch*.

The provincial society is composed of country and town and it is clear that while in the country rank is the primary consideration of social status, in the town social hierarchy is structured on a financial basis. Education, though necessary to social climbing, is not by itself sufficient. For example, Mrs. Garth is well-educated, but looked down upon by Mrs. Vincy and even though Mr. Farebrother ignored "the Middlemarch discrimination of ranks," (*MM,* 438) the narrative voice explains the actual situation:

> Still, you see, he spent his evenings at the Vincys," where the matron, though less of a lady, presided over a well-lit drawing-room and whist. In those days human intercourse was not determined solely by respect. (*MM,* 439)

The landed gentry consisted mainly of Chettam, Casaubon and Mr. Brooke, whom the narrator describes as not "exactly aristocratic." (*MM,* 29) This obviously means that he fell a trifle short of the aristocracy, yet in the Middlemarch world the three families are the leading lights. While in Jane Austen, this class alone is knowable, Eliot extends her attention to other inhabitants of the country who were lower down the social ladder. The Cadwalladers, for instance, are impecunious but Mrs. Cadwallader was born into the aristocracy and had gone down socially by marrying the Rector. Featherstone of Stone Court is a "gentleman farmer" (*MM,* 131) but socially inferior to Casaubon who was Rector of Lowick parish and owner of the estate, whereas Mr. Tucker, his curate was an inferior clergyman. Thus even within the country community there are gradations of social status.

Similarly, in Middlemarch, the Vincys and the Bulstrodes are the elite. Lydgate can be taken as superior to the rest of the medical community in town on account of his connections with Sir Godwin. Drs. Sprague and Minchin are physicians educated at the ancient Universities and therefore "gentlemen" whereas Toller and Wrench, by virtue of being surgeon-apothecaries,are lower down the social scale which plunges lower still to include Mr. Gambit, who has had little education. In their prosperous days, the Garths shared a "slight connection" (*MM,* 263) with the Vincys but:

> Even when Caleb Garth was prosperous, the Vincys were on condescending terms with him and his wife, for there were nice distinctions of rank in Middlemarch; and though old manufacturers could not any more than dukes be connected with none but equals, they were conscious of an inherent social superiority which was defined with great nicety in practice, though hardly expressible theoretically. (*MM,* 263)

But of all the people depicted on the lower social rungs of town and country, who for the most part remain caricatures, it is Caleb and Mary Garth that are depicted at length. It might seem as if the Garths are set up as the moral paradigms within the story, but of the two, it is only Mary who is always morally right. Even Caleb is not exempt from his mistakes as is evident from his well-intentioned but hapless money-lending to Fred Vincy. Mary, on the other hand, takes a stand in favour of what is right even if her attitudes may seem harsh. She does not fulfil the dying Featherstone's raving demands, nor does she relent in the case of Fred's lax ways. She is virtuous, hard-working, selfless and her actions are not determined by financial considerations.

It is clear that the Garths are not working-class people in the sense that they are neither urban nor rural labourers nor is Caleb Garth an entrepreneur. He is an estate manager whose wife had at one time been a teacher. Mary earns her living in looking after the ailing Featherstone. According to Neale's model, Lydgate and the Garths would both belong to the "middling" class which consisted of "petit bourgeois, aspiring professional men, other literates and artisans."[62] The Garths are a typical instance of what can be termed "genteel poverty" that has been often idealized by Victorian novelists. Therefore, in *Middlemarch,* there are no workers except as we have seen, *en masse* like a chorus at the Tankard or the rural labourers briefly rallying in mistaken opposition to the railway agents who surveyed the land. (*MM,* 56)

Even within this middling class, there is no uniformity but a system of hierarchy that is not rigid but mobile. Money is an important contributing factor in status, but is not yet paramount, for it is still rank in terms of birth that is the ultimate criterion of social standing. Education also contributes to a rise in the social scale but is not the ultimate determinant. Fred is the Mayor's son, has been to University, but the moment he takes up the assignment as Garth's assistant, his social standing falls. As Mr. Vincy tells him, "You've thrown away your education, and gone down a step in life." (*MM,* 613)

Therefore, it is clear that the limits of Eliot's world do not stretch beyond the socially "knowable" which are beginning to include the educated elite. The Garths, though poor, are all educated and by introducing the Fred-Mary relationship, Eliot is reversing conventional notions of desirable marriage settlements as found in the novels of Jane Austen. For Mary has neither beauty nor money, and Fred though "a fine fellow" lacks the competence and independence that wealth and position give to the conventional hero. In the cases of both Dorothea and Mary, Eliot makes unconventional marriage settlements which is her way of breaking the limits of what is socially "knowable." As we have seen, Williams's concept of "knowable community" has been useful in unravelling the various narrative strands that are interwoven with such complexity.

Williams's concept of the "knowable community" is useful by nature of its flexibility. It is a descriptive rather than an evaluative category, embodying not only the depiction of social experience but also its articulation in language that is seen as "historically and socially constituting."[66] It is primarily helpful in dealing with realist literature. However, its efficacy in dealing with modernist fiction is debatable. Williams explains that from the 1890s to 1914, there is the growing awareness of the split between the individual and society. The isolated consciousness creates its own community and this is manifested in the "internal disturbances of language and form." (*TEN*, 124) The language that emerges to articulate this experience is then ordinary for it has divested itself of conventional forms, as in *Ulysses* which Williams praises for its "community of speech." By this Williams is referring to "that wider human speech which has been screened and strained by the prevailing social conventions." (*TEN*, 167) On the other hand, the community of *Middlemarch* is seen in terms of actual human relationships. Kettle believes that the "richness of *Middlemarch* lies in a consideration of individual characters firmly placed in an actual social situation." (*I*, 168) Yet he feels that the novel is not finally moving because:

> this sense of social interpenetration, so remarkably revealed in the exploration of the individual dilemma and so consistently and consciously sought after by George Eliot throughout the novel, does not in fact infuse the book as a whole. (*I*, 170)

The reasons that Kettle assigns for the above objections will be examined in the next section.

IV

> *Middlemarch* as a whole is not a deeply moving book. The total effect is immensely impressive but not immensely compelling. Our consciousness is modified and enriched but not much changed. (*I*, 168)

This observation is descriptive in that it categorizes *Middlemarch* as a certain kind of novel, evaluative as it implies judgement, and finally prescriptive, for it imposes a certain norm whereby novels can be judged as successful or not. The criticism in this passage rests upon one factor--that is, change of consciousness. It is evident that Kettle does not settle for "modification," which according to the Chambers dictionary would be "to alter slightly," but wants "change" which the same dictionary defines as "to alter or make different; to make to pass from one state to another." Hence "change" is more total than "modify," and it would seem as if Kettle is implying that the success/failure of a novel would depend upon its ability or otherwise to change the reader's consciousness. Thus Kettle's view of the function of art is qualitatively different from that of the thirties's Socialist Realists, who attributed to art the function of urging the individual to goal-oriented ends. It is also somewhat different from that of Leavis. Kettle believes that the novel must depict "life" in a concrete way but it must also act upon our consciousness in order to change it. This is an advance over Leavis's position, for whom it is enough that the consciousness is "enriched," that is, the sensibilities are refined and "fitness for a humane existence" is ensured, but Kettle is thinking in more revolutionary terms. As for the terms "moving" and "compelling," they are imprecise and lead to the problem of what Peter Jones calls "epistemological egoism." According to him:

> It is held that "the world" of each individual is essentially mediated by his perceptions or "feelings" . . . and that this "world" may be said to be a function of his viewpoint, psychology and knowledge. In this way each man's world is different.[64]

And hence the concept of what constitutes "moving" may differ not only individually but also temporally. However, what, according to Kettle, is the missing factor? He explains:

> For all her intellect, all her human sympathy, all her nobility and generosity of mind, there is something of life that eludes her. (*I*, 171)

Not only does "life" have resonances of Leavis's aesthetic criteria, but it also seems to echo the preoccupation of Lord David Cecil:

> She sacrifies life to art. Her plots are too neat and symmetrical to be true. We do not feel them to have grown naturally from their situation like a flower, but to have been put together deliberately and calculatedly like a building.[65]

Though Leavis quotes the above passage, he disagrees with its judgement. Taking the clue from the above passages, is it possible to identify the alleged blind-spot in Eliot's narrative method? Or is it possible that in her concern for Life she has missed out on "life"?[66] According to Kettle, what the novel lacks is "that final vibrant intensity of the living organism." (*I*, 171) This statement then implies that there is a lack of organic unity in the novel. Kettle justifies this, saying that this happens because the novel changes from "the story of Dorothea"

(*I*, 167) to that of "old provincial society" (*I*, 167) and thus "the background has become the subject." (*I*, 168) It is interesting to relate this to Williams's observation in relation to the historical novel as transformed by the romantic imagination when, "Society . . . could be seen . . . as an agency, even an actor, a character." Here, Williams is making an objective analysis whereas in the case of Kettle, this fact of society becoming the "subject" is identified as the weak-spot in the novel. Kettle further relates this weakness of *Middlemarch* to the fact "that the various stories within the novel, though linked by the loose plot, have no organic unity." (*I*, 171-72) On the other hand, Mark Schorer in his essay "The Structure of the Novel" says that "in spite of a loose mechanical plot [*Middlemarch* is] a highly integrated novel."[67] He then goes on to say that the most obvious unifying factor is that in every book most of the representatives of the five stories are brought together. It would be unfair to ignore the fact that Kettle points out that "many of the chief characters are related by blood, but their artistic relationship is not fully realized." (*I*, 172) The word "artistic" has an "aesthetic nimbus"[68] surrounding it in the manner of Benjamin's "aura." Having already dealt with "artistic relationships" in the first two sections of this chapter, I will now deal with the question of organic unity in its formal aspect. Like Schorer, Kettle agrees that the unifying subject of the book is its central Saint Theresa theme which Schorer identifies as the contrast between social idealism and self-absorption. He then points to the organizing role of metaphors which serve three functions--expressive, interpretive and structural.[69] Schorer then concludes:

> The material is fused in a moral-philosophical view and is enlarged by a particular method of observation and dramatization. That method has a positive and crucial part in our experience of what we feel to be a work of proportions at once generous and unified, for the proportions no less than the unity are not in the breadth of scene or range of character, finally, but in the mind that views these.[70]

The critical strategy involved in these interpretations is clearly one that retails the view that the text is a unified whole--not simply on account of who is related to whom, or the frequency of the character's appearances, but in the overall perspective and consciousness of the narrator.

The use of an omniscient narrator is a crucial convention of nineteenth century fiction. According to J. Hillis Miller:

> The theological overtones of the word "omniscient" suggest that such a narrator is like a god, standing outside the time and space of the action, looking down on the characters with the detachment of a sovereign spectator who sees all, knows all, judges all from a distance.[71]

Conscious echoes of this stance can be found in *The French Lieutenant's Woman* when Fowles views this technique from a twentieth century perspective. He says:

> The novelist is still god, since he creates . . . what has changed is that we are no longer the gods of the Victorian image, omniscient and decreeing; but in the new theological image, with freedom our first principle, not authority.[72]

The narrator can be omniscient in three ways--temporally, spatially and psychologically. In *Middlemarch,* the narrator exploits all three kinds of omniscience, moving from past to future, being at different places at the same time and being able to move in and out of the character's minds. In *Middlemarch*, the narrator is not only omniscient but she is intrusive as well, passing "judgements on characters, remarks on how the story is being told, direct addresses to the reader, and generalizations and miscellaneous observations on a variety of subjects."

Kerry McSweeney, however, does not view the omniscience of the narrator as "god-like" but as "generational," for he says that "the novel is narrated from the point of view of middle-age looking back on youth."[73] However, it may be pointed out that "god-like" and "generational" need not be mutually exclusive or in opposition--in fact, the authority assumed by the older generation is "god-like." And this view is somewhat corroborated by the following passage from the text:

> If youth is the season of hope, it is often so only in the sense that our elders are hopeful about us; for no age is so apt to think its

> emotions, partings and resolves are the last of their kind. Each crisis seems final, simply because it is new. . . . To Dorothea, still in that time of youth . . . that morning's parting...seemed to be the close of their personal relations. (*MM,* 521)

It is this digressive method that has often been criticized. Wayne C. Booth makes a distinction between "telling" and "showing" which corresponds roughly to Plato's "diegesis" and "mimesis"--the former entails narrating in one's own voice, while the latter refers to imitating the speech of another. In the 1920s, Percy Lubbock articulated the belief:

> the art of fiction does not begin until the novelist thinks of his story as a matter to be *shown,* to be so exhibited that it will tell itself.[74]

Booth does not admit the superiority of "showing" over "telling" but has a position similar to that of David Lodge who says:

> the classic realist novel "mixes" the two discourses in a more fundamental sense: it fuses them together, often indistinguishably and inextricably, through the device of free indirect speech by means of which the narrator, without absenting himself entirely from the text communicates the narrative to us coloured by the thoughts of a character.[75]

This method is making constant demands on the reader's attention in the Barthean sense of being *scriptible.* This method, as employed by Eliot, is characterized by Williams as "a critic's fiction" (*TEN*, 91) and one which he states, is quite different from that of Charlotte or Emily Bronte. For example, in *Jane Eyre*, the method of direct appeal to the reader is described by Williams as "the fiction of special pleading." On the other hand, Emily Bronte tells a story within a story. Quoting a passage on Mrs. Cadwallader, Kettle questions the method "in which George Eliot turns her moral gaze direct upon the reader and beckons to his personal conscience" wondering if it is possible to "isolate a weakness in her method and put our finger on a note in *Middlemarch* which may justly be described as a shade flat?" (*I*, 163) This "putting our finger on" tactic is one that Kettle shares with Leavis, as pointed out earlier.

Commenting on the same passage on Mrs. Cadwallader, Kettle underscores the crude irony implicit in the sentence:

> Let any lady who is inclined to be hard on Mrs. Cadwallader inquire into the comprehensiveness of her own views; and be quite sure that they afford accommodation for all the lives which have the honour to coexist with hers. (*I*, 163)

And he further asks, "In what sense is 'honour' to be read? Against what is the irony directed? The ambiguity betrays a weakness." (*I*, 163) While Kettle is taking a negative view of "ambiguity," most modern readings regard it as generative of a plurality of meanings. As Lodge puts it:

> because the narrator's discourse is never entirely ambiguous, predictable and in total interpretive control of other discourses in *Middlemarch* that the novel survives, to be read and re-read, without ever being finally closed or exhausted.[76]

This passage not only acts as a corrective to Kettle's reading but it is also contrary to McCabe's interpretation of the narrative voice as a "metalanguage" which controls and judges other discourses thereby putting the reader in a dominant position over the characters and their stories. However, as we have seen earlier, coexisting with the metalanguage, are various other discourses that subvert the final authority of the dominant discourse.

The narrator sees her/himself as a historian, "unravelling certain human lots, and seeing how they *were* [my italics] woven and interwoven." (*MM,* 137) The narrator's voice cannot be equated with that of the historical subject, that is, the author as Leavis does in *The Great Tradition.*[77] The narrator is a separate entity and an androgynous one in *Middlemarch*. And even if the identity of the narrator as a male/female could be established, the question would still remain whether the writer was speaking as "George Eliot" or "Mary Ann Evans." What is significant here is that instead of trying to organize contemporary events, the narrator has chosen to go back forty years and therefore impose order on a settled series of events. As Lukacs says, "The use of the past tense is thus a basic technique prescribed by reality for achieving artistic unity and organization."[78]

Nevertheless, for Kettle even this attempt at unity fails because of Eliot's "mechanistic philosophy and her moral view of the world as an udder." (*I*, 173-74) His observations become increasingly prescriptive:

> The point here, it is worth insisting, is not that her moral concern should be consistent and explicit, not that she should continuously refer us back to our own consciences, but that she should do so in a way which weakens the tension of the scene she is describing and places her characters at a distance which makes an intimate conveying of their feelings difficult. (*I*, 173)

On the next page, Kettle continues that we feel oppressed by the fact that we are taken from one moral crisis to another. No doubt there are several moral crises in the novel but the distancing effect is induced by the digressions of the narrator's voice. Just as Brecht's songs interrupt the action, thereby distancing the audience, it seems to me that there is this constant mechanism of distancing at play in Eliot's method, for example, in Chapter 80, after Dorothea's night of suffering, we are told, "On the road there was a man with a bundle on his back and a woman carrying her baby." (*MM*, 750) and at once the tension is dissolved.

What Kettle is looking for in the novel is evidence to fit his dialectical world-view. He says:

> Because her outlook is mechanistic and not revolutionary no one can fight Middlemarch or change it. The most they can do is to improve it a little. (*I*, 174)

This brings us back to the statement with which we started and the notion of "change" in consciousness. Kettle's strictures of what Eliot should or should not have done seem to constitute the basic weakness in his critical practice. To look at Eliot's whole enterprise--her characterization and narrative technique from only the angle of her "mechanistic philosophy" is to overlook the artistic achievement of the whole. Williams, on the other hand, analyzes her enterprise in positive terms:

> For this is George Eliot thinking beyond, feeling beyond, the restrictions and the limitations she has so finely recorded; thinking into mobility not as dislocating but as liberating; with

> some anxiety, certainly--some registered qualified anxiety--but following a thread to the future, as she tried in *Daniel Deronda,* a single thread that has come loose from the web, but that she insists is there, running beyond Middlemarch as she herself ran beyond it. (*TEN,* 93)

V

As we have seen, Kettle and Williams approach *Middlemarch* from different perspectives though both agree that it is a great novel. Williams considers it "a superb presentation" (*TEN,* 91) and Kettle believes that "the novelists of the future will turn to *Middlemarch* more often than to any other English novel." (*I*, 177) Both critics centre their analysis of the novel on Eliot herself--Kettle referring frequently to her philosophy and intention, while Williams analyzes the development of her method.

It is interesting to note that like Heathcliff, it is clear that Ladislaw as a character can be categorized as the "other." He is alienated not on account of his skin colour but in more subtle ways relating to birth, rank and money. Thus Eliot, by proposing an unconventional hero, is inserting an oppositional discourse within an otherwise conventional classic realist text. However, as we have seen, most critics fail to see this aspect of his character and continue to debate about the validity or otherwise of his existence and relationship with Dorothea. Kettle follows the general consensus in condemning Ladislaw whereas Williams, although he does not categorize him as the 'other,' comes fairly close to defining him as a modernist hero--"coming from 'nowhere,' belonging 'nowhere,' he is able to move, to relate and so to grow in ways that the others are not." (*TEN,* 93)

Dorothea's character is seen by most critics as idealized but this effect is countered by the fact that she is presented through many perspctives – the ironic and the idealized,[79] the romantic and the realist. A feminist reading shows that in spite of the advantage she has in terms of class position, she is still a victim of a patriarchal society. By adopting a male pseudonym, it is not as if Eliot is submitting to male standards and values, but by positing herself within them, she is able to carry out a searching analysis of male values and thereby to expose them. Neither Kettle's nor Williams's models allow for this aspect of the text.

As Williams has rightly pointed out, Eliot has extended the sense of community as Jane Austen had not, and this community is further extended in the case of Hardy, as we shall see. Society is seen as a web where each thread is interconnected and one can see the relation between this image and the organic imagery of Spencer's evolutionary theory. To Kettle's charge that Middlemarch society is static, textual evidence proves otherwise and it is evident that Eliot goes to a deeper level of society than manifest historical or political events can indicate.

The discussion in the last section leads us to conclude that though there is artistic unity within the book, there is an interplay of perspectives at a thematic level. The narrative voice is not only producing a distancing effect by "telling" but creates a dramatic rapprochement by "showing." Thus the "mimetic" and "diegetic" are held in tension. The narrative voice cannot be equated with the writer's nor can it be placed in terms of gender. At best, it can be seen as androgynous.

It is evident that Kettle's literary criticism falls in line with the tradition of the critic being the ultimate authority in passing judgements that are somewhat democratized by enlisting the reader's assent. This goes contrary to his avowed ideological position. By defining the effect of *Middlemarch* as "not moving," Kettle is resorting to "subjective" as opposed to "objective" criticism. Moreover, this kind of criticism, while making useful observations and opening interesting avenues for discussion is, in the last analysis, prescriptive. Williams's concept of the "knowable community" is useful because it is analytic and not prescriptive, and as we have seen, used in analysing *Middlemarch* though not *Wuthering Heights,* where the action is limited to a single set of characters at any given time. On the other hand, in *Middlemarch* while the drama of the lives of five different sets of characters is closely knit together, the focus does not fall in any single direction. As we have seen, Kettle attributes the failure of Ladislaw, Dorothea and the novel to Eliot's "mechanistic philosophy" which is restrictive to the extent that it proposes what "should be" as opposed to what "is."

The form, scope and technique of *Middlemarch*, then, is quite different from that of *Wuthering Heights*. *Wuthering Heights,* as we have seen, "provide[s] a bridge from Richardson and the Romantics to modern psychological literature, to the experiments of James and Lawrence's transcendentalism."[80] *Middlemarch* can be said to belong to the highwatermark period of Victorian fiction, whereas *Tess of the d'Urbervilles* can be said to bridge the gap between Victorianism and modernism. It will now be relevant to see how this novel marks a further stage in the development of the nineteenth century novel as a whole, as a point of transition into modernist fiction, and how adequately Kettle and Williams deal with it within the context of their models.

NOTES

1. "Notes of Form in Art" (1868), *Essays of George Eliot,* ed. Thomas Pinney (N.Y: Columbia University Press, 1967), p. 432
2. Virginia Woolf regards it as "the magnificent book which for all its imperfections is one of the few novels written for grown-up people." *The Common Reader,* First Series (London: Hogarth, 1968), p. 213.
3. Holmstrom and Lerner, eds., *George Eliot and Her Readers* (London: The Bodley Hogarth, 1966), p. 117.
4. "Realism and the Cinema: Notes on Some Brechtian Theses," *Screen,* Summer 1974, Vol. 15, No. 2, p. 8.
5. "George Eliot's *Middlemarch,*" *The Galaxy,* March 1873, *A Century of George Eliot Criticism,* G.S. Haight, ed. (London: Methuen, 1965), p. 83.
6. *The Great Tradition* (London: Chatto and Windus, 1962), p. 75.
7. *The English Novel* (Harmondsworth: Pelican, 1982), p. 233.
8. McCabe, p. 19.
9. Leavis, p. 75.
10. *Loc. cit.*
11. "Re-reading the Great Tradition," *Re-reading English,* Peter Widdowson, ed. (London: Methuen, 1982), p. 126.
12. Quoted in Holmstrom and Lerner, p. 87.
13. *Ibid.*, p. 111.
14. *Middlemarch* (Harmondsworth: Penguin, 1982), pp. 442-43. Hereafter cited as *MM.*
15. *The Art of George Eliot* (London: Chatto and Windus, 1961), p. 170.
16. London, 29 Oct. 1876, *Letters VI,* Gordon S. Haight, ed. (Yale: University Press, 1955), pp. 301-2.

17. "George Eliot in *Middlemarch,*" *Critical Essays on George Eliot,* B. Hardy, ed. (London: Methuen, 1970), p. 148.
18. *The Long Revolution* (London: Chatto and Windus, 1961), p. 278.
19. Williams, *Problems in Materialism and Culture* (London: Verso, 1980), pp. 40-42.
20. Barthes's death of the author.
21. "Representation and the Colonial Text," *The Theory of Reading,* F. Gloversmith, ed. (Brighton: Harvester, 1984), p. 100.
22. "George Eliot's 'eminent failure': Ladislaw," *This Particular Web,* Ian Adam, ed. (Toronto: University Press, 1975), p. 24.
23. As asserted by Henry James in "George Eliot's *Middlemarch,*" *The Galaxy,* March 1873, *A Century of George Eliot Criticism,* p. 83.
24. *Critical Practice* (London: Methuen, 1980), p. 52.
25. *The Madwoman in the Attic* (New Haven: Yale University Press, 1979), pp. 528-29.
26. Leavis, p. 76.
27. Harvey, p. 197.
28. Gilbert and Gubar, pp. 529-30.
29. McCabe, p. 16.
30. "George Eliot's *Middlemarch,*" *A Century of George Eliot Criticism,* pp. 81-82.
31. Leavis, p. 75.
32. *Ibid.*, p. 72.
33. *Ibid.*, p. 74.
34. See Chapters 2 and 3.
35. Goldmann, *Towards A Sociology of the Novel,* Alan Sheridan, trans. (London: Tavistock, 1975), p. 6.
36. In this case and in his analysis of *Oliver Twist,* Kettle says, "But the weaknesses--which may be summed up as the inadequacy of Dickens's conscious view of life--are in the first eleven chapters of *Oliver Twist* almost obliterated by the strength." (*I,* p. 119)
37. Haight, p. 82.
38. *The English Novel,* p. 231.
39. Gilbert and Gubar, p. 450.
40. *Ibid.*, p. 466.
41. *Westminster Review,* LXVI, Oct. 1856, pp. 442-61.
42. *Essays of George Eliot,* Thomas Pinney, ed. (New York: Columbia Univ. Press), p. 303.

43. *Ibid.*, p. 324.

44. Holmstrom and Lerner, pp. 15-16.

45. *Literary Women* (London: Women's Press, 1976), pp. 194-95.

46. Casaubon's statement is strongly reminiscent of the hierarchical caste system that existed in Hindu society and which was further reinforced by the fatalistic ethic which preached that the *summum bonum* of the individual consisted in doing one's duty unquestioningly.

47. *The Art of George Eliot*, p. 179.

48. *Politics and Letters*, p. 247.

49. This has been discussed at greater length earlier.

50. Jacob Korg, Rev., *TEN, Modern Fiction Studies* (18), p. 263.

51. *The Country and the City* (London: Chatto and Windus, 1975), p. 203.

52. *Loc. cit.*

53. Leavis, p. 61.

54. Richard P. Appelbaum, *Theories of Social Change* (Chicago: Markham, 1970), p. 32.

55. *Culture and Society* (Harmondsworth: Penguin, 1982), p. 118.

56. *Ibid.*, p. 119.

57. J. Hillis Miller, *The Form of Victorian Fiction* (Indiana: Notre Dame, 1968), p. 119.

58. *Criticism and Ideology* (London: NLB, 1976), p. 120.

59. *Problems in Materialism and Culture*, p. 47.

60. Jerome Beaty, "History by Indirection: The Era of Reform in *Middlemarch*," *A Century of George Eliot Criticism*, p. 313.

61. A further discussion of the organic unity of the novel will be found in Sec. IV. Here I will only deal with the community within the novel.

62. "Class and Class Consciousness in early Nineteenth Century England, 3 classes or 5?," p. 23.

64. *Marxism and Literature* (Oxford: University Press, 1977), p. 44.

65. *Philosophy and the Novel* (Oxford: University Press, 1975), p. 10.

66. Leavis, p. 6.

67. Kettle refers to this distinction between "life" and "Life." (*I*, 161)

68. *Middlemarch: Critical Approaches to The Novel*, B. Hardy, ed. (London: Athlone Press, 1967), p. 22.

69. W. Benjamin, *Understanding Brecht*, Anna Bostock, trans. (London: NLB, 1977), p. xvii.

70. "The Structure of the Novel," *Middlemarch: Critical Approaches*, pp. 13-22.

71. Schorer, p. 24.
72. *The Form of Victorian Fiction,* p. 63.
73. Fowles, *The French Lieutenant's Woman* (London: Granada, 1984), p. 86.
74. K. McSweeney, *Middlemarch* (London: George Allen and Unwin, 1984), p. 73.
75. Quoted in Wayne C. Booth, "Telling and Showing," *The Nineteenth Century Novel,* p. 54.
76. Lodge, p. 236.
77. *Loc. cit.*
78. Discussing Lydgate, Leavis says: "Only those," his creator tells us, "who know the supremacy of the intellectual life--the life which has a seed of ennobling thought and purpose in it--can understand the grief of one who falls from that serene activity into the absorbing soul-wasting struggle with wordly annoyances." (*TGT,* p. 65)
79. "Narrate or Describe?," *The Nineteenth Century Novel,* p. 73. George Eliot's practice for setting her novels back in time is interpreted by Stephen Marcus as a "defence mechanism," "constructed to control . . . sexual passion . . . social conflict and . . . a world without sense, meaning or intelligibility." (*Representations: Essays on Lit. and Society,* N.Y., 1975, pp. 206-7).
80. G. Hemstedt, "The Novel," *The Victorians,* L. Lerner, ed. (London: Methuen, 1978), p. 12.

Tess of the d'Urbervilles

Without going into all the ideological implications of the changing fashions in Hardy criticism, a brief examination of the various stages through which it has developed will be a useful starting point here. According to Eagleton, Hardy, during his lifetime, was regarded as the "charming supplier of rural idylls" whereas with the publication of *The Dynasts,* he came to be seen as "the melancholic purveyor of late nineteenth century nihilism."[1] In the forties and fifties, his reputation suffered a setback at the hands of the formalists (in America) and the "Scrutineers" especially F.R. Leavis, who quotes with approval Henry James's letter to R.L. Stevenson, which reads: "The good little Thomas Hardy has scored a great success with *Tess* which is chock-full of faults and falsity."[2] However, the forties also saw a shift towards a sociological perspective while in the sixties and seventies there is a marked tendency towards formalist criticism. Eagleton sums up:

> he [Hardy] has been phenomenologized, Freudianized, biographized, claimed as the true guardian of "English" liberal-democratic decencies against the primitivist extremism of emigre modernists.[3]

In referring to this consensus, the intention here is to locate Kettle and Williams within the third stage, that is, the sociological, though in both cases the emphasis is different. For example, Kettle defines the novel as a "social document" (*II*, 45) whereas Williams locates the social and ideological crisis in interpersonal relationships.[4]

That Hardy is popular in the 1980 s is evident from Antonia Byatt's article "Hardy Rules O.K.," wherein she publishes the result of a survey on 500-520 students asked to list their favourite authors in order of preference. Hardy ranked first with 194 votes, followed by Austen (165), Lawrence (158), Dickens (124), the Brontes (106),

Orwell (103) and George Eliot (69). Byatt says that the change could be a result of the shift in teaching policy and wonders if this generation discovered Hardy for themselves, "Or does the rural nostalgia ally itself to the more simple, back-to-earth emotions that led to the passion for Tolkien?"[5] Byatt offers no simple answers and all these factors could possibly contribute to the phenomenon.

It is crucial to consider these shifts in Hardy's case because as Williams points out:

> The tone of social patronage, that is to say, supported by crude and direct suppositions about origin, connects interestingly with a tone of literary patronage and in ways meant to be damaging with a strong and directing supposition about the substance of Hardy's fiction. (*TEN,* 100)

In his essay, "Hardy in History," Widdowson asserts that late nineteenth century criticism measured Hardy by the yardstick of "character and environment"--a term used by Hardy himself.[6] This was consistently reinforced by twentieth century critics (David Cecil, to name one), and the "minor" fiction was sifted from the "major." It is because Hardy's "minor" fiction does not answer to the "discourse of liberal-humanist realism"[7] that it has been totally ignored. Exposing the politics of the critiographical enterprise, Widdowson says that by challenging "realism," Hardy is calling into question the practice of the dominant ideology:

> For realism is not just a matter of literacy form; it is the common-sense expression in aesthetic terms of an ideology in which the unified individual human subject "makes sense" of his/her world by negotiation with external forces--Nature, Society, etc. which presupposes a universe that *can* be made sense of and an always potentially self-determining human subject. . . . Realism, in effect, is the writing of the unified human subject onto the immensities of time, process and history, and as such is a crucial instrument in this ideology's naturalizing function. When the essential fiction of bourgeois realism--the illusion of truth--comes to be believed as the literal truth, then fiction and ideology are working very closely together, and the deception of their "truthfulness" must be sustained at all costs.[8]

Widdowson's definition of "realism" with its philosophical and political implications, unravels the complexity of the literary-ideological construct "Hardy." It is also quite different from the definition of realism put forward by Kettle and Williams. For Widdowson, "bourgeois realism" is a confining category while for both Kettle and Williams, it is a test of great literature. How far, then, Kettle and Williams conform to the dominant system, is a question that will be dealt with in the course of the discussion.

The issues of the construction and re-construction of "canons" will be dealt with in relation to *Tess of the d'Urbervilles,* which was first published in three volumes by Osgood, McIlvane and Co. in November 1891.[9] The discussion in Section I will initiate from Kettle's statement regarding Alec d'Urberville's status as a villain of Victorian melodrama. As we have seen, the majority of critics condemn non-realist modes like melodrama, romance, the gothic. From a radical 1980s perspective, melodrama would be seen as a mode of subversion operating against the "realist" discourse, but does Kettle take this position? The question then is to examine how Kettle, with his focus on realism regards the accommodation of various modes within a realistic framework, and to what extent Hardy's technique differs from that of Eliot's.

Section II will concentrate on the novel in relation to its sociological context. Kettle designates *Tess* a *roman a these* and a moral fable and looks at it as symbolizing the "actual fate of millions of working-women." (*II*, 51) This analysis is strongly reminiscent of Heathcliff's alleged representation of the proletariat, but this leads to an examination of Kettle's changed position on the novel as stated in The Open University Course Unit. The discussion will also focus on Williams's approach to the novel and whether he makes use of his concepts of the "knowable community" and "structure of feeling" in his analysis of it.

Section III will deal with the problem of language in *Tess.* Kettle looks at the linguistic strategy in terms of narrative technique, and the question that now arises is how he squares this analysis with his overall reading of the novel. Williams looks at this problem in terms of the customary/educated dichotomy which links Hardy to Eliot before him and to Lawrence after. Can the novel be termed "polyphonic" is an allied question also to be discussed at this stage.

In the final section, I will try to clarify some of the issues raised here and in the discussion that follows. I will also try to sum up the relation between the three novels featured in this book in terms of the development of the Victorian novel leading to modernism and finally, how far the methodology of Kettle and Williams achieves a satisfactory and useful reading of the texts.

I

> The only blot on this otherwise excellent work is the absurdly melodramatic character of that "villain of the deepest dye," Alec d'Urberville.[10]

Alec d'Urberville has been generally dismissed as a "bounder" and as the "stock villain of Victorian melodrama." Kettle goes along with this consensus, but considers it in a positive light:

> It seems to me that almost the whole point about d'Urberville is that he is indeed the archetypal Victorian villain. Far from being weakened by the associations of crude melodrama he in fact illuminates the whole type. . . . It is the very typicality of d'Urberville that serves the purpose of the novel. (*II*, 55)

Is this the only dimension to the character of Alec and how far does he fit within the framework of realistic fiction? How he serves the purpose of the novel and to what extent his portrayal was dictated by the need to cater to popular taste are some questions that will be discussed in this section. The major issue however, is the insertion of non-realist modes like melodrama within a realist framework.

Melodrama (in theatre) was a phenomenally popular form of entertainment in Victorian times. Due to rapid industrial expansion, a huge working-class with a low level of literacy, were demanding sensational yet cheap entertainment. As Michael Booth explains:

> Essentially, melodrama is a simplification and idealization of human experience dramatically presented. For its audiences, melodrama was both an escape from real life and a dramatization

> of it as it ought to be, uncomplicated, easy to understand, sufficiently exciting to sweep away petty cares.[11]

Regarding the relation of the nineteenth century novel to theatre, Booth says:

> The whole question of the relation of the novel to the stage in the nineteenth century is a large one; suffice to say here that hundreds of melodramas were taken from novels.

According to Booth, the villain is more important than the hero who is merely a passive creature. He adds that "black remains the villain's colour; hair, complexion and moustache are tokens of his trade."[12] In *Tess of the d'Urbervilles,* Alec is first introduced in the following words:

> He had an almost swarthy complexion, with full lips . . . above which was a well-groomed black moustache with curled points.[13]

As we have seen earlier, black, with its associations of villainy, suggests undercurrents of racism in a nation passing through a dominant phase of imperialism. However, the elements of racism in melodrama are older than Victorian times, and the association is more with other European foreigners like the Spaniards, Italians and the gipsies. It also suggests the commonly-held dichotomy between white and black, the colours signifying good and the forces of evil respectively. The audiences, (mainly the working-classes and the peasants) hissed the villains who were generally "wealthy employers and noblemen,"[14] thus indicating anti-upper-class attitudes. However, the educated elite were obviously not so enthusiastic about such stereotypes.

No doubt Alec is the archetypal Victorian villain with roots that can be traced back to the Morality plays, but to discern the extent to which the myth is "displaced" in the interest of compatibility to the realist mode, a reference to Frye's theory of myths is necessary here. According to Frye:

> In myth we see the structural principles of literature isolated, in realism we see the *same* structural principles (not similar ones) fitting into a context of plausibility.[15]

Frye rejects what he terms the "representational fallacy" and believes that literature is not based on life but on literature itself. Realism, according to him, is not "likeness" to an object, but likeness to conventions one is familiar with.[16] Frye relates the archetype to a closed system of myths while Kettle relates it to the society in which it was popular.

In *Tess*, Alec is not the only literary stereotype. As Howe has pointed out, Tess is the typical Victorian heroine--"self-sacrificing," "doomed aristocrat"[17] and the long-suffering submissive woman idealized by Victorian society. Tess conforms to the dominant image of femininity, that is, the Madonna, whereas Arabella in *Jude the Obscure* belongs to the other category, the whore. Kate Millett points out the three images of women dominant in nineteenth century fiction--women placed on a chivalric pedestal, the *femme fatale,* and finally the "realistic" character who emancipates herself from her traditional role. There are elements of all three types in Tess, but Hardy basically sees her as the "pure woman," for he feels:

> The beauty or ugliness of a character lay not in its achievements, but in its aims and impulses; its true history lay, not among things done, but among things willed. (*Tess,* 433)

This is a fact that Angel does not recognize when he rejects Tess. According to Hardy, "Angel is a *type* of a certain class of the modern young man,"[18] [my italics] embodying the double standard of values that still exist in patriarchal societies. Merryn Williams comments on Angel:

> He is a typical representative of that Victorian society in which intellectuals complained about how much they would like to believe in God, if they only could, and which idealized woman and the home in the most fulsome language at a time when the number of prostitutes in England was greater than ever before.[19]

This then brings us to the question of "typicality" and how Kettle's use of it (in this context) differs from that of Lukacs.[20] Lukacs uses "typical" in the sense of the individual in society whereas Kettle is merely referring to it in regard to literary convention. The closest Kettle comes to Lukacs is in his emphasis that *Tess*:

> is the expression of a generalized human situation in history and neither (what it is generally assumed to be) a purely personal tragedy nor (what Hardy appears to have intended) a philosophic comment on life in general and the fate of Woman in particular." (*II*, 53)

How this "typicality" of Alec serves the purpose of the novel is clear from Kettle's earlier statement that the novel is about the "destruction of the peasantry." (*II*, 54) At a symbolic level, Alec can be seen as representative of the *nouveau riche* "aristocracy," thus highlighting the fact of social mobility that had reduced Tess, the daughter of a life-holder and trader, to the level of manual labour. At a formal level, it proves Kettle's awareness of the fact that Hardy was not writing in one mode alone. *Tess of the d'Urbervilles* incorporates a plurality of modes–melodrama, the folk-tale, and Greek tragedy. As P.N. Furbank puts it, Hardy is "almost as free as an Elizabethan dramatist to move from one mode to another."[21] When such flexibility is acknowledged by the critic, most charges of "improbability" and "unrealism" are waived. In any case, "our very use of the term 'realism' acknowledges that realism is not reality, but merely another convention for the representation of reality."[22] And instead of attempting photographic realism, Hardy is aiming for a synthesis between the commonplace and the unusual, his thesis being:

> A story must be exceptional enough to justify its telling. We tale-tellers are all Ancient Mariners, and none of us is warranted in stopping Wedding Guests . . . unless he has something more unusual to relate than ordinary experience of every average man and woman.[23]

This somewhat forestalls the objections to Hardy's unusual tales that are usually criticized on grounds of excessive coincidence.

Tess of the d'Urbervilles has the same relentless quality that is found in Sophoclean tragedy. Like Oedipus, Tess is unable to escape the hounds of fate. But the main factor that lifts the novel from the level of melodrama to "tragedy" is the final affirmation of human dignity that is manifested in Tess's last act. A human being may be defeated but not destroyed is the experience transmitted. The Chorus, (so essential to classical tragedy) in the shape of rural characters, is not as prominent in *Tess of the d'Urbervilles* as it is in *The Mayor of Casterbridge* and *The Return of the Native.*[24] This synthesis of the novelistic and dramatic elements places Hardy in the tradition of Fielding and his followers. As David Cecil points out:

> The setting and characters of their stories were carefully realistic but they were fitted into a framework or non-realistic plot derived from the drama, consisting of an intrigue enlivened by all sorts of sensational events--conspiracies, children changed at birth, mistakes of identity.[25]

This problem of reconciling diverse modes is noted by Eagleton:

> The formal problem of how to reconcile these conflicting literary modes--is Alec d'Urberville bourgeois *arriviste,* pantomime devil, melodramatic villain, symbol of Satanic evil?--is the product of Hardy's unusually complex mode of insertion into the dominant ideological formation and its span of possible literary modes.[26]

The relation of Hardy's conscious philosophy to his awareness of social processes and his class position will be discussed in Sections II and III respectively. As we can see neither Alec nor Angel is represented in purely black and white terms. It is only D.H. Lawrence who, in his "Study of Thomas Hardy" complains that Hardy is unjust to Alec, the physical man, believing that, in Manston, and Troy and Fitzpiers, and Alec d'Urberville, there is good stuff gone wrong.[27] To decide whether Alec was really "good stuff gone wrong," it is necessary to decide whether Tess was raped or seduced. The event is first described:

> Why was it that upon this beautiful feminine tissue . . . there should have been traced such a coarse pattern as it was doomed to receive. . . . Doubtless some of Tess d'Urberville's male ancestors rollicking home from a fray had dealt the same measure even more ruthlessly towards peasant girls of their time. (*Tess,* 101)

From this passage it is clear that this is a case of rape. But doubts arise when one realizes that it is only in late October Tess leaves Trantridge whereas the "rape" had taken place in September. The parting conversation between Alec and Tess seems to confirm this. Says Tess:

> If I had gone for love of you . . . I should not so loathe and hate myself for my weakness as I do now. . . . My eyes were dazed by you for a little but that was all. (*Tess,* 105)

Here it would seem as if it was seduction after all. Tess is a passionate woman who writes a desperate letter to Angel saying, "I am so exposed to temptation." (*Tess,* 359) This ambivalence continues in the conversation between Marian and Izz who are worried about Tess's future, "His [Alec's] having won her once makes all the difference in the world. "Twould be a thousand pities if he were to tole her away again." (*Tess,* 387)[28]

Does Hardy then represent Tess as a pure woman? Contemporary readers felt that Tess was "depraved"[29] and could not reconcile her final act with the concept of purity. But according to Hardy, who in a conversation with Raymond Blathwayt, says:

> I still maintain that her innate purity remained intact to the very last; though I frankly own that a certain outward purity left her on her last fall. I regarded her then as being in the hands of circumstances . . . a mere corpse drifting.[30]

No doubt Hardy has represented Tess faithfully but he has failed her in that he has attributed all her troubles to Fate/the President of the Immortals. This reference to a determining fate diffuses the impact of Hardy's social commentary. What he has not consciously emphasized is that Tess is doubly marginalized--because of her class and because of her gender. The "fate" of Tess is not due to Alec alone but also because of her economic condition and her final abandonment by Angel. Having been brought up in a patriarchal society, Tess is used to fulfilling certain roles--as daughter, mother, wife and when Angel leaves her, a vacuum is created into which Alec inevitably rushes. Her whole life is beset by turmoil and only when she goes to the gallows, a strange calm descends upon her--for she can now abandon all roles to which she had been hitherto consigned.

In his critique of *Tess of the d'Urbervilles,* Kettle says that it is not about the "fate of Woman in particular" (*II*, 53) but about "a generalized human situation in history." (*II*, 53) But while gender distinctions exist, it is difficult to speak of a "generalized human situation" for that would ultimately read "generalized male situation."

This reading may go contrary to authorial intention, but as Alison Light aptly points out:

> The literary text works as a process of the production of meaning, one which can be reproduced differently in history at each time of reading.[31]

With the growing awareness of women to their subordinate position, a feminist reading has inevitably developed--a position that both Kettle and Williams do not approach. As we have seen in the earlier chapters, the various discourses embodied in a text are unravelled according to the interests of the historical moment. However, in general terms:

> The realistic novelist of the nineteenth century . . . possessed a double equipment. On the one hand, he inherited a series of literary techniques. . . . On the other hand are the new ambitions of the panoramic novel, the new fidelity of realistic dialogue, the new belief that the personal can be explained in social terms. The struggle between these two modes, between literary tradition and social awareness, is fought in each novelist and in each novel, often with great complexity, and it is never (if the book is any good) a total victory for either.[32]

This "struggle" is not highlighted by Kettle, who praises the characterization of Alec, not as a subversive force but in the manner of Lerner, as a tried and effective convention. While Angel can be taken as representing the dominant Victorian value of respectability, the hollowness and hypocrisy of this is brought into sharp focus by Alec's outright villainy. Thus Alec is not just a brilliantly actualized conventional model, but a subversive force that unveils the double standards of society. And when Tess finally goes to the gallows, it is not Alec, but Angel and the "respectable" society he represents, that are responsible.

In addition to this, Kettle's critical methodology entails an examination of the author's conscious philosophy in terms of its progressiveness or otherwise (as we have seen in his analysis of George Eliot) and the world-view that emerges in the novel. How in spite of Hardy's pessimistic philosophy, *Tess of the d'Urbervilles* is regarded as a great novel by Kettle, will now be discussed.

II

As we have seen in the last section, *Tess* incorporates various fictional modes, and this sometimes encourages emphasis on one particular aspect of the novel which then results in partial appreciation or severe condemnation of it. For example, if the novel is taken solely as a manifestation of Hardy's deterministic philosophy deriving the cue from recurrent references to the President of the Immortals, the significance of the social context and the complex processes that Hardy has depicted are totally lost. It is this latter aspect of the novel that both Kettle and Williams highlight with varying emphases.

Kettle's position is evident from his discussion of the conversation between Tess and Abraham where Tess likens the world to a "blighted star," saying that if it had been a "sound one" her father would have been free from physical irritants like "coughing" and "creeping" and her "Mother wouldn't have been always washing and never getting finished." (*II*, 51) Most critics, including Kettle, agree that a peasant girl would hardly talk in this manner and that the philosophy of life is too facile to be convincing. However, Kettle interprets:

> It is the kind of life her parents lead that drives Tess to her feelings of despair and it is the sentence about her mother never getting finished that in fact saves the scene. For here is no pretentious philosophy of fatality but a bitterly realistic recalling of the actual fate of millions of working women. (*II*, 51)

Tess here is clearly not thinking in metaphysical terms but in terms of actual social conditions.[33] In his enthusiasm to stress the social aspect, Kettle simply says that *Tess* is a *roman a these,* the thesis being "the disintegration of the peasantry." (*II*, 45) Can the term "peasantry" serve as a blanket-term to signify the working-classes in the country? Williams explains:

> Where Hardy lived and worked, as in most other parts of England, there were virtually no peasants, although "peasantry" as a generic word for country people was still used by writers. (*TEN,* 100)

A rather interesting comment on the use of the term is made by Merryn and Raymond Williams in an essay "Hardy and Social Class" (1980):

It is interesting that after it had lost any precise meaning in English rural society, following the rise of capitalist agriculture, it was reintroduced to express a more totalizing view: one which suppressed the crucial actual relations and variations. The reintroduction was essentially political, in the reaction which followed the French Revolution. A crucial text is Cobbett, in 1830:

> Pray, my readers, attend to these things, and then (if you be Catholics) *cross yourselves* when you hear Peel and Knatchbull say, the fires *do not proceed from the peasantry, a new* name given to country labourers by the insolent borogh-mongering, and loan-mongering tribes. But if it be not the "peasantry," who is it?[34]

John Durbeyfield, for instance, is not a peasant but a life-holder and small-dealer. Tess is not "an unapprehending peasant woman" (as Angel seems to think (*Tess,* 297) but is educated up to the Sixth Standard and if she slides further down the social scale becoming a wage-labourer involved in heavy field-work, her condition is symptomatic of the volatile social situation of the period. As Merryn Williams points out:

> The society which Hardy presents in his novels is not feudal, not a rigid caste system which denies all mobility, but a developing capitalist society, in which it is possible for families either to sink or rise from their original status.[35]

The old aristocracy was being replaced, not necessarily by a "meritocracy," but by a class of *nouveau riche* Carlylean "captains of industry" masquerading as their predecessors under borrowed illustrious names. Alec d'Urberville's father, enriched by trade, acquires an ancient name and a country seat. But instead of an old country manor, his house is of "recent erection" (*Tess*, 62) and in his estate "everything looked like money--like the last coin issued from the Mint." (*Tess,* 63) A similar process in reverse, is also evident. As Angel observes, "it is surprising how many of the present tillers of the soil were once owners of it." (*Tess,* 217) The fact of social mobility is true not only in class terms but also in terms of geographical mobility, for example, the Old Lady Day migrations when "work-folk" were headed towards new farms and assignments. And as Hardy said, "all the mutations so discernible in village life did not originate entirely in the agricultural unrest. A depopulation was also going on." (*Tess,* 375) Commenting on this passage Williams says:

> Here there is something much more than the crude sentimental version of the rape of the country by the town. The originating pressures within rural society itself are accurately seen and are given a human and social rather than a mechanical dimension.[36]

Within literature, there have been two traditions of country writing--"pleasant fictions of the Arcadian school" and those "which dealt realistically with the facts of destruction and destitution."[37] In *Tess*, the latter tradition dominates though elements of the former are evident in places, for example Tess's sojourn at Talbothays could somewhat resemble Arcadia and Hardy seems to reinforce the image:

> Rays from the sunrise drew forth the buds and stretched them into long stalks, lifted up sap in noiseless streams, opened petals and sucked out scents in invisible jets and breathings. (*Tess*, 156)

However, Hardy does not concentrate on idyllic images alone, but subtly inserts the elements of class-consciousness that even a relatively communal place like Talbothays is not exempt from:

> When milking was finished for the evening they straggled indoors, where Mrs. Crick, the dairyman's wife--who was too respectable to go out milking herself, and wore a hot stuff gown in warm weather because the dairymaids wore prints--was giving an eye to the leads and things. (*Tess*, 140)

On the whole, Talbothays still operates on the feudal values of respect and care. On the other hand, Flintcomb Ash embodies the process of dehumanization and reification, with the cash nexus as the sole link in human relationships. As Irving Howe says:

> What Marx wrote about the working day and the outrage of female labour becomes tangible and immediate. Tess as a woman, Tess as a distinctive person hardly exists; she has become a factor in the process of production.[38]

But to look at the novel in terms of the pastoral tradition alone or to read in it only elements of documentary social realism, is to do it injustice. Williams offers a *via media*, one that Kettle approvingly quotes in the Open University Course Unit:

> We then miss most of what Hardy has to show us if we impose on the actual relationships he describes a pastoral convention of the countryman as an age-old figure, or a vision of a prospering countryside being disintegrated by Corn Law repeal or the railways. . . . It is also that the social forces within his fiction are deeply based in the rural economy itself . . . in what happens to people and to families in the interaction between general forces and personal histories. . . . This is his actual society, and we cannot suppress it in favour of an external view of a seamless abstracted country "way of life." (*TEN,* 112-13)

This reveals a sophisticated understanding of the complex process of the mediation between "life" and "art," and by accepting this analysis, Kettle repudiates his earlier position of seeing *Tess* "simply as a *roman a these* or *Tendenzroman* or moral fable with a didactic emphasis."[39] Explaining this shift, Kettle says:

> At that time [in 1951] I wanted to stress the socio-historical nature of Hardy's novel . . . but I grew fairly quickly to see it as an inadequate reading of the book.[40]

An adequate reading would naturally involve a recognition of the various modes and conventions that the novel embodies (as we saw in the first section). *Tess of the d'Urbervilles* is realistic but not in the sense of naturalism, in "which every detail that occurs is supposed to be a precise fictional equivalent of what would 'really' happen in life."[41] For Kettle, realism does not consist in giving factual details but in dealing with the "actual problems and values of life" (*I*, 28) and thus the task before the nineteenth century novelists was "to achieve realism, to express . . . the truth about life as it faced them." (*I*, 88)[42] But in order to achieve this, Kettle believes that they had to overcome the false consciousness engendered by the capitalist structure of society and therefore they had to become rebels:

> It was not of course always a conscious intellectualized rebellion; very seldom was it based on anything like a sociological analysis. It was rather a rebellion of the spirit, of the total consciousness, and it was often indirectly reflected in the lives the writers led. (*I*, 89)

It is clear that the rebellion in each case was different. Emily Bronte can be taken as the typical case of "rebellion of the spirit" which manifested itself in withdrawal from the actual world into that of the Angria and the Gondal poems. Eliot's rebellion is of a more aggressive nature as it overtly transgresses social norms (her relationship with G.H. Lewes) while Hardy subverts the dominant values of his time in his fiction. (*Tess* ends with Angel and Liza Lu holding hands, whereas this kind of relationship between sisters and brothers-in-law was considered legally incestuous until 1906.) This "rebelliousness," however, is described differently by Lukacs:

> This ruthlessness towards their own subjective world-picture is the hallmark of all great realists, in contrast to the second-raters who nearly always succeed in bringing their own *Weltanschauung* into "harmony" with reality, that is forcing a falsified or distorted picture of reality into the shape of their own world-view.[43]

Kettle apparently agrees with this view:

> A pessimistic and determinist view of the world in which man (and even more, woman) is at the mercy of an unyielding outside Fate, is the conscious philosophy behind the novel. (*II*, 52)

Yet *Tess* achieves greatness in the manner of Tolstoy's novels, for Hardy's great understanding of social processes far transcends his conscious philosophy. It is interesting to note that Kettle relates the weakness in *Middlemarch* to George Eliot's conscious philosophy, that is, "its failure to incorporate a dialectical sense of contradiction and motion." (*I*, 190) But whereas Hardy's redeeming feature is his "deep instinctive comprehension of the fate of Wessex peasants," (*II*, 55) Eliot "tried to convey the interrelatedness of social life or the changing nature of individuals and their relationships." (*I*, 190) It is clear then that Kettle's pattern of analysis is based on the abstract philosophy/concrete social understanding dichotomy that accounts for the failure/success respectively of the whole novel somewhat in the manner of Leavis who would separate Gwendolen Harleth as the better part of *Daniel Deronda*, discarding the title story.[44]

It would seem as if Hardy had literally and metaphorically reserved the last word in the novel for his philosophy featuring the President of the Immortals, yet Kettle does not see it as such. He says that instead of urging the reader to accept Tess's fate as inevitable, Hardy "is arousing in the reader's mind a deep sense of indignation."[45] I do not think that the final effect, whatever Hardy's intentions, is either one of passive acceptance or militant indignation but rather one of awareness of the unjust social system and the pronounced degradation of women within it.

There is a greater awareness of the woman question in Kettle's analysis of 1982 as compared with that of 1951. For instance, when Tess confesses her past experience, Angel recoils from her saying "the woman I have been loving is not you." (*Tess*, 255) Kettle takes this as proof of the "process of idealization of women so deep in the Victorian ethos."[46] But the double standards are also evident, for the same lapse in Angel is forgivable whereas in Tess it is not.

In literary convention, the woman is broadly depicted as the Madonna or the whore. While Dorothea clearly belongs to the former category, Tess belongs to neither. She is described as a fresh, virginal, pagan child of nature who finally hardens into accepting a position as kept mistress. By designating her a "pure woman" contrary to societal convention, Hardy is clearly taking a stand in favour of women in Tess's position. At one level, it might seem as if Tess is passively accepting her lot, but at another, it is evident that by recuperating after each blow dealt to her, (not by "blind fate" but by society) she is quietly but heroically coming to terms with her situation. She cannot change the world, but she changes her own situation as best as she possibly can, culminating in her final act of self-assertion, the murder of her seducer, which can be taken as her rejection of the society that has nothing better to offer to women like her.

Tess, abandoned and destitude, when sleeping in the woods, becomes aware of the pheasants dying around her. This image of the hunted pheasants makes us realize, as Kettle points out, that:

> the pure woman is in fact a victim not just of predatory male hunters but of situations and attitudes which the society in which she lives thinks of and justifies as "natural."[47]

In spite of her condition, Tess is able to transcend her feeling of self-pity and is full of sympathy for the beautiful mangled birds. Her response is somewhat akin to that of Dorothea in *Middlemarch*, when after her night of suffering, she looks out of her window, realizing the narrowness of her concern. While the responses of both women can be said to be similar, their position within Victorian society is not so. Dorothea is the upper class Saint Theresa, the Madonna, whereas for the working-class Tess no such vocation is possible. However pure or noble her intentions might be, socio-economic pressures have dragged her almost to the level of whore.

By comparing Kettle's 1982 essay on *Tess* with his analysis in *An Introduction to the English Novel,* it is obvious how far he has developed as a critic. As Kettle himself said in his essay "Marxism and Literature" (1939):

> Literary standards, like others, depend on social developments. Marxism helps you to realize the futility of erecting absolute standards of judgement. It puts literary critics, like social systems, in their place.[48]

This is as true today as it was forty five years ago. *An Introduction to the English Novel* is overtly Leavisite, Williams's *Reading and Criticism* being more so. In the Open University Course Unit, Kettle discards the cruder concepts of "moral fable" and "*roman à thèse.* He is incorporating several approaches--biographical, formalist and feminist though the overall emphasis is sociological. While in *An Introduction to the English Novel,* Kettle is content to take the novel as having "the quality of a social document," (*II*, 45) in the Open University Course Unit, he shifts his emphasis:

> The essence of *Tess*, as Hardy himself recognized when he added his sub-title after reading the novel in proof, is that it is the story of "a pure woman."[49]

However, as pointed out earlier, the Course Units have limited accessibility and Kettle's changed stance remains, for the most part, unknown. *An Introduction to the English Novel* marks the development of a single position whereas in the Course Units, it is more a question of arbitrating and summarizing various approaches with a view to making them accessible to as many students as possible. Having dealt with the social background of *Tess*, I will now take up Hardy's relation to Wessex, the tension between the "customary" and the "educated" and its allied linguistic and ideological implications.

III

Reviewing *Tess* in April 1892, Mowbray Morris accuses Hardy:

> of writing like a man "who had been at a great feast of languages and stolen the scraps," or, in plain English, of making experiments in a form of language which he does not seem to clearly understand, and *in a style for which he was assuredly not born*. [my italics][50]

The tone of "literary patronage" (*TEN*, 100) is closely connected with a tone of social snobbery--a continuing trend in Hardy criticism--and one that Williams so perceptively exposes. Critics with "elitist" tendencies like Henry James and Leavis have written Hardy out of the "great tradition" whereas, interestingly enough, most Left-Wing critics like Fox, Caudwell, Kettle, Williams and Eagleton have tried to redeem his position. Fox says:

> One cannot, however, think passionately even about English country and the English earth if one is unable to see that this earth is not free, that the heritage of every Englishman is being wantonly deformed and destroyed by a tiny group of ignorant and conscienceless landlords. Hardy had the ability to see this and Lawrence had not, so, though Lawrence wrote better English, it is Hardy's vision of the English country which is more compelling.[51]

Caudwell believes:

> Hardy's novels have affinity with earlier novelists such as Dickens and George Eliot, precisely because the rustic economy in which he developed was backward and close to theirs, and it was a homogeneous, self-contained countryside. The fact gives Hardy his rural foundation--his gnarled epithets, his gaunt, simple characters, the reality of his rural background and its interrelatedness.[52]

Kettle in the Open University Course Units, by his own admission, is almost "falling over backwards"[53] to defend Hardy while Williams does this not only in *The English Novel* but also in *The Country and The City* and *Writing in Society*. Similarly, Eagleton analyzes Hardy's work to advantage in *Criticism and Ideology* and *Walter Benjamin: Towards a Revolutionary Criticism*. The politics of the critical enterprise is obvious here.

In *An Introduction to the English Novel, Vol. II,* Kettle does not touch upon the problem of Hardy's language, but in *The Open University Course Units 17-18* (1982), commenting upon the incongruity of Hardy's prose style, he concedes that "there is . . . a distinct gap between the novelist's language and the consciousness he is evoking."[54] However, he continues that the inclusion of classical allusions is not a device to engage the "educated" reader (as commonly supposed), but is used to "deepen" the effect and help the reader see the situation in its many dimensions.[55] As Kettle says:

> most of the linguistic features which we nowadays tend to respond to unsympathetically are a part of Hardy's strategy in varying the pace and function of his narrative and contriving the confrontation which is at the heart of the text.[56]

Kettle explains the linguistic devices in terms of the writer's conscious narrative strategy. On the other hand, Williams sees the problem in a different context:

> It would be easy to relate Hardy's problem of style to the two languages of Tess: the consciously educated and the unconsciously customary. But the comparison . . . is inadequate. . . . The marks of surrender to each mode are certainly present in

> Hardy but the main body of his writing is a more difficult and complicated experiment. (*TEN*, 107)

And the complexity arises from the fact that Hardy:

> sees as a participant who is also an observer; this is the source of the strain. For the process which allows him to observe is very clearly in Hardy's time one which includes, in its attachments to class feelings and class separations, a decisive alienation. (*TEN*, 110)

Williams rightly locates Hardy's novels in the social crisis of his time, and his position within that set-up, a point I will return to later. Here I will refer to David Lodge's remark about the two languages of Hardy, that is remarkably similar to Williams's observation:

> Tess, we are told, "spoke two languages. . . ." To some extent the same is true of Hardy as narrator. There is the Hardy who can recreate dialect speech with flawless authenticity . . . and there is Hardy speaking . . . in orotund sentences of laboured syntax...who studied *The Times*, Addison and Scott to improve his style.[57]

Lodge doe not think that either mode imposes on the other but that each is indispensable:

> For while one aspect of the novelist's undertaking in *Tess* demands a quality of immediacy, of "felt life," achieved through his empathic identification with his characters . . . other aspects demand a quality of distance both of time and space, through which the characters can be seen in their cosmic, historical and social setting.[58]

In spite of the similarity between the two critics, the emphasis is different—in Williams's case socio-linguistic, whereas it is literary-linguistic in the case of Lodge. Moreover, Williams stresses the complexity of the problem while Lodge points out its dichotomy. According to Williams, the "tension" in Hardy's writing arises neither because of his status as an "awkward countryman," nor in his position as an "autodidact" but it arises "when the observer holds to educated procedures but is unable to feel with the existing educated class."[59]

Williams also points out that "One of the marks of a conservative society is that it regards style as an absolute"[60] but his own proposal is that:

> good prose and style are not things but relationships; that questions of method, subject and quality cannot be separated from the changing relations of men which are evident elsewhere in changing institutions and in a changing language.[61]

Seen from this angle, most of the conventional criticisms of Hardy's style are set aside. No doubt Hardy is given to using a consciously studied literary style as is evident from his use of phrases like "noctambulist's face," (*Tess*, 197) and "pachydermatous king" (*Tess*, 198) but it is justifiable when seen in the context of his curious relationship with his educated readers, when he caters to them but cannot ultimately feel with them. The novel carries ample proof of the fact that Hardy exposes various Victorian values and institutions. When Angel's brothers are described as "such unimpeachable models as are turned out yearly by the lathe of a systematic tuition"(*Tess*, 204), it is clear that the irony is directed at the state of education. Similarly, the novel exposes the institution of marriage, religion and the values of respectability and purity that were so paramount in the Victorian ethos. In addition, there is the distinction between education and class as is evident from the speech of the two brothers educated at University and Angel who has adopted the rhetoric of Froom valley. When he takes a present of black pudding and mead from Mrs. Crick for his family, he finds that while the pudding had been given away in charity, the mead had been put aside in his mother's medicine chest on account of being "extremely alcoholic." (*Tess*, 207) Regretfully, Angel happens to remark that "'that mead was a drop of pretty tipple.' 'A what?' said Cuthbert and Felix both," (*Tess*, 207) making Angel blush and immediately apologize "Oh-'tis an expression they use down at Talbothays." (*Tess*, 207) The shocked reaction of the brothers and the mother's excess of principle but lack of feeling underscore the differences in attitudes even within the "same" class.

It is clear then that the above analysis is facilitated by the use of the model proposed by Williams. What had previously been considered failings in Hardy are now re-assessed as a necessary complexity of his fictional practice. Williams undertakes to re-chart the map of the

English novel with Hardy's position secure within it. Not only Williams, but Merryn Williams with her book *Thomas Hardy and Rural England* (1978) and several articles on Hardy has tried to redress the balance. In fact, Williams is responsible for re-defining the "great tradition" from Dickens and George Eliot to Hardy and Lawrence, for:

> These are novelists all separated, in different degrees, from what was becoming and formally still stands as the dominant social and literary culture.[62]

The significant point of contact between Eliot, Hardy and Lawrence is "the problem of the relation between customary and educated life" (*TEN*, 97) which inevitably surfaces in each writer's use of language. For example, in Eliot there is "the break . . . between the narrative idiom of the novelist and the recorded language of her characters" (*TEN*, 79-80) whereas in Lawrence "the language of the writer is at one with the language of his characters." (*TEN*, 173) The variation in the use of language in the case of all three novelists points to the development in the English novel, for example, in Eliot, the community is extended (as compared to that of Austen) to include working people, but these are a mere chorus, whereas in Hardy's case "work" becomes a major theme and with it comes in the individuation of the working people although the breach still remains. The reason, Williams suggests, may be that Hardy occupied a middle position between the workmen and the middle/upper classes to whose tastes he was catering. For the tension created for a person of modest origins looking up the social scale can manifest itself in several ways in creative work. In the case of Lawrence, Williams points out that he is "feeling with his people, not of them or about them . . . he is simply writing where he lived." (*TEN*, 173) He links the three writers on the basis of how they extended the community "which their life-experience gave them; in the inclusion in their novels of people hitherto unwritten about, or at best observed from a distance." (*TEN*, 171)

A related though different way of looking at the issue of language is indicated in Williams's essay "Notes on English Prose," wherein Williams traces the development of prose in the novel from 1780 to 1950 stating that "In descriptive power, prose was already mature. . . . But now two other uses were remarkably developed" namely "the power of sustained analysis of a situation or state of mind" (79) and "the incorporation . . . of spoken as opposed to written rhythms and constructions"[63]--developments evident in the writing of Hardy.

Williams is also responsible for demystifying the old myth of the "timeless order" of nineteenth century rural England and of Hardy as the dispenser of such conventions. According to Williams, the country/city polarity is not absolute--just as the country is not simply a place "of peace, innocence, and simple virtue," so also the city is not only the site of "learning, communication, light." Nor is the city simply a place of "noise, worldliness and ambition"; and the country synonymous with "backwardness, ignorance, limitation."[64] Besides there are many settlements between the two polarities of country and city--"suburb, dormitory town, shanty town, industrial estate."[65] What Hardy has dramatized is the process of change in country living by pressures within it and outside it. (*TEN*, 102) Therefore, it is unfair to call him a regional novelist because as Williams puts it, his novels:

> reveal the major crises of late nineteenth century England. He could reach a very wide range of social experience through a series of relations which were wholly unknown to him in manifest ways, and which he could render concrete in his fiction.[66]

The use of the word "concrete" is significant here for it links Williams not only to Kettle but to Leavis before him. As pointed out earlier, Williams owes a certain debt to Leavis but while Leavis treats Hardy, the novelist, like a country yokel, Williams puts up a conscious opposition to him. In 1930, in his *Mass Civilization and Minority Culture* pamphlet, Leavis had stated:

> The minority capable not only of appreciating Dante, Shakespeare, Donne, Baudelaire, Hardy (to take major instances) but of recognizing their latest successors constitute the consciousness of the race (or a branch of it) at a given time.[67]

This makes the subsequent dismissal in *The Great Tradition* seem somewhat paradoxical. However, the earlier reference is perhaps to Hardy the poet rather than to Hardy the novelist, for he appears in a gallery of writers who are predominantly poets.[68] Williams explains the paradox:

> Hardy is very disturbing for someone trying to rationalise refined, civilized, balancing judgement. Hardy expresses so much which cannot be displaced from its social situation, particularly in later books.[69]

This defence can be linked with Williams's own autobiographical experience:

> To many of us, now, George Eliot, Hardy and Lawrence are important because they connect directly with our own kind of upbringing and education. They belong to a cultural tradition much older and more central in this country than . . . the public schools. (*TEN,* 96)

For both Hardy and Williams belong to the "border country" between the "customary" and the "educated." It is interesting to note that Gerda Charles, in her review of *Border Country* likens Williams to Hardy:

> Mr Williams has an architectural, Hardy-like feeling for landscape, strong insights into the processes of social change.[70]

This is no doubt true but Williams lacks the dramatic power of Hardy and the ease of the story-teller that is so clear in Hardy's technique. Williams, the grammar-school boy, broke class barriers to enter Cambridge as Hardy's Jude could not enter Christminster. Hardy himself was largely self-educated though in the *curriculum vitae* that he himself prepared for *Who's Who*, he says, "Education: Dorchester, King's College, London." Norman Page has pointed out that the reference to King's College is not strictly true, for Hardy had attended "an evening class in French there for a 'term or two,' apparently in 1865-66."[71] However, Hardy's reference emphasizes the desirability of the prospect, even though he is aware of the alienation caused by esoteric and pedantic institutions. Williams quotes from *Tess*:

> If these two noticed Angel's growing social ineptness, he noticed their growing mental limitations. Felix seemed to him all church, Cuthbert all college. (*TEN*, 110)

What Hardy is aiming at in his novels, is not this pedantic one-sidedness but a complex interaction between the "customary" and the "educated," "between work and ideas, between love of place and an experience of change." (*TEN*, 98)

At a thematic level, in both *Tess of the d'Urbervilles* and *Border Country*, one can see the whole process of change in the community. In *Border Country,* Williams calls for a "common culture," which is as worthy of respect as an "elite culture." Williams also believes that the common usage of language has as much merit as standard language, thus attempting to break down the linguistic hierarchy.[72] The tension between the two languages of Hardy would be termed heteroglossia in Bakhtin's epistemology. For Bakhtin, the tension between various discourses is the very characteristic feature of the novel:

> the narrator's story or the story of the posited author is structured against the background of normal literary language, the expected literary horizon. Every moment of the story has a conscious relationship with this normal language and its belief system, is in fact set against them, and set against them *dialogically*: one point of view opposed to another. . . . This interaction, this dialogic tension between two languages and two belief systems, permits authorial intentions to be realized in such a way that we can acutely sense their presence at every point in the work. The author is not to be found in the language of the narrator, not in the normal literary language to which the story opposes itself . . . but rather, the author utilizes now one language, now another . . . in order that he himself might remain neutral with regard to language.[73]

This "dialogism" is evident not only between the speeches of different characters and opposing viewpoints but can also be found within the same character at the level of language, values, ideology, as evident from the following examples, which also refer to the gender question that is overlooked by Williams. Tess tells her mother:

> Had it anything to do with father's making such a mommet of himself in thik carriage this afternoon? Why did 'er? I felt inclined to sink into the ground with shame! (*Tess*, 46)

The first two sentence are spoken in the Wessex dialect while the last one in standard language revealing Tess's educated status. Besides, her "dialect" and "standard speech" are not really separate but can easily intermingle. Her reference to "shame" betrays not only her characteristic sensibility but also her "gentility," a social acquisition closely connected with her education--unlike her mother's "vulgarity" who dismisses the incident saying, "That wer all a part of the larry!" (*Tess*, 46)

Further, the double standards prevalent in Victorian society are evident from the following exchange between Tess and Angel:

> "Forgive me as you are forgiven! I forgive *you*, Angel. . . ." "O Tess, forgiveness does not apply to the case! You were one person, now you are another. My God--how can forgiveness meet such a grotesque--prestidigitation as that!" (*Tess*, 255)

This also speaks for the idealization of women--"you were one person, now you are another!" It exposes the humane facade that Angel has hitherto kept up. H.M. Daleski points out that Angel's use of a word like "prestidigitation" at this precise moment suggests that he takes refuge in words.[74] In the absence of moral conviction, Angel uses high-flown words to suggest his superior status educationally and thereby socially, for as we gather from *Jude the Obscure*, education was still only available to the elite. By using a word like "prestidigitation," Hardy is emphasizing the distance that his class values have immediately imposed between him and Tess. Tess's mother, though disappointed at her predicament dismisses the event stoically saying, "Tis nater after all and what do please God!" (*Tess*, 104) In church, Tess noticed, that upon observing her people "whispered to each other" (*Tess*, 107) but they did not make an issue of her misfortune by ostracism which would have been inevitable in Angel's social circle whose standards of the ideal woman were met in the personality of Mercy Chant. In fact, Angel commends Tess to his parents's approval on the basis that:

> she was a regular church-goer of simple faith; honest-hearted, receptive, intelligent, graceful to a degree, chaste as a vestal, and in personal appearance, exceptionally beautiful. (*Tess*, 210)

Instead of accepting Tess as she is, Angel, in keeping with the Victorian standards, is aspiring to the ideal. That standards of morality are more rigid among the middle-classes is evident here as is also obvious the fact that Hardy is questioning these at every juncture. It is this alternative sense of values that causes the tension in his use of language. And Williams can relate to Hardy on the basis of his marginal position to the dominant.

Leavis, on the other hand, does not have the same sympathy with Hardy's situation. As pointed out earlier, Hardy's exclusion from the canon has been the result of several causes. From the perspective of early modernism, and its avant-garde movements, Hardy is not aesthetically interesting enough. Firstly, he was taken more seriously as a poet than as a novelist. As a novelist, he had to contend with the exciting new fictional experiments of Woolf, Joyce and Forster while as a poet he was counterposed against Eliot and Pound. Secondly, the whole modernist movement placed his "Englishness" and parochialism into question. Thirdly, Hardy was attempting to situate himself outside the dominant values and with his attacks on the Church, the educational system and the institution of marriage (as pointed out earlier) could hardly aspire to become part of bourgeois literary ideology. "Literary" here signifies Balibar's use of the term:

> The "literary" is an ensemble of linguistic practices, inscribed in certain institutions, that produce appropriate "fictional" and ideological effects, and in doing so contribute to the maintenance of linguistic class-divisions.[75]

Therefore, Hardy was unacceptable to critics committed to the "literary" not because of how he wrote but because "of the ideological disarray that his fictions, consciously or not, are bound to produce."[76] This calls into question the politics of the critical enterprise and proves that Hardy's exclusion from the literary canon is partly the result of the prejudices of the established system and its attitudes to those that would challenge its hegemony.

While Kettle's position vis-a-vis *Tess* has undergone a major change from *An Introduction to the English Novel* (1951) to the Open University Course Units (1982) Williams has maintained his position on Hardy fairly consistently since 1964. For example, Williams wrote an essay "Thomas Hardy" in *Critical Quarterly*, Vol. 6, Winter 1964, which was reproduced in nearly the same form and with exactly the same substance in *The English Novel* (1970) and the same essay can be found, with minor variations, as "Wessex and the Border Country" in *The Country and the City* (1973). In fact, some of the issues discussed in this essay, that is, the notion of the "peasantry" again find their way in the essay "Hardy and Social Class" (1980) written in collaboration with Merryn Williams. This does not signify that Williams's position is outdated. On the contrary, his insights have helped demolish the myths surrounding Hardy. His term "knowable community," does not appear even once in the chapter on Hardy. Yet it is significantly present in Williams's analysis of the novel and his reference to the customary/educated polarities. If it is to be applied in this case, it is clear that instead of an interactive community, there is the relative insularity of the middle-class in its relations with the "lower" orders. For example, Angel genuinely tries to make incursions into the community at Talbothays, yet cannot bridge the class-division for it is clear that he receives preferential treatment in the sense that he is habitually addressed as "sir" (*Tess*, 142-43) and it is class values that induce him to reject Tess. Similarly, Alec's relation to Tess, as we have seen, is exploitative and expedient yet he is different from the former in that he is not posing behind a mask of "gentlemanly" virtue.

Kettle, in the Open University Course Unit, analyzes several isolated passages for evaluative purposes and in his chapter on Hardy, Williams uses a similar method. This is not the normal practice of either Kettle or Williams but in Hardy's case, Williams makes an exception saying that "a close reading was relevant there."[77] Nevertheless it is clear that in other aspects, the analysis differs. Kettle proceeds from a fairly simplistic Marxist humanist perspective to a pluralist one while Williams relate the tension within Hardy's fiction to his complex location within his ambiguous class position.

IV

This chapter has raised several questions not only about Hardy's fictional strategy but about the nature of critical practice in general. By tracing the rejection of Hardy through the decades, it is clear that his reputation has now risen to rank as almost the primary Victorian. (Fowles in *The French Lieutenant's Woman* sets Hardy up as the paradigm of the nineteenth century novelist by setting his own novel in

Dorset, and Sarah Woodruff seems remarkably like Eustacia Vye in *The Return of the Native*.) The reason for this could lie in several directions, but the primary reason apart from the availability of the copyright and its significance to publishing (Widdowson), seems to be in the ideological shift that has taken place and how Left-Wing critics occupying key positions in institutions of power, that is Universities, journals, schools have reconsidered the value of Hardy's works and ensured their dissemination via courses starting at the school level.[78] Williams goes so far as to say, "Hardy is our flesh and our grass." (*TEN*, 118)

Tess of the d'Urbervilles is not the model classic realist text. As we have seen in Section I, it incorporates various modes with great success and can be taken as pointing towards modernism. Focusing on the question of whether Alec is a successfully-realized character or a mere stereotype of melodrama, the answer would lie in neither direction, for he incorporates the two modes. In this sense, it is right to conclude that there is no *one* meaning that the text generates or the meaning that the author intended to suggest. The text embodies a plurality of significations decoded differently at different stages.

Thirdly, it is clear that Kettle's position with regard to the text has been a changing one, pointing to the development of the critic. Williams has fairly consistently championed the cause of the writer, laying great stress on his social situation relating the rupture in his linguistic practice to his ways of seeing and feeling. (*TEN*, 110)

Kettle is consistent in his critical practice of evaluating a writer according to his/her conscious philosophy whereas Williams's method is flexible to the extent that though his concerns can be stated in general terms as those of "knowable community" and "structure of feeling" yet these terms do not assume conceptual rigidity. As Williams states in connection with "structure of feeling":

> The point of the deliberately contradictory phrase, with which I have never been happy, is that it was a structure in the sense that you could perceive it operating in one work after another which weren't otherwise connected – people weren't learning it from each other; yet it was one of feeling much more than of thought – a pattern of impulses, restraints, tones, for which the best evidence was often the actual conventions of literature or dramatic writing.

> To this day . . . I keep coming back to this notion from the actual experience of literary analysis rather than from any theoretical satisfaction with the concept itself.[79]

While Kettle points to Tess's situation as the pure woman, he does nothing to substantiate it. Both critics ignore the feminist perspective and also fail to take into account the fact that one of the reasons for Alec's dismissal is closely tied up with the fact of his "otherness." Their allegiance to a form of "classic realism" once again limits their analysis and paradoxically points to the "conservative" element in their thought, a dominant cultural value, which can be fully consistent with mainstream liberal humanism.

NOTES

1. Eagleton, "Liberality and Order: The Criticism of John Bayley," *New Left Review*, 110, July-August 1978, p. 35.
2. 19 March 1892, quoted in *Thomas Hardy and His Readers: A Selection of Contemporary Reviews*, Lerner and Holmstrom, eds. (London: Bodley Head, 1968), p. 85.
3. *Ibid.*, p. 36.
4. ". . . the relation between the changing nature of country living, determined as much by its own pressures as by pressures from 'outside,' and one or more characters who have become in some degree separated from it yet who remain by some tie of family inescapably involved." (*TEN*, p. 102)
5. *Times Educational Supplement*, 28.1.81, p. 12.
6. Hardy divided his novels as: I *Novels of Character and Environment--Under the Greenwood Tree, Far from the Madding Crowd, The Mayor of Casterbridge, The Return of the Native, Tess* and *Jude*. II. "Romances and Fantasies": *A Pair of Blue Eyes, The Trumpet Major, Two in a Tower, The Well-Beloved*. III. "Novels of Ingenuity": *Desperate Remedies, The Hand of Ethelberta, A Laodicean*. Norman Page explains: "This grouping was made for the collected edition of 1912, and there is evidence (in an unpublished letter) that Hardy did not set great store by the categories he devised. Although the first group contains all the major novels, they were certainly not planned as a series." *Thomas Hardy* (London: Routledge and Kegan Paul, 1977), p. 37.
7. *Literature and History*, Vol. 9:1, Spring 1983, p. 13.
8. *Ibid.*, pp. 13-14.
9. *Tess of the d'Urbervilles* appeared in serial form in *The Graphic* with isolated parts like "The Midnight Baptism, a Study in Christianity" published

in the *Fortnightly* May, 1891, and "Saturday Night in Arcady," printed in a literary supplement of the *National Observer* of Edinburgh, 14 Nov. 1891, in Lerner and Holmstrom, p. 58.

10. *Punch*, 27 Feb. 1892, in Lerner and Holmstrom, p. 84.
11. *Hiss the Villain,* (London: Eyre and Spottiswoode, 1964), p. 9.
12. M. Booth, *English Melodrama* (London: Herbert and Jenkins, 1965), p. 20.
13. *Tess of the d'Urbervilles* (London: Macmillan, 1974), p. 64. Hereafter cited as *Tess.*
14. *Hiss the Villain*, p. 16.
15. *Anatomy of Criticism* (New Jersey: Princeton, 1965), p. 136.
16. *Ibid,* p. 132.
17. Ellen Moers, "Tess as Cultural Stereotype," *Twentieth Centuty Interpretations of Tess of the d'Urbervilles,* Albert J. LaValley, ed. (N.J., Englewood Cliffs: Prentice-Hall, 1969), p. 99.
18. Merryn Williams, *Thomas Hardy and Rural England* (London: Macmillan, 1978), p. 96.
19. *Loc. cit.*
20. *Studies in European Realism* (London: Grosset and Dunlap, 1982), p. 6.
21. *The Nineteenth Century Novel,* A. Kettle, ed. (London: Heinemann, 1982), p. 264.
22. Jeanette King, *Tragedy in the Victorian Novel* (Cambridge: University Press, 1978), p. 161.
23. J.O. Bailey, "Changing Fashions in Hardy Scholarship," *Thomas Hardy and the Modern World: A Symposium,* F.B. Pinion, ed. (Dorchester: Thomas Hardy Society, 1974), p. 144.
24. Kettle also refers to the element of tragedy in *Tess* saying that Hardy achieves "in his two final novels, *Tess* and *Jude* tragedy which . . . bitterly and poignantly captures a central truth of the era in which he lived." (*II*, p. 52)
25. *Hardy the Novelist* (London: Constable, 1969), p. 37.
26. *Criticism and Ideology* (London: NLB, 1976), p. 131.
27. *Selected Literary Criticism: D.H. Lawrence*, Anthony Beal, ed. (London: Heinemann, 1969), p. 197.
28. This question is dealt with by H.M. Daleski in his essay "*Tess of the d'Urbervilles*: Mastery and Abandon," *Essays in Crit*, Vol. 30, 1980. According to Daleski: "Hardy, apparently, both wishes it to be clear it is not only a rape that is in question (if it is a rape at all) and wants to minimise the extent of Tess's transgression. He is led into inconsistency, it seems to me, not so much because he is intent on presenting Tess as 'a pure woman,' as has been asserted, as because he wants her to be seen as

a victim." p. 333. David Lodge assets that "it is important to realize that she is seduced, not raped." *Language of Fiction* (London: Routledge and Kegan Paul, 1967), p. 185.

29. *The Independent,* 25 Feb. 1892, Lerner and Holmstrom, p. 81.
30. Lerner and Holmstrom, p. 95.
31. "Feminism and the Literary Critic," *LTP Journal of Literature Teaching, Politics,* No. 2, 1983, Sussex, p. 74.
32. Laurence Lerner, *The Literary Imagination* (Brighton: Harvester, 1982), pp. 120-21.
33. It is interesting to note that Kettle's analysis of this passage remains nearly the same, thirty years later, in the Open University "The Nineteenth Century Novel and its Legacy" Course Units 17-18 (1982).
34. *Tess, The Nineteenth Century Novel and its Legacy,* OU Course Units 17-18 (Portsmouth: Open University Press, 1982), p. 17.
35. Merryn Williams, *Thomas Hardy and Rural England* (London: Macmillan, 1978), p. 115.
36. *The Country and the City* (London: Chatto and Windus, 1975), p. 252.
37. Merryn Williams, p. 17.
38. Irwing Howe, *Thomas Hardy* (London: Weidenfeld, 1968), p. 125.
39. Open University Course Units 17-18, p. 21.
40. *Ibid.*, p. 5.
41. *Ibid.*, p. 26.
42. It is interesting to note that in the Open University Course Unit, Kettle does not view the novel in solely realistic terms but says, "it is doubtful whether it is appropriate to treat *Tess* as a 'nineteenth century realist' novel at all; and if the convention Hardy is writing in is recognized as no more literally 'realist' than, say, a Greek or Shakespearean play, most of the force of this particular complaint disappears." (22)
43. *Studies in European Realism* (New York: Grosset and Dunlap, 1964), p. 11.
44. Leavis, *The Great Tradition* (London: Chatto and Windus, 1961), p. 80.
45. OU Course Units 17-18, p. 24.
46. *Ibid.*, p. 18.
47. *Ibid.*, p. 34.
48. *University Forward,* Vol. 5: 32, 1939, p. 9.
49. OU Course Units 17-18, p. 34.
50. *The Quarterly Review,* April 1892, in Lerner and Holmstrom, pp. 86-87.
51. *The Novel and the People* (London: Lawrence and Wishart, 1944), p. 99.

52. *Romance and Realism*, Samuel Hynes, ed. (New Jersey: Princeton, 1970), p. 91.

53. OU Course Units 17-18, p. 32.

54. *Ibid.*, p. 30.

55. *Loc. cit.*

56. *Ibid.*, p. 32.

57. "Tess, Nature and the Voices of Hardy," *The Language of Fiction* (London: Routledge and Kegan Paul, 1966), p. 168. Williams says in *TEN*, pp. 106-7: "We know that he [Hardy] was worried about his prose and was reduced by the ordinary educated assumptions of his period to studying Defoe, Fielding, Addison, Scott and *The Times*, as if they could have helped him." This first appeared in an essay "Thomas Hardy" published in the *Critical Quarterly*, Vol. 6, Winter 1964, whereas Lodge's book *The Language of Fiction* came out in 1966.

58. *Ibid.*, p. 168.

59. "Notes on English Prose," *Writing in Society* (London: Verso, 1984), p. 106.

60. *Ibid.*, p. 73.

61. *Ibid.*, p. 118.

62. R. Williams, "Thomas Hardy," *Critical Quarterly*, Vol.6, Winter 1964, p. 351.

63. *Writing in Society*, p. 79.

64. *The Country and the City*, p. 9.

65. *Ibid.*, p. 10.

66. *Politics and Letters*, p. 247.

67. The Arden Library, 1979, 1st published, Cambridge: The Minority Press, 1930, pp. 4-5.

68. See *New Bearings in English Poetry* (London: Chatto and Windus, 1959), pp. 56-61.

69. *Politics and Letters*, p. 246.

70. Review of *Border Country*, *New Statesman*, 19 Nov. 1960.

71. Norman Page, p. 2.

72. However, Williams's own use of language in his critical discourse conforms to the literary register and his long sentences hardly ensure facility in comprehension.

73. Bakhtin, *The Dialogic Imagination*, Michael Holquist, ed., Caryl Emerson and M. Holquist, trans. (Austin: University of Texas Press, 1981), p. 314.

74. "Tess of the d'Urbervilles: Mastery and Abandon," *Essay in Criticism*, Vol. 30, Oxford, 1980, p. 339.

75. Eagleton, *Walter Benjamin: or Towards a Revolutionary Criticism* (London: NLB, 1981), p. 129.
76. Widdowson, p. 4.
77. *Politics and Letters,* p. 265.
78. Byatt, *T.E.S.*, 28.1.81, p. 12.

Conclusion

> Each stage is necessary, and therefore justified for the time and conditions to which it owes its origin. But in the face of new, higher conditions, which gradually develop in its own womb, it loses its validity and justification. . . . For it (dialectical philosophy), nothing is final, absolute, sacred.
>
> Engels, *Basic Writings on Politics and Philosophy*

As we have seen, this process is evident from the historical reconstruction of the literary critical trends from the thirties to the "moment" culminating in the work of Kettle and Williams. The work of Williams superseded that of Kettle and is itself somewhat overshadowed within radical literary criticism by that of Eagleton in *Criticism and Ideology*, who shifts the site of the text's value from achieved "realism" to its conditions of production. In both cases, the criterion is "pre-emptive" to the extent that the text is seen as an "achieved" artefact, whereas as Tony Bennett points out:

> The problem of value is the problem of the social production of value; it refers to the ever ongoing process whereby which texts are to be valued and on what grounds are necessarily matters for debate and, indeed, struggle. Value is not something which the text has or possesses. It is not an attribute of the text, it is rather something that is produced for the text.[1]

This process has been illustrated in the course of the discussion, particularly with reference to Hardy. The concern with value shifts from the inherent 'universality' of 'great' literature to it being seen as historically, culturally and ideologically variable. From a mid-eighties perspective of the predominant Formalist, feminist and colonial theories, the three selected texts have yielded a plurality of perspectives which have marginalized the earlier standpoints, yet the earlier stage was a necessary precondition within this dialectical process. The formation of 'canons' is an ideological process and as Eagleton points out:

> ...there is no such thing as yet which is "really" great, or 'really' anything, independently of the ways in which that writing is treated within the specific forms of social and institutional life.[2]

Nevertheless, this does not explain the fact why, all things being equal, some texts are preferred to others. To answer this, it is necessary to follow Eagleton's argument that:

> Literary criticism selects, processes, corrects and rewrites texts in accordance with certain institutionalized norms of the "literary" – norms which are at any given time arguable, and always historically variable.[3]

The current proliferation of literary theories has resulted in a "Copernican decentring"[4] of literary criticism. René Wellek believes that "The profession divides, inevitably, into at least three distinct branches: the historians, the interpreters, and the theorists."[5] Wellek argues for a "'respect for tradition" while Paul de Man calls this not simply "civilized conservatism" but "moral indignation."[6] While within Western academia, critical theory is paramount to the extent that there are special courses on the subject, in most English departments elsewhere, in the Anglophone world and particularly in India, as noted in the introduction, which follow a step or two behind, various shades of Leavisism are still thriving. This "deferral" then is another reason for the choice of the present subject, as already stated at the outset.

The importance of Kettle's enterprise then, within this context, is apparent. His achievement and influence can be summed up mainly in practical terms. His correlation of literature and life, brings it from a rarified plane to one of quotidian reality; his simple use of language makes his work extremely accessible and relevant to non-native students of English. Kettle's book deals with most of the major canonical texts that feature in the curricula of Indian universities and hence it is regarded as a fairly all-embracing guide. The tone of the text is authoritative enough to appeal to the widespread mentality that is an offshoot of the residual colonialism inculcated and reinforced by a plagiaristic educational system. This gives rise to the contradiction at the heart of literary studies—that is, the emphasis on subjective judgement based on the student's "originality," "imagination" and "creativity"[7] and the need for objectivity, the increasing demand for "the science of the text" as opposed to "intuitionism."

Though Williams's literary criticism shares some aspects of Kettle's enterprise, it has a different character in that it does not offer evaluative"'touchstones." The categories for fictional criticism proposed by Williams are a useful way of analyzing not only the novel but drama as well. The tripartite distinction of the residual-dominant-emergent is particularly helpful in capturing the complex structure of feeling of a specific period in a particular text. Williams's recent position as pointed out earlier, incorporates not only a consideration of the historical and material conditions of cultural production but also the social and historical conditions of the reader's response. Not only in India, but even within the context of British academia, Williams's theoretical concepts are requisitioned, modified, developed but certainly not ignored. Williams thus is a 'live' presence as evident from the fact that even Eagleton, an earlier critic of Williams has apparently returned to the fold:

> When structuralism and semiotics were the most in fashion, Williams abided by his concern with the "non-discursive" only to see the erstwhile devotees of structuralism rejoining him in their discovery of Voloshinov and Foucault. While other materialist thinkers, including myself, diverted into structuralist Marxism, Williams sustained his historicist humanism only to find such theoreticians returning under changed political conditions to examine that case less cavalierly, if not to endorse it uncritically.8

Broadly, both the books under study could be categorized as "socialist-humanist," which is in many more ways akin to the liberal humanist criticism practised by traditional critics rather than radical Marxists and hence their popularity within a culture that largely subscribes to this particular ideology. While both writers focus on class concerns, they ignore areas dealing with gender and race relations, areas that have been consigned to marginality, dispossession and subordination to the extent that this suppression has irrupted in militant forms of feminism and anti-imperialist criticism.

Literary criticism has perhaps always been an ideological "apparatus" in the twentieth century, increasingly developed by the academic institution to adjudicate in matters of what constitutes the "canon," what literature should be taught, who should be elevated and who dethroned. In the face of such institutional hegemony, the need for subversive insurgency within its stronghold from deprived sub-cultures is all the more important. The strategy is first to find a *via media* between empiricism and a purely theoretical approach. For if theory is invalid without practical reference, by the same logic, practice without theory is without direction or organization. Secondly, literary criticism cannot divorce itself from other disciplines but must continually draw upon politics, philosophy, history, linguistics and allied subjects. The novel especially, by its very nature, cannot be contained within a comprehensive "poetics."[9] Walter L. Reed has suggested two necessary elements for the formation of a poetics—"a tendency towards system or structuration" and "a tendency to establish literary norms and a literary canon."[10] As we have seen, both these "tendencies" are based on a set notion of realism, which has further been exposed as an "ideological operateur," to borrow a phrase from Macherey and Balibar. As such, it can be concluded that "the novel declares its independence of poetics, the fictionalist strategy of incorporation and transcendence."[11]

Furthermore, literary criticism should neither be ahistorical nor transcultural, for the production and distribution of a text is part of a specific historical and cultural moment. Much present criticism, as has been discussed in the earlier chapters, is predominantly phallocentric as well as anglo-centric. It is on account of this process of institutionalization that male writing and Euro-American writing is set up as a paradigm, reverently followed by Asian, African and Latin-American writers. It is only recently that Indian writing in English is coming into its own, but with the hegemony of English literature in academic curricula, this writing only reaches the Indian public via the West. The problem is too complex to be discussed here, but Indian writers in English primarily address a Western readership and hope for a publication in the West. For example, Anita Desai's winning the indigenous *Sahitya Akademi Award* counts far less than winning a nomination for the Booker prize. This lack of a readership within India exacerbates the problem which could be rectified to an extent by introducing these texts for study in the prescribed courses – a process which has started but not yet gained momentum. This imbalance is evident from the fact that most people have read/seen *A Passage to India*, but how many people in either India or England have heard of Nirad C. Chaudhri's *A Passage to England* ?

Therefore future literary theories, in order to have global relevance must address themselves to questions of race and gender. Especially in a racist and sexist society like India, the importance of this project cannot be over-stressed. Racism is directed primarily against the Dravidian while the 'ideal' Indian woman, projected in film and mass-media is humble, submissive, self-sacrificing, modest and home-loving and this "sphere" is not different from that proposed by Sarah Ellis to *The Women of England* in 1839, "You have deep responsibilities; you have urgent claims; a nation's moral worth is in your keeping." This ideology has been quietly subverted by both Bronte and Eliot by "giving emphasis to female capability."[12] Catherine is too aggressive to fit the ideological configuration of the Victorian stereotype of ideal womanhood which is set up in the character of Isabella and promptly demystified. Similarly, Dorothea is far from the conventional Victorian heroine and if she marries Ladislaw it is because he has a "direct, instinctive, powerful sexual presence, and in matters of sex they [Eliot's heroines] are driven to know what they desire and to develop love from desire."[13] If the men in women's fiction have been condemned as inadequately portrayed, it is because male critics have "applied male standards to the men imagined by women as men their heroines might love, and they have often found them wanting."[14] Miller continues: "It is not that men have not been at a disadvantage in writing about women, but they have not needed to see themselves at a disadvantage."[15]

The dominant Victorian ideology is aptly summed up by Joan Rockwell:

> The requirement of success in the novel – the hero or heroine must move upwards in society and in wealth – Work! Venture! Succeed! It is to be noted that the success in question is an individual success, not the rise to power of a clan or class.[16]

However, the conjunction of love and money, the closure of the "happy family" situation are all questioned at various levels in the texts under analysis. In *Wuthering Heights,* young Catherine and Heathcliff look into the beautiful Linton home, the seemingly ideal family situation, yet there is a slippage, for there is disruption in the form of the children quarrelling and crying. Catherine's marriage to Linton is desirable in terms of money but not in terms of love. Similarly, Dorothea marries Ladislaw for love, not money. This disjunction is the reverse of Austen's love/money settlements. Tess goes up the social scale in her marriage to Angel but opposing class values disrupt this "desirable" situation.

It is this "dialogism" that disturbs the seemingly organic unity of the Victorian novel. "Dialogism," as we have seen, can mean different things at different times – at the level of plot, perspective, conflicting value-systems and the positing of generic modes. At its simplest, Paul de Man defines it as:

> double-talk, the necessary obliqueness of any persecuted speech, that cannot, at the risk of survival, openly say what it means to say: there is ample evidence from what is known of Bakhtin's biography.[17]

This meaning, it is evident, is applicable to all three writers under discussion, in terms of their marginal positions – gender in the case of Bronte and Eliot, and the charge of provincialism, an offshoot of class snobbery, in Hardy's case.

Middlemarch has been set up as the *locus classicus* of the classic realist text, not only because it encourages such readings, but:

> institutionally, not only in the Universities but . . . in those multitudes of contemporary practices which reproduce and sustain an ideology of realism.[18]

All this is part of the general effort to search for the "indispensable centre . . . for expressing a main intention."[19] *Wuthering Heights* is dialogic not only because it has double plots and a multiple narrative but because it does not head towards a resolution of perspective. According to Garrett:

> What distinguishes the major Victorian multi-plot novels . . . is the way their multiple narratives and frequent thematic parallels or oppositions are subject to a dialogical play of perspectives

> which prevents them from resolving into any single stable pattern or meaning.20

In order to detect such subversions inscribed within the text, the privileging of realism must be re-examined. Rather than calling for the death of the author, it would seem that the Althusser-Machereyan proposition might well be viable:

> The author as mysterious genius has disappeared, but has been replaced by a worker transforming a given raw material through the methodical employment of determinate means of production21.

However, literary production cannot be placed at par with the production of basic commodities like food, shelter and clothing. In present society, literary activity constitutes a privileged sphere and cannot be satisfactorily explained in the above terms. Moreover the emphasis on the importance of literature differs in affluent societies from that in developing ones. In England, the creation of a consolidated reading public is possible on the basis of a common language whereas in countries like India, no such 'public sphere' (as used by Eagleton pace Habermas) can be created. So far, within departments of English, Western critical practice is being adopted unquestioningly. The next step would be to modify this to suit specific needs, finally leading to a situation when innovative theories would engender a fruitful East-West dialogue, which would be mutually beneficial in the interests of critical practice.

NOTES

1. *Formalism and Marxism* (London: Methuen, 1978), p. 173.
2. *Literary Theory* (Oxford: Basil Blackwell, 1983), p. 202.
3. *Ibid.*, p. 203.
4. Belsey, *Critical Practice* (London: Methuen, 1980), p. 133. Belsey, however, is referring to the "death" of the author, and I have used it in a different context.
5. "Respect for Tradition," *Times Literary Supplement,* 10 Dec. 1982, p. 1356.
6. *Ibid.*, p. 1355.

7. These constitute the "terminology trap" and along with "genius" are the four main Romantic words used repeatedly by Leavis, as pointed out by Philip Hobsbaum HETE Conference, Lecture: "Eeconstructing Literature."

8. *The Function of Criticism* (London: Verso, 1985), p. 109.

9. A "poetics" of the novel can be constructed on the basis of narrative, linguistics and even dialogism, but at best, such attempts would be "monologic," for they would privilege one form over another.

10. "The Problems With a Poetics of a Novel," *Towards a Poetics of Fiction,* Mark Spilka, ed. (Bloomington: Indiana University Press, 1977), p. 62.

11. *Ibid.,* p. 70.

12. Judith Lowder Newton, *Women, Power and Subversion: Social Strategies in British Fiction 1778-1860* (London: Virago, 1986), p. 6.

13. Antonia Byatt in Jane Miller, *Women Writing about Men* (London: Virago, 1986), p. 41.

14. Miller, p. 141.

15. *Ibid.,* p. 41.

16. *Fact in Fiction* (London: Routledge, 1974), p. 93.

17. "Dialogue and Dialogism," *Poetics Today,* Vol. 4:1, 1983, p. 100.

18. *James Joyce and the Revolution of the Word* (London: Macmillan, 1981), p. 26.

19. Henry James, "Preface" to *The Tragic Muse, The Art of The Novel,* quoted in Peter K. Garrett, "Double Plots and Dialogical Form in Victorian Fiction," *Nineteenth Century Fiction,* No. 32, 1977-78, p. 1.

20. *Ibid.,* p. 4.

21. Belsey, p. 138.

APPENDIX

An Interview with Arnold Kettle
4 March 1985

I. On the years at Cambridge and political involvement

Well I became involved in politics very much through the peace and anti-fascist movements and joined the Party in 1936 and by 1938-39 was secretary of the Socialist Club which was a very large organization and where I learnt active politics. And the point I was going to make was that it was very much on the basis of building up unity among the anti-fascist students and people, and seeing this as the way forward to socialism that I became involved whereas Raymond, who was a few years younger, came into a more complicated situation. He came up to Cambridge just as the War began and at that time the politics was very different everywhere, including Cambridge. I always think that our different ways of approach came from that. I've always felt it very important to write in a way that would be meaningful and understandable to a large number of people and not just to Marxists. I've never been much of a theoretician. My politics was very much based on the practical sense of the economic crisis in England and the role of the Chamberlain government as well as the rise of fascism in Spain and Germany.

II. On Leavis and his influence

Leavis was certainly very important in Cambridge. He had a lot of influence on all of us. It's interesting now to look back and ask why. I think it was because although Leavis did not have a progressive attitude yet he took literature seriously and he was concerned to link the judgement of literature to the judgement and values of life – not exactly in the same way as a Left-winger or Marxist would do though a lot of the Leavisites were also Left-wing.

III. On the relationship between *Scrutiny* and the thirties's Marxists

They overlapped. Quite a number of the *Scrutiny* people were themselves members of the Communist party and thus the relationship was quite complicated, for example, Boris Ford who was active in *Scrutiny* was a member of the C.P. Knights was not a member but was certainly sympathetic to the Left. Leavis was not an entirely reactionary force. Why did so many progressive students flock to *Scrutiny* and Leavis? It was because Leavis did take literature seriously. He wasn't an aesthete--he wanted to link literature with moral values. This was what appealed to us. At the same time, we are very critical of him.

IV. On whether the writing of *An Introduction to the English Novel* was a conscious attempt to synthesize the strands of Marxism and Leavisism

It was not conscious at all. There were these two influences--the Marxist and Leavis--important to me and indeed to Raymond whose first book [*Reading and Criticism*] is much more Leavisite than mine. On the other hand, what I did get from Leavis was this sense that I didn't want to make too general statements about literature. I wanted to examine particular pieces of literature and felt that it was very important to emphasize if the book had any personal impact on you rather than just an ideological one. Our encounters with the Communist party have had their effect but they were both in some ways theoretically contradictory. But in practice, I would write about one novel, rather than give a general impression, e.g. *Oliver Twist*, applying that kind of consideration that one associates with Leavis though ideologically from a different point of view. My own aim was that it should be comprehensible to a large number of people rather than elitist. I suppose I've got partly from Leavis my feeling that literature was more than ideology--was of course affected by ideology but literature has a reality of its own. I don't find myself sympathetic to later neo-Marxists who see literature as simply or primarily something which a ruling class ideology is forcing onto people, and who see the literary canon as something entirely suspect. There are plenty of suspect things about choice of books and literature courses and things like that. What's considered "good" has more political significance than the people who choose them realize. On the other hand, it's not meaningless to talk about "good" literature. Good literature has a particular value because of the way the language is used and the effect it produces on the reader. I thought this was very important.

V. On the impetus behind the writing of *An Introduction to the English Novel*

Basil Willey, who was editor of the literary section of the Hutchinson's University Library and English don at my college Pembroke, asked me if I'd like to write a book about the novel. It's most interesting how little I thought about the theoretical implications of what I was writing. What I wanted was to write literary criticism which was closely bound up with life, which was comprehensible to a large number of people, and the part literature could play in making the world more progressive. This was the general principle. For example, in my first chapter, I developed something about literature and life. I've always realized that philosophically this was not very deeply thought out and was very vulnerable. The last thing I had in mind was to write Marxist literary criticism – it would be a pretentious thing to do. I wanted to put my abilities to the service of the Communist movement and was hoping to break down the separate compartments of literature and life that many intelligent readers kept.

VI. On his role as educator

I've always been a very keen educator wanting to help people improve their lives, to become more conscious and because of the Open University, which I joined in 1970, I had particular opportunities to do this. For example, people said they'd no idea they could write an essay on Emily Bronte. This discovery of new possibilities in people's lives, their feeling of self-esteem is very important.

VII. On influences from Europe and the Soviet Union

From Europe hardly at all, though a bit more from the Soviet Union. Lukacs began to be translated in the fifties I think, whereas in the thirties and forties he was very esoteric. I've been influenced by Lukacs now and have great admiration for him. He's a bit theoretical for my taste, but I do tend to turn to him. Benjamin was scarcely known by us in the thirties though I like his book on Brecht and have read essays on him. But I feel I haven't mastered him. I don't know enough about Goldmann. We knew about the thirties's Socialist Realists. At Cambridge, there was a group of us on whom the main influence was Alick West. We met and talked about socialist literature and socialist criticism. He was the main single influence on me because he too combined this great respect for literature because of its quality of the use of language and the need to analyze particular pieces of literature rather than to make general statements about them and he combined this with a Marxist outlook. My work was affected by the whole atmosphere of the thirties. I realized, as I grew older, how much we're the products of the thirties.

VIII. Attitudes to the Soviet Union

We were sympathetic to the Soviet Union as a Socialist state. I don't think we were nearly as Stalinist as later people came to assume. I did not leave the Party in 1956, not because I was a hundred percent convinced that the Russians were right but on the whole, life had become better in Hungary. But the same cannot be said of Czeckoslovakia in 1968. I'm rather pragmatic in my view about these things and in general take a fairly liberal kind of stance. I regard Marxism as a humanist philosophy though "humanism" is regarded as a wicked word by contemporary Marxists.

IX. On feminist criticism

It is the most important trend in the last 10 years. I wouldn't like to make a very general statement but obviously it's done a terrific job in making readers and writers more conscious of the whole problem of women and their struggles and we are all being affected by this whether consciously or not. Some narrowly feminist books are not very sympathetic to me. But on the whole, they're doing a fine job in bringing back into the reading public's consciousness, a whole lot of women writers who had been forgotten. I think theoretical feminism, like every other theory, if separated from actual practice, can be ridiculous.

X. On Raymond Williams and *The English Novel from Dickens to Lawrence*

I liked the book. I don't find Raymond a very accessible writer. I find that I rather have to push my way through his books. He says interesting things but I wish he would say them a little more directly and less in the passive voice. His criticism is not very different from mine. I think he is more consciously suspicious of the merely subjective than I am. *Border Country* is a very nice novel.

XI. On whether the twentieth century novel is in a state of decline

I don't think it's in a state of decline. There are certain developments in the last fifty years--certain good and certain not so good--but all are bound up with social developments. I'm neither a socialist realist nor an anti-realist as I know young Left-wing critics tend to be. Many of them feel that because you can't have literal realism, they condemn the whole concept as misleading. I don't do that and I don't think Raymond does, either.

XII. The definition of "positive values"-- an oft-recurring term in *An Introduction to the English Novel*

I define "positive values" as life-enhancing values very much in terms of changing historical and social reality.

XIII. On second thoughts regarding *An Introduction to the English Novel*

I don't think I would want to reverse judgements in a theoretical way but I would write many chapters differently, for example, if you compare my chapters on *Tess* with the Open University Course unit, you'll see that they're very different. I've been influenced by Marxist structuralist criticism. I would not analyze Heathcliff as the proletariat--which is crude. There's scarcely a chapter of that book which I wouldn't write differently but not that I reject the whole thing. I hope it has been useful and its great advantage is that students understand it.

XIV. On whether *An Introduction to the English Novel* would be his claim to fame

More than anything else, I would like to be associated with the material I have prepared for the Open University. That has been my most productive period and a task I was suited to do.

A select Bibliography of the works of Arnold Kettle has been compiled by W.R. Owens, in Douglas Jefferson and Graham Martin, eds., *The Uses of Fiction* (Milton Keynes: Open University Press, 1982).

Bibliography

I. PRIMARY SOURCES

1. ARNOLD KETTLE

"Marxism and Literature," *University Forward*, Vol. 5, 32, Part 9, 1939.
"Report from America," *University Forward*, Vol. 8 (5), 1943.
"The Artist and Politics." *Marxism Today*, Vol. 3, No. 5, May 1951.
"Talks with Soviet Writers," *Anglo-Soviet Journal*, Vol. XIII, 3, 1952.
An Introduction to the English Novel. Vol. I (1950), Vol. II (1953). London: Hutchinson, 1977, 2nd ed. 1967.
"A Blow for Humanism," rev. *The Emperor's New Clothes*, Kathleen Nott, *The Marxist Quarterly*, Vol. I 3, 1954.
"Life and the Novel," rev. D.H. Lawrence, Novelist, F.R. Leavis, *The Gryphon*, Jan. 1956.
"Two Working-Class Novels," *The Marxist Quarterly*, Vol. 3 (4), 1956.
"Leeds: Impressions of a Provincial University," *Twentieth Century*, Vol. 159, 1956.
"Rebels and Causes: Some Thoughts on the Angry Young Men," *Marxism Today*, Vol. 2, No. 3, March 1958.
"Rocco and his Brothers," *Marxism Today*, Vol. 6, No. 3, March 1962.
"Charles Dickens: The Novelist and the People," *Marxism Today*, Vol. 7, No. 2, Feb. 1963.
Karl Marx: Founder of Modern Communism. 1963, 2nd ed., 1968.
Ed. *Shakespeare in a Changing World*. London: Lawrence and Wishart, 1964.
"The Early Victorian Social Problem Novel," *The Pelican Guide to the English Novel*. Vol. 6, Boris Ford, ed. Harmondsworth, 1964.
Communism and the Intellectuals. London: Lawrence and Wishart, 1965.
Hardy the Novelist: A Reconsideration: The W.D. Memorial Lecture. University College of Swansea, 1966.
"The Future of the Left," *Marxism Today*, Vol. 10, No. 1, Jan. 1966.
Ed. *The Nineteenth Century Novel: Critical Essays and Documents*. London: Heinemann, 1981, 1st ed., 1972.
The Late Nineteenth Century Novel, Open University Course Unit No. 23. Milton Keynes: Open University Press, 1973.
"Lawrence, Leavis and Life," *Marxism Today*, Vol. 21, No. 9, Sept. 1977.
Tess, The Nineteenth Century Novel and Its Legacy, Open University Course Units 17-18. Portsmouth: Open University Press, 1982.

2 RAYMOND WILLIAMS

Reading and Criticism (1950). London: Frederick Muller, 1966.
Culture and Society (1958). Harmondsworth: Pelican, 1976.
Border Country. London: Chatto and Windus, 1960.
The Long Revolution. London: Chatto and Windus, 1961.
Second Generation. London: Chatto and Windus, 1964.
"Thomas Hardy," *Critical Quarterly*, Vol. 6, Winter 1964.
The English Novel from Dickens to Lawrence (1970). London: Hogarth, 1984.
The Country and the City. London: Chatto and Windus, 1973.
Keywords. London: Fontana, 1976.
Marxism and Literature. Oxford: University Press, 1977.
"Lecture on Realism," *Screen*, Vol. 18, No. 1, Spring 1977.
The Volunteers. London: Eyre Methuen, 1978.
The Fight for Manod. London: Chatto and Windus, 1979.
Politics and Letters. Interviews with NLR (1979). London: Verso, 1981.
Problems in Materialism and Culture. London: Verso, 1980.
"The Sadder Recognition," Sue Aspinell talks to Raymond Williams, *Screen*, Vol. 23, Nos. 3-4, Sept-Oct. 1982.
Writing in Society. London: Verso, 1983.
Loyalties. London: Chatto and Windus, 1985.

3 NOVELS

Emily and Anne Bronte, *Wuthering Heights and Agnes Grey*. London: Smith Elder, 1910.
William M. Sale Jr., ed., *Wuthering Heights: An Annotated Text With Essays in Criticism*. New York: W.W. Norton, 1963.
George Eliot, *Middlemarch*. Harmondsworth: Penguin, 1982.
----"Silly Novels by Lady Novelists," *Westminster Review*, LXVI, Oct. 1856.
----*Essays of George Eliot*, Thomas Pinney, ed. New York: Columbia University Press, 1963.
----*The George Eliot Letters*, 9 Vols., Vol. 6, 1874-1877, Gordon S. Haight, ed. Yale: University Press, 1955.
Thomas Hardy, *Tess of the d'Urbervilles*. London: Macmillan, 1967.

II. SECONDARY SOURCES

4 ON WILLIAMS

Barnett, Anthony. "Raymond Williams and Marxism: A Rejoinder to Terry Eagleton," *New Left Review*, Sept.-Oct. 1976.
Bilan, R.P. "From Leavis to Marx," *Queens Quarterly*, 87.
Charles, Gerda. Rev. *Border Country*, *New Statesman*, 19 Nov. 1960.

Duckworth, Alastair M. "Raymond Williams and Literary History," *Papers in Language and Literature,* Vol. 11, 1974.

Green, Michael. "Raymond Williams and Cultural Studies," *Cultural Studies,* Vol. 6, Spring 1975.

Johnson, Leslie. *The Cultural Critics.* London: Routledge and Kegan Paul, 1979.

Knoepflmacher, V.C. Rev. *The English Novel from Dickens to Lawrence, Victorian Studies,* 14.

Korg, Jacob. Rev. *The English Novel, Modern Fiction Studies,* 18.

Lockwood, Bernard. *Four Contemporary British Working-Class Novelists.* Unpublished DPhil thesis, Wisconsin.

Pechey, Graham. "*Scrutiny,* English Marxism and the Work of Raymond Williams," *Literature and History,* Vol. 11, 1, Spring 1985.

Watkins, Evan. "Raymond Williams and Marxist Criticism," *Boundary,* Vol. 2, 4, 1976.

Watson, Garry. "Criticism and the English Idiom: the Significance of Raymond Williams," *New Universities Quarterly,* Vol. 31, No. 4, Autumn 1977.

----. *The Leavises, the "Social" and the Left.* Swansea: Brynmill, 1977.

Ward, J.P. *Raymond Williams.* University of Wales Press, 1981.

5 ON KETTLE

Jefferson, Douglas and Graham Martin, eds. *The Uses of Fiction: Essays on the Modern Novel in Honour of Arnold Kettle.* Milton Keynes: The Open University Press, 1982.

6 ON EMILY BRONTE

Allott, Miriam, ed. *Wuthering Heights: A Casebook.* London: Macmillan, 1970.

Barker, Francis. "*Wuthering Heights* and the Real Conditions," *Red Letters,* Vol. 3, Autumn 1976.

Collins, Clifford. "Themes and Conventions in *Wuthering Heights," The Critic,* Vol. I, No. 2, Autumn 1947.

Craik, W.A. *The Bronte Novels.* London: Methuen, 1968.

Eagleton, Terry. *Myths of Power.* London: Macmillan, 1975.

G rin, Winifred. *Emily Bronte*: A Biography. Oxford: Clarendon, 1971.

Ohmann, Carol. "Emily Bronte in the Hands of Male Critics," *College English,* Vol. 32, No. 8, May 1971.

7 ON GEORGE ELIOT

Adam, Ian. ed. *This Particular Web: Essays on Middlemarch.* Toronto: University Press, 1975.

Bennett, Joan. *George Eliot: Her Mind and Her Art.* Cambridge: University Press, 1948.

Haight, Gordon S. *A Century of George Eliot Criticism*. London: Methuen, 1966.

Hardy, Barbara, ed. *Middlemarch: Critical Approaches to the Novel*. London: Athlone Press, 1967.

----. *Critical Essays on George Eliot*. London: Routledge and Kegan Paul, 1970.

Harvey, W.J. *The Art of George Eliot*. London: Chatto and Windus, 1961.

Hertz, Neil. "Recognizing Casaubon," *Glyph*, Vol. 9, 1979.

----. "Why Feminist Critics are Angry With George Eliot".

Holmstrom, J. and Lerner, L. eds. *George Eliot and Her Readers*. London: Bodley Head, 1966.

McSweeney, Kerry. *Middlemarch*. London: George Allen and Unwin, 1984.

8 ON THOMAS HARDY

Abercrombie, Lascelles. *Thomas Hardy: A Critical Study*. London: Martin Secker, 1919.

Bayley, J.O. *An Essay on Hardy*. Cambridge: University Press, 1979.

Byatt, Antonia. "Hardy Rules O.K.," *Times Educational Supplement*, 28.1.81.

Cecil, David. *Hardy the Novelist*. London: Constable, 1969.

Daleski, H.M. "*Tess of the d'Urbervilles*: Mastery and Abandon," *Essays in Criticism*, Vol. 30, 1980.

Gregor, Ian. *The Great Web*. London: Faber, 1974.

Hardy, Florence Emily. *Life of Hardy*. London: Macmillan, 1962.

Howe, Irving. *Thomas Hardy*. New York: Collier, 1973.

LaValley, Albert J. ed. *Twentieth Century Interpretations of Tess of the d'Urbervilles*. N.J. Englewood Cliffs: Prentice Hall, 1969.

Lerner, L. and Holmstrom, J. eds. *Thomas Hardy and His Readers: A Selection of Contemporary Reviews*. London: Bodley Head, 1968.

Miller, J. Hillis. *Thomas Hardy: Distance and Desire*. Harvard: University Press, 1970.

Page, Norman. *Thomas Hardy*. London: Routledge and Kegan Paul, 1977.

Pinion, P.B. ed. *Thomas Hardy and the Modern World: A Symposium*. Dorchester: Thomas Hardy Society Ltd., 1974.

Widdowson, Peter. "Hardy in History," *Literature and History*, Vol. 9:1, Spring 1983.

Williams, Merryn. *Thomas Hardy and Rural England*. London: Macmillan, 1978.

Index